D0917099

"Leader, this book is a deep, transforming well. Draw from it and drink the water of divine wisdom. Dive in, splash around, drink again, swallow slowly, and savor. Daniel Montgomery and Jared Kennedy don't offer you their collected leadership wisdom—they offer you your Lord. He is the water that not only quenches a leader's thirst but also quiets his heart and transforms the way he leads. I wish I had this book forty years ago!"

Paul David Tripp, President, Paul Tripp Ministries; author, *Dangerous Calling*

"*Leadership Mosaic* is easily the most stimulating book I've read on leadership in the past ten years. What grabbed my attention and heart the most was Daniel Montgomery's commitment to ground leadership culture in the dynamic life and beauty of the Trinity. To acknowledge that each of us has been made in the image of God is to affirm that *we* have been made in the image of God—not just individually but collectively as the people of God. Revealing our God as leaders is way more important than simply delivering our product. Thank you, Daniel, once again, for turning my thoughts heavenward."

Scotty Smith, Teacher in Residence, West End Community Church, Nashville, Tennessee

"I've interviewed thousands of pastors over the years and know that Daniel Montgomery is a rare find. *Leadership Mosaic* reflects Daniel's unique combination of artistic and intuitive talent with systematic thinking. Reading this book will expand your leadership and give you a system for constant growth."

William Vanderbloemen, CEO and President, The Vanderbloemen Search Group; author, *Next: Pastoral Succession That Works*

"I've been in some form of leadership in the local church for almost twenty years, but I've often wondered if I was 'doing it right.' What makes a godly leader effective? Daniel Montgomery helps us answer that question with perceptiveness and nuance. Writing from a place of vulnerability and honesty, he offers hard-won leadership insights, gleaned from both wins and losses across a sustained season of ministry. And his answer makes room for leaders of all kinds to recognize and effectively deploy their unique gifts in service to the church."

Jen Wilkin, author, *Women of the Word* and *None Like Him*

"Daniel Montgomery is a leader of great ability and theological conviction. For over a decade he has faithfully led Sojourn Community Church and the Sojourn Network of churches planting other churches. *Leadership Mosaic* is a careful and compelling portrait of leadership built on doctrinal principle. This book is a much-needed resource for evangelical leaders and an articulate call to biblical leadership."

> **R. Albert Mohler Jr.,** President, The Southern Baptist Theological Seminary

"Books, both secular and religious, on leadership principles and practices abound. Christian leaders are searching for help in leading their churches and the teams that work in them toward successful ministry. Most of the books can be categorized as 'somewhat helpful'—you know, the sort of thing that CEOs of corporations first learned in their MBA classes. But *Leadership Mosaic* is different. Taking the paradigm of the Trinity, Montgomery has crafted a truly God-centered model of leadership based on the love, mutual respect, submission, and unity found among the Father, Son, and Holy Spirit as they work as one to bring about the salvation of souls and the glorification of one another. I'm really thankful for this book and hope that it will foster a revival of unified, other-centered ministry in our churches."

> **Elyse Fitzpatrick,** author, *Counsel from the Cross*

"*Leadership Mosaic* is a creative and challenging book about leadership and life. Author Daniel Montgomery connects leaders and their leadership to our great eternal God. Montgomery not only helps us understand leadership, but also shows us how to lead in this critical hour in the church and in America. If you want to grow in your life and as a leader, then read this book. It is worth sharing with your friends and colleagues!"

> **Ronnie Floyd,** Senior Pastor, Cross Church, Springdale, Arkansas

"Have you ever considered how the Trinity relates to leadership? I hadn't—until now. Montgomery takes us on a theological journey into leadership that both challenges and inspires. He helps us identify the type of leaders we are, some of our pitfalls, and the beauty in the way God has made each of us for his glory. This book envisions holistic leaders who embody each of the aspects of leadership while also embracing our differences so we might be a beautiful mosaic."

> **Trillia Newbell,** author, *Fear and Faith* and *United: Captured by God's Vision for Diversity*

"In *Leadership Mosaic*, Montgomery calls us to leadership that is simultaneously convictional, creative, courageous, collaborative, and contemplative. No small order, to be sure. But unlike other paradigms that rely on our will, charisma, or natural giftedness, Montgomery calls us outside ourselves to a vision of leadership that reflects the nature of the triune God. If you're looking for gimmicks or magic formulas, move along. This is nothing less than spiritual formation. Nothing less than being transformed into the image of Christ himself."

Hannah Anderson, author, *Made for More: An Invitation to Live in God's Image* and *Humble Roots: How Humility Grounds and Nourishes Your Soul*

"*Leadership Mosaic* shines a light on key insights for leading in a manner that honors Christ above all. By making the practice of leadership a theological issue, this book makes the 'how' of leading an opportunity to spotlight the beauty of God as Trinity. I am confident that this book will not only improve the way we lead our churches, families, and organizations, but also shape our hearts for the glory of God."

Kevin Peck, Lead Pastor, The Austin Stone Community Church, Austin, Texas; coauthor, *Designed to Lead*

"In *Leadership Mosaic*, Daniel Montgomery and Jared Kennedy provide a top-notch Christian leadership resource that builds its case on the nature and character of God, not selected proof texts from a few Scriptures. This book is a gift to the church and its leaders."

Ed Stetzer, President, LifeWay Research; author, *Subversive*

"Writing from his unbounded enthusiasm, creative clarity, and doctrinal convictions, Montgomery connects Trinitarian theology to leadership in a way that makes sense, makes disciples, and makes a difference. If you're aspiring to leadership or looking to improve your leadership, the next step is in your hands!"

Dave Harvey, Executive Director, Sojourn Network; Founder, AmICalled.com

"Using a fivefold leadership model grounded in the doctrine of the Trinity, *Leadership Mosaic* helps us connect theology and practice. I'm grateful for the ways this book has challenged my paradigm of leadership, and I'm confident it will do the same for you."

Bob Thune, Lead Pastor, Coram Deo Church, Omaha, Nebraska

"Christian leadership is a topic jumbled with a cacophony of competing voices, each one claiming to have found the key that everyone else has missed. In *Leadership Mosaic*, Daniel Montgomery and Jared Kennedy avoid such overblown claims and speak with clarity, calmness, and grace. They don't pretend to offer any magical keys to leadership. Instead, they trace the complex contours of a wisdom that the triune God has woven into his creation and exemplified supremely in Jesus Christ. The result is a settled and substantive exploration of leadership to which you will return again and again."

Timothy Paul Jones, Associate Vice President for the Global Campus, The Southern Baptist Theological Seminary

"Combining a theology of leadership with practical ways to understand more of yourself as a leader, *Leadership Mosaic* helps us identify the complex issues facing Christian leaders, orders them into helpful categories, and offers the resources and ideas necessary to learn how to implement different leadership styles in your ministry. This book will make you think deeply, and it will help you lead effectively."

Kyle Idleman, Pastor, Southeast Christian Church, Louisville, Kentucky; author, *Not a Fan*

LEADERSHIP
MOSAIC

5 LEADERSHIP PRINCIPLES FOR MINISTRY
AND EVERYDAY LIFE

DANIEL MONTGOMERY

WITH JARED KENNEDY

FOREWORD BY RUSSELL MOORE

:: CROSSWAY®

WHEATON, ILLINOIS

Leadership Mosaic: 5 Leadership Principles for Ministry and Everyday Life

Copyright © 2016 by Daniel Montgomery

Published by Crossway
    1300 Crescent Street
    Wheaton, Illinois 60187

All rights reserved. No part of this publication may be reproduced, stored in a retrieval system, or transmitted in any form by any means, electronic, mechanical, photocopy, recording, or otherwise, without the prior permission of the publisher, except as provided for by USA copyright law. Crossway® is a registered trademark in the United States of America.

Cover artwork: Luke Stockdale for Side Show Design Co.

Cover design and illustration: Don Clark for Invisible Creature, Inc.

First printing 2016

Printed in China

Unless otherwise indicated, Scripture quotations are from the ESV® Bible (The Holy Bible, English Standard Version®), copyright © 2001 by Crossway, a publishing ministry of Good News Publishers. Used by permission. All rights reserved.

Scripture quotations marked KJV are from the King James Version of the Bible.

Scripture quotations marked NASB are from The New American Standard Bible®. Copyright © The Lockman Foundation 1960, 1962, 1963, 1968, 1971, 1972, 1973, 1975, 1977, 1995. Used by permission.

Scripture references marked simply NIV are taken from The Holy Bible, New International Version®, NIV®. Copyright © 1973, 1978, 1984, 2011 by Biblica, Inc.™ Used by permission. All rights reserved worldwide.

Scripture references marked NIV1984 are taken from The Holy Bible, New International Version®, NIV®. Copyright © 1973, 1978, 1984 by Biblica, Inc.™ Used by permission. All rights reserved worldwide.

Scripture quotations marked NLT are from the Holy Bible, New Living Translation copyright © 1996, 2004, 2007, 2013 by Tyndale House Foundation. Used by permission of Tyndale House Publishers Inc., Carol Stream, Illinois 60188. All rights reserved.

Scripture references marked RSV are from The Revised Standard Version. Copyright © 1946, 1952, 1971, 1973 by the Division of Christian Education of the National Council of the Churches of Christ in the U.S.A.

All emphases in Scripture quotations have been added by the author.

Hardcover ISBN: 978-1-4335-5255-7
ePub ISBN: 978-1-4335-5258-8
PDF ISBN: 978-1-4335-5256-4
Mobipocket ISBN: 978-1-4335-5257-1

Library of Congress Cataloging-in-Publication Data

Names: Montgomery, Daniel, 1974– author.
Title: Leadership mosaic : 5 leadership principles for ministry and everyday life / Daniel Montgomery with Jared Kennedy.
Description: Wheaton : Crossway, 2016. | Includes bibliographical references and index.
Identifiers: LCCN 2016005314 (print) | LCCN 2016024333 (ebook) | ISBN 9781433552557 (hc) | ISBN 9781433552588 (epub) | ISBN 9781433552564 (pdf) | ISBN 9781433552571 (mobi)
Subjects: LCSH: Christian leadership. | Trinity. | Leadership—Religious aspects—Christianity. | Reformed Church—Doctrines.
Classification: LCC BV652.1 .M65 2016 (print) | LCC BV652.1 (ebook) | DDC 253—dc23
LC record available at https://lccn.loc.gov/2016005314

Crossway is a publishing ministry of Good News Publishers.

RRDS   26   25   24   23   22   21   20   19   18   17   16
15   14   13   12   11   10   9   8   7   6   5   4   3   2   1

To

Mr. K., a sixth-grade teacher
who inspired a wild child.

My mother,
who welcomed a prodigal home.

Ed Stetzer, who gambled on
a twenty-four-year-old church planter.

Rich Plass, who helped a desperate pastor
find his first love again.

The pastors of Sojourn and Sojourn Network,
who have made it all worth it.

CONTENTS

FOREWORD

Most of the leaders I know face one of two temptations. Some leaders are tempted toward a kind of reckless confidence. They see their power as inhering within some quality that makes them special. This can be beneficial in some ways, fighting back the paralysis that accompanies fear. But it comes at the cost of a lack of accountability and community. This sort of leader grows more and more prideful, and more and more isolated, until he or she falls.

Some leaders are tempted toward a lack of confidence. These leaders constantly compare themselves with others who they feel have more natural talent or seem to have everything together. Seeing this, the confidence-lacking leaders believe themselves to be imposters, making things up as they go along, fearful of ever being exposed as not quite the experts they seem to be. This can sometimes be beneficial too, keeping organization-compromising risks from happening. But, again, the cost is too high. These leaders typically operate out of fear and risk aversion, which lead to paralysis.

Most of us find ourselves, at some point or another, in both of these categories. That's why most of us, whatever we are called to lead, need some wise counsel when it comes to leadership. And that's why I'm grateful for this book, written by two men who don't just know the theory of Christian leadership but also have modeled it in remarkable ways.

Leadership Mosaic is a look at how the gospel and biblical theology provide us with five reliable principles of leadership. These principles are founded on scriptural truth and are illuminated with insights from theologians, leadership experts, and social scientists. As you read, you will see yourself and the challenges you face, along with practical wisdom about how to improve your leadership. You will also recognize that, whatever your situation, you are not alone.

Each chapter comes with a set of exercises at the end, small tasks to help you absorb and put into practice the content. This key feature of the book is designed to build habits, starting small, in ways that can grow into a life of renewed leadership.

This book can benefit Christian leaders of all sorts. Some lead, as these authors do, in churches and networks. Others lead in workplaces or in their homes or in community organizations or on mission fields. This book presents practical wisdom that can be applied in a variety of settings and contexts. The ultimate goal, though, is not leadership for the sake of leadership. It is to see leaders conformed into the image of Christ Jesus, the one who taught us to lead by serving, and to serve by leading.

Russell Moore

The mind of the Christian is not satisfied until every form of existence has been referred to the Triune God and until the confession of the Trinity has received the place of prominence in our thought and life.

Herman Bavinck, *The Doctrine of God*

The triune nature of this God affects everything from how we listen to music to how we pray: it makes for happier marriages, warmer dealings with others, better church life; it gives Christians assurance, shapes holiness and transforms the very way we look at the world around us. No exaggeration: the knowledge of this God turns our lives around. Spooky, huh? There is, of course, that major obstacle in our way: that the Trinity is seen not as a solution and a delight, but as an oddity and a problem.

Michael Reeves, *Delighting in the Trinity*

Christians believe that the Triune God created the world, and that should have some implications for the kind of world that it is. Many Christians have acknowledged the perichoretic shape of the life of the Trinity, and that in particular should leave some trace in the world that has been made and remade by the Father, Son, and Spirit.

Peter J. Leithart, *Traces of the Trinity*

As we take up our journey on the Sea of Complexity, we find that organizations also can no longer be considered as machines built component by component and then reliably and predictably "run" by talented managers. Instead, we find that organizations themselves are agents in the quantum world where they are understood best as organisms that reside within a complex web of internal and external relationships with myriad other agents.

Jack Burns, *Organizational Leadership*

Introduction

THE COMPLEXITY OF LEADERSHIP
AND OUR TRIUNE GOD

Summary: *There is a leadership crisis in the local church. When we look around, we see different visions of leadership competing for our devotion. We set these visions against one another—the convictional theologian against the soulful contemplative, for example. We choose the one we think is best. Living from insecurity, we exaggerate our favorite leadership image, and it crowds out the others. God didn't intend this. If we step back, we can see that God's own leadership is a beautiful mosaic. God's own complexity is the most appropriate model for leadership in a complex world. This book unpacks a fivefold vision of leadership rooted in the Trinity. You will see that God's redemptive leadership in the world is the basis for understanding the nature, purpose, and eternal impact of our own leadership.*

It had been a busy, fun week in Chicago.[1] My wife, Mandy, wanted just one more thing before we left town—cupcakes. I ran out to fulfill her last wish before our exciting time in the city came to a close. She saw sacrificial valor. I saw an opportunity to go for a run in the early morning haze and bustle of downtown. I wanted to run along the lake, clear my head, and burn off a hearty dinner from the night before.

The run began well. I found the lake, and its breeze left a gentle mist on my face as I paced myself. Then I turned back to find coffee—perhaps the greatest of coffees—Intelligentsia. With my coffee in hand, I cautiously sipped and ran.

As I write this now, it seems ludicrous. Why run with coffee? It was not the best idea. But with caffeine coursing through my veins, I headed for the cupcakes. I ran and ran. Google Maps shouted directions. *Turn here. Turn there. Dodge taxi. Avoid nicely dressed folks who don't want a splash of my coffee.*

Then I realized the light overhead was gone. I was running through a tunnel. This can't be right. Wait? Where am I? How far is this cupcake boutique? Surely Google knows. I stopped. I tried to recalibrate my map app. My mind wandered as I paced, trying to find my bearings and strength. But once cell-tower reception was back, I found myself checking the fiber content on the cupcakes. Should my wife and I split one *or* should I get two for all this effort? Distracted, I tried to refocus and analyze the map. Then the texts started.

MANDY: "Daniel, our flight is in 90 minutes. Are you almost back to the hotel?"

With urgency I took off with the latest Google directions. No matter how far I ran or how many turns I made, the "how long to cupcakes" timer didn't budge. The texts increased in frequency, but my pride and shame kept me from texting back. Nearing exhaustion, I found the cupcake shop, ordered four cupcakes (lay off—there was a discount for four), swiped my credit card, trashed the coffee, and set off toward the hotel. I opened Google again, *but wait . . . what's the name of the hotel?*

MANDY: "Daniel, where are you? Are you lost? Come back. The hotel is at 33 W. Illinois St. We only have an hour before our flight!"

I was over a mile away and wiped out. Saved by grace and a rational, loving wife, I hailed a cab.

So let's start here: we are all lost in Chicago.

You are a church leader. And this means you're a sojourner on the road of leadership. As you look ahead, you can see that this road has many challenges. The journey will be difficult.

Maybe you're just starting out, fresh off your first internship. Now you're three months into your first church role. You are asking, "What is my identity? What will I do with this role? Who am I becoming as a leader? How do I handle this new responsibility I've been given? Wait a minute. *Am* I a leader? Around what person or organization or conviction should I organize my life?"[2] You've been in ministry just long enough to realize you never had a class on how to help your team see eye to eye. Managing conflict is one thing, but giving direction when you are discovering that your new team has major philosophical differences is another.

Maybe you've been in ministry for a while and you feel like you're moving from crisis to crisis—marriages failing one after another or a fellow minister and friend bailing on the faith. The number of funerals has caught up with the number of marriages. Your authority is increasing, but the creative juices that were there at the beginning are no longer there. You're asking, "How do I cope with the demands being made on me? How do I teach on being a great husband or dad when I'm short with my wife and yelling at my kids? Why am I so disappointed in others and myself? Am I making a difference? Am I making a contribution?" How do you process your own grief and limitations and still press on? Where do you find the motivation to keep leading week after week when you're so exhausted? You're realizing that the work rhythms that got you this far won't be able to sustain you as you move forward.

Maybe you're nearing the end of the road, and you're putting together a transition plan. You're asking, "Why is time moving so fast? Why don't I have the time to do all the things I want to do? When do I stop doing the things that have defined me?"

Too often ministers are lost on the road of leadership—wandering down streets they don't know and hoping not to be struck down by a motorist who is texting and driving.

Looking for Direction

Think about the last time you got lost. Maybe you were at a leadership conference looking for that elusive breakout session tucked away in a hidden corner. You're looking for room 217, and you've walked past 216 and 218 at least three times. Where could it be? One of our first inclinations when we're walking around lost is to look for someone to follow. You say to yourself, "He looks like he could be going to that breakout, and he's walking pretty confidently. I'll follow him—maybe not actually ask him for directions, but see where he's going."

When we're lost, we look for leaders. After all, they seem to know where they're going. The trouble is that as you look at other leaders, they all seem to be going in different directions.

We live in a world of pictures. People spend hours watching television and surfing the Internet. George Cladis has argued that this "flow of images across our brains is training our minds to think more in images than in words."[3] Whether we know it or not, we all have an image in our heads that drives our work as leaders. I argue that, more often than not, our image of leadership is adapted from the images of leadership we see around us. Like young children acting out the latest Disney movie as they play, we've followed after the culture and we don't even realize it.

There are five distinctive images of Christian leadership in the American church:

1. *The theologian.* He's a thinking man. His congregation sits eagerly and attentively to hear his nuanced insights about the Bible. He also has convictions of steel. His mantra: "Here I stand." You admire how his tribe knows what is right and stays committed to truth in the midst of a hostile culture. Back when you were in seminary, this was the person you aspired to be.[4]

2. *The innovator.* He's the young cutting-edge guy whose teaching is engaging and relevant. He doesn't just preach it. He lives a life of creative contextualization, effectively reaching others and doing the work of an evangelist. This leader always has new ideas for reaching his community, and they always seem to work.

3. *The activist.* She's the millennial dream packaged up as a professional minister.[5] Her rapidly growing nonprofit feeds the homeless, cares for crisis pregnancies, or wins prostitutes to Jesus. When you're tempted to become a complacent Christian, you hear her cry, "Take the hill!" Her passion is inspiring.[6]

4. *The good manager.* He's a business executive who could do anything but has decided to order his church like a well-oiled machine. His motto: "Get it done." Does your church have budget troubles? Marriages falling apart? Kids misbehaving? He has a discipleship program for that. Since you picked up a book called *Leadership Mosaic,* it's likely you're attracted to his team-based, collaborative approach. Do you have more business leadership books on your shelf than books on pastoral care? Maybe you could follow this organizational CEO.[7]

5. *The soulful leader.* She hasn't been to a conference in years, but everyone at the Christian retreat center knows her by name. Her prayer life is powerful. Her life is marked by radical transparency, deep vulnerability, and holy desire. Her constant prayer is "Abba Father, I trust you." You admire her, because she always seems to be at the pinnacle of emotional health.

These differing visions of leadership are all necessary within the church, but unfortunately they often compete for our devotion. It's easy to set them against one another and then choose the one we think is best—the convictional theologian against the soulful contemplative. Whenever we exaggerate one version of leadership, it crowds out the others. Soon we see there's something missing. The truth is we're still lost.

From Complicated to Complex

We're lost because the church-leadership world is complicated. How can a minister lead with truth, relational connection, a missional focus, solid management skill, and depth? We can't all be omnicompetent.

We're even more lost because the world we live in is changing. Researchers suggest that Christians in American are about to become a distinct minority group.[8] Church leaders—even really competent

Five Contemporary Images of Christian Leadership*

Theologian
All about: Truth

Conviction
Clear beliefs
Propositional/analytical thinking
Theological purity

Innovator
All about: Connection

Creativity
Relevance
Cultural engagement
Community contextualization

Activist
All about: Mission

Courage
Change
Visionary strategy
Social advancement

Good Manager
All about: Organization

Efficient collaboration
Process
Team-based strategy/management
Planning/structure

Soulful Leader
All about: Depth

Communion
Relationships
Contemplation/reflection
Emotional health

* Adapted from Gary Bredfeldt, *Great Leader, Great Teacher: Recovering the Biblical Vision for Leadership* (Chicago: Moody Press, 2006), 163.

ones—find themselves less and less in a position of power in society. We need more than greater competency to handle it all. We need a new way of thinking in a changing world.

Similar shifts are taking place in the worlds of science, business, and even warfare. Science has moved from the modern, reductive, and efficient ways of Newtonian physics to the complex, indeterminate, and integrated models of quantum mechanics. The business world has moved from scientific and bureaucratic management systems with clear, top-down authority and bottom-line results to systems of process and responsibility where minimum-wage workers are empow-

Strategic Paradigm Shifts

	Old-School Paradigms	*New-School Paradigms*
Science	*Newtonian thinking*: atomistic, fragmented, reductive, determinate	*Quantum thinking*: holistic, integrated, both–and, indeterminate
Business	*Scientific and bureaucratic management*: top-down authority, results-oriented, decisions made remotely, bullet-proof strategic plans	*Lean management*: empowerment, process-oriented, decisions made on the spot with facts, organic strategy based in contingency and systems theory
Military	*Modern military*: race for newest and mightiest technology, chess match for greatest efficiency, decisions made by the brass	*Counterinsurgency*: long duration of engagement that seeks to change hearts and minds in order to change the political situation, each unit empowered to create strategy

ered to stop the assembly line for the sake of quality control and safety. Even the military looks less like a top-down chess match. Nations now fight with counterinsurgency methods. The days of throwing money at problems or simply thinking technology will solve all the problems are coming to an end. Conducting business as usual in a way that lacks understanding and empathy or using merely complicated solutions to attack complex problems is no longer viable.[9]

What we learn from these changes is that leadership in the world today is more complex than it was before the information age. We've moved from a merely complicated world to a complex and unpredictable one. The difference between a complicated system and a complex one, according to General Stanley McChrystal, is akin to the difference between a car and ocean currents.[10] A car should work if all its parts are in working order. A failure of one part, like the fuel pump, has a predictable outcome: the car stalls. On the other hand, ocean currents can be so complex that, in one situation, the migration path of a pod of whales may change the direction or force of a current, and in another situation, the same pod will change nothing. The number of factors is so vast and their interactions so complex that any prediction is defied.

Complexity and unpredictability can make a leader anxious. It's frustrating when old ways of leading stop working. What is a leader to do? Should we fight against the change or embrace it? Donella H. Meadows describes the tension we feel:

> There's something within the human mind that is attracted to straight lines and not curves, to whole numbers and not fractions, to uniformity and not diversity, and to certainties and not mystery. . . . Another part of us recognizes instinctively that nature designs in fractals, with intriguing detail on every scale from the microscopic to the macroscopic. That part of us makes Gothic cathedrals and Persian carpets, symphonies and novels, Mardi Gras costumes and artificial intelligence programs, all with embellishments almost as complex as the ones we find in the world around us.[11]

As our world increases in complexity, I believe that Christians should be on the leading edge of embracing and even celebrating this change. We cannot simply grow in our competency to fix predictable ministry problems. We need a new way of seeing. We need this paradigm shift because the complexity of the world is a witness to the complexity and greatness of our God.

God Is Our Master Image

An artist gathers together pieces of stone and glass. Each piece has a different shape and color. Slowly she arranges the pieces into a bigger picture—a *mosaic*—that gives shape and meaning to variegated tesserae. Some images—what George Cladis describes as controlling or master images—"can have a profound, though sometimes subtle, effect on how we perceive reality . . . an effect on how we order the world around us."[12] That's what we need. We need a master image that can provide a clear and practical critique of our own leadership journey and the competing contemporary visions of Christian leadership.

But we need even more. I gravitate toward studying leadership because I was born into a leadership crisis. My mom raised me by herself for the first nine years of my life. My father wasn't present. I grew up in a broken home, sandwiched between the suburbs of Orange County, California, and the barrio. All the chaos I experienced as a child has given me a burden for leadership in life, home, and church. But I wasn't able to put the complexity together on my own. I needed more than a master image to order my life around. I needed the Master.

Paul S. Fiddes writes, "A complex God is the most appropriate creator of a complex world."[13] In other words, a God-sized world needs God-centered leadership. When we look to the Bible, we shouldn't merely look for a theology of leadership. We must look for the Trinitarian God who leads.

Herman Bavinck was a theologian possessed with a God-sized vision of the world. This is what he wrote about the place of the Trinity in the Christian life:

> The thoughtful person places the doctrine of the Trinity in the very center of the full-orbed life of nature and mankind. The [Trinitarian] confession of the Christian is not an island in mid-ocean but a mountain-top overlooking the entire creation. And the task of the Christian theologian is to set forth clearly the great significance of God's revelation for (and the relation of that revelation to) the whole realm of existence. The mind of the Christian is not satisfied until every form of existence has been referred to the Triune God and until the confession of the Trinity has received the place of prominence in our thought and life.[14]

Our Trinitarian doctrine of God is not a mathematical formula we must solve in order to pass an orthodoxy test. That makes it sound like the Trinity is optional. Rather, God—in all of his complexity—must be the operating system for our lives and our leadership. Only he can empower us to lead meaningfully in every situation and circumstance. That's why the apostle Paul writes, "Be imitators of God" (Eph. 5:1).

But don't think this is merely our confession. It's a beautiful vision. The glory of this truth is that God has lived eternally in community. When he made mankind in his image, he invited every human person to participate in his mission and leadership in the world. Leadership at its source is relational and not merely functional. As Christians, we don't simply lead *like* God. We lead *with* God.

The Trinity, Our Mosaic

Persecution often forced early Christians into secrecy and seclusion. But when Constantine won control of the Roman Empire in the early fourth century AD, he eventually elevated Christianity to favored status. Soon Christian leadership began to build beautiful meeting places. By the end of the fourth century, Christians were adorning the walls, ceilings, and open aisles of their basilica-style buildings with the mosaic art form. At Santa Costanza in Rome, you will see mosaic depictions of cherubs gathering grapes and making wine. You can visit the Church of the Nativity in Bethlehem and find an original mosaic floor with geometric patterns in the Roman style. At the vaulted Tomb of Julii near the crypt below St. Peter's Basilica, you can find mosaics that tell the stories of the Good Shepherd with his sheep and Jonah and the great fish.

But those mosaics might never have been built if it hadn't been for a pastor in Alexandria whose enemies called him "the Black Dwarf." The pastor's name was Athanasius. Within the first decade of Constantine's rule, a young pastor by the name of Arius began teaching that the Son—Jesus—was a created being, not eternally divine. "If God is the cause of all," he argued, "then how can the Son, who received his being from the Father, be uncaused?" Arius was persuasive and popular. Many followed him. It seemed like the whole world would go astray. Athanasius dedicated his life to proving just how catastrophic Arius's teachings were for healthy Christian living.[15] "Our redemption isn't possible," he wrote, "unless Christ himself is eternal—the image of the eternal Father."[16]

To forge unity, Emperor Constantine gathered the contending parties and representatives from throughout the empire to a council in the city of Nicaea in 325. Standing alongside Athanasius was a mosaic of

Christian leaders who both articulated Trinitarian doctrine and modeled it in their unity and love for truth. Bishop Alexander represented the embattled old guard from the West. He'd endured bloody persecution under Emperor Gaius and slander in his own parish.[17] St. Nicholas—yes, indeed, *that* St. Nicholas—was part of a fiery contingent from the East. They were a diverse crew. Yet, in the end, they stood together with conviction and courage; out of more than three hundred representatives from churches throughout the world, only two bishops sided with Arius against the biblical and apostolic understanding of Jesus. Through the unity that emerged from this diversity came a beautiful and biblical affirmation of faith that developed over time into the Nicene Creed. The Arian heresy was defeated. Trinitarian orthodoxy had won the day.

The Council of Nicaea shows us that we need diverse personalities and leadership styles to contend for the faith. Like assorted pieces of rock and stone, leaders come in all shapes and sizes. If you're searching for a vision of leadership that encompasses the whole, it's easy to get lost. My prayer is that *Leadership Mosaic* will help you see how God holds all the diverse pieces together.

Leadership Mosaic is a fivefold vision of leadership rooted in five Trinitarian doctrines. The Trinity is our mosaic. The triune God himself, the Master, is our master image. In theological terms, we say that our God is transcendent and immanent. He's the God of the big picture and the God of the details. He allows us to see the beauty of the whole and the beauty in the pieces.

When we look to the Trinity, we find that God's mission transcends every cultural change and yet speaks to us immanently—in time, in place, in body. He is God over every leadership image in the Bible, in the culture around us, and even in our personal history.

He is the God who forms the church in his image. Church leaders don't simply have to compare themselves to one another or parrot the leadership images they see around them. We don't have to choose between being maverick parachurch leaders or sycophants in a megachurch system. We can find our vision of leadership by looking to God wherever we serve. His redemptive work in the world is the basis for understanding the nature and purpose of our leadership.[18] When we think of leadership, our first thought should be the triune God.

Just think. You have all kinds of leaders at your church. When the board meets, you have some guys who come in wired to lead as CEOs. Other guys—maybe staff members—think more pragmatically. Others are theologians. If you have seven different leaders, there are seven different family histories. There are seven different ways of viewing the world. And—whether we recognize it or not—there are probably seven thousand different principles driving their leadership. We don't have simple solutions that can cut through all of that complexity, but we know the One who can.

The goal of *Leadership Mosaic* is to dive deeper into the doctrine of God in order to understand how the Trinity—Father, Son, and Holy Spirit—*informs* and *transforms* our life as leaders. Leadership is knowing where people need to go and taking the initiative to get them there in God's way and by God's power.[19] God is our model for leadership because God the Father shows us where to go. Jesus has already taken the initiative to get us there. We have the power to join him because the Holy Spirit goes with us on our way.

I believe only the Trinity is big enough to address everything leadership involves. A pastor recently told me: "I have a robust theology over here and a robust ministry philosophy over there. But it's hard to see how they connect. There is only pixie dust in between." I believe God not only defines doctrine but also guides leadership. He is big enough to knit together our theology and our church budgets. He can join a leader's spiritual life and his strategic planning.

Leadership is knowing where people need to go and taking the initiative to get them there in God's way and by God's power.

Over this book's five chapters, I will unpack five perspectives on leadership. My goal isn't to compare and contrast them. Don't pick just one. Rather, I believe each of these leadership visions can be rooted and redeemed in our doctrine of God. The best leaders exemplify them all. The best teams are those where each of the strengths is present.

- First, *convictional leaders* embody their beliefs. Many leaders are blown and tossed around by the latest ministry fads. But when God speaks, he is always true to himself. We need conviction to listen to God's voice and get in line with what he says.
- Second, *creative leaders* imagine the way forward. God has a plan to take your leadership chaos and make it beautiful. He has given us imagination so we can inspire others to follow his redeemed vision for the future.
- Third, *courageous leaders* take risks. Since God has sent us and the Spirit empowers us, we can leave behind what hinders and step out in faith. We can move forward to meet the challenges within and the challenges ahead.
- Fourth, *collaborative leaders* empower others. They know that working with others is better than leading alone. God has created us for community. We need a team to grow, develop, and strengthen one another for bigger and better things.
- Finally, *contemplative leaders* are fully awake to God. For leadership to be sustainable over the long haul, we need communion. We must abide in God in order to encourage the hearts of those we lead.

Christian leader, are you lost? If you are, I have an invitation for you. Stop chasing simplistic and reductionistic leadership philosophies; instead taste and see that the Lord has a better way forward. Gaze with me—not merely at the diversity of leaders we find in the world but at the varying ways the triune God himself leads his people. Take a step back and take in his complexity. Behold him.

Now consider. Piece by piece, he's transforming you into his own image. Gazing at him is the pathway to growth. Beholding is the way to becoming. The big picture—the whole mosaic—for how we lead is found in him.

Leadership Mosaic

Leadership is	*This requires*
knowing where people need to go	a convictional leader, a creative leader,
and taking the initiative to get them there	a courageous leader,
in God's way and by God's power.	a collaborative leader, a contemplative leader.

Part 1

THEOLOGICAL VISION

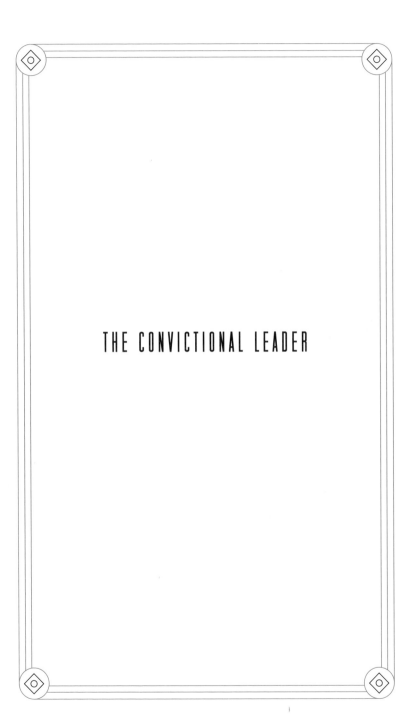

THE CONVICTIONAL LEADER

In the creation of the universe by the triune God lies the guarantee that nature also, as far as it extends, provides a trustworthy revelation of the being of God. It is not as if the natural revelation must lead to Unitarian results and then suddenly, in a totally unprepared fashion, the idea of the Trinity appears before us on the basis of God's supernatural revelation. The more and better we get to know nature, the more will we be brought face to face with the triune God.

Geerhardus Vos, *Reformed Dogmatics*

A purely mental life may be destructive if it leads us to substitute thought for life and ideas for action. The activity proper to man is not purely mental because man is not just a disembodied mind. Our destiny is to live out what we think, because unless we live what we know, we do not even know it. It is only by making our knowledge part of ourselves, through action, that we enter into the reality that is signified by our concepts.

Thomas Merton, *Thoughts on Solitude*

Behavior from important people in an organization, contrary to the vision, overwhelms all other forms of communication.

John Kotter, *Leading Change*

If a person does not become what he understands, he does not really understand it.

Søren Kierkegaard, *The Diary of Søren Kierkegaard*

Knowing and doing, hearing and obeying are integrally connected for people whose convictions are truly and deeply Christian.

Steven Garber, *The Fabric of Faithfulness*

Every man of humane convictions must decide on the protest that best suits his convictions, but we must all protest.

Martin Luther King Jr., "Beyond Vietnam"

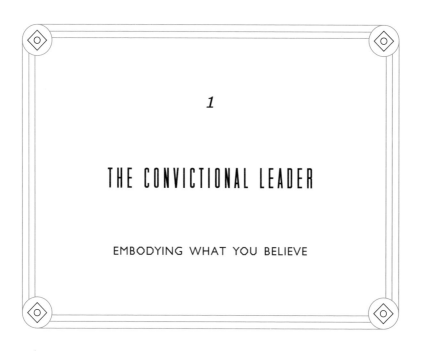

1

THE CONVICTIONAL LEADER

EMBODYING WHAT YOU BELIEVE

Summary: *We live in the information age, a world awash with data. Our culture believes that if we mine this data for the right solutions, we'll solve all the world's problems. But we don't necessarily need more information. We need God's revelation. Wisdom for leadership begins with the conviction that God speaks. He makes himself known through his world, Word, and works. Because the Father is sovereign over his world and the Son's salvation is revealed in his Word, we have a grid for understanding reality—in all its complexity and particularity. Because the Holy Spirit still works today, the first step for leaders is listening for God's voice. When a leader has heard from God, he can move beyond mere values to deep convictions felt in his heart and embodied in his life.*

In the first two weeks after the September 11, 2001, terrorist attacks, the FBI asked the nation to provide potential leads to the case; the response was an avalanche of information. Over 260,000 tips were received from concerned citizens via the Internet and phone calls in the first twenty-one days. As a result, approximately four thousand agents were reassigned nationwide to assist in chasing the new leads.[1] Within a matter of weeks, the FBI had to adjust from not having enough information to information overload.

In our age of technological advancements—faster processors, expanding memory, and wireless Internet—there has been an explosion of data and consumers with insatiable appetites for more. In 1971, the average American was targeted by at least 560 daily advertising messages. Twenty years later, that number had risen sixfold. From 1980 to 1990, there were nearly three thousand new magazine startups. By 2003, the Internet boasted three hundred million web pages.[2] *The New York Times* now contains more information than the average man or woman in seventeenth-century England was likely to come across in a lifetime,[3] and the paper doesn't print all that's written for its website. According to *Science Daily*, 90 percent of the world's data has been generated over the past two years.[4]

Let's be real. The information age has provided us with instant access to information, but there is more information than we can handle. In 2010, Basex, a technology watchdog group, conducted a survey of knowledge workers—those whose daily tasks focus on creating content, thought, and reflection, sharing knowledge, and networking.[5] Over 50 percent believed that the amount of information they were presented with each day was detrimental to productivity. Ninety-four percent of those surveyed had at some point felt overwhelmed by information to the point of incapacity. Researchers suggest that the stress of information fatigue causes weakened vision, high blood pressure, and heart disease.[6]

Solutionism

How should leaders respond to this info-glutted, fact-bogged world? Google, Amazon, and the other Internet-based companies in Silicon Valley have made an industry out of it. Order with one click and the newest book is at your door in two days—or on your device in seconds.

Search engines and Wikipedia are so popular because they help individuals make sense of the increasing mass of data (at least in theory). Technology has been so successful that Silicon Valley executives are now giddy about the potential for the future. Eric Schmidt, the executive chairman of Google has said: "In the future, people will spend less time trying to get technology to work . . . because it will just be seamless. It will just be there. The Web will be everything, and it will also be nothing. It will be like electricity. If we get this right, I believe we can fix all the world's problems."[7]

Schmidt is an optimist and a technological futurist. He believes tomorrow is bright. If you listen long enough to the tech companies' hopes and dreams, you might think that we can solve all of humanity's problems—obesity, insomnia, global warming, etc.—if we can just create the right apps. After all, tech companies like Google have plans for improving everything under the sun: politics, publishing, cooking, and even garbage collection. The need to fix things runs high.[8] Evgeny Morozov, author of *To Save Everything, Click Here*, observes that "'Fitter, happier, more productive'—the refreshingly depressive motto of the popular Radiohead recording from the mid-1990s, would make for an apt welcome sign in the corporate headquarters of [Silicon Valley's] many digital mavens."[9]

Morozov has a name for the tech sector's utopian ideology. He calls it *solutionism*.[10] He explains:

> I borrow this unabashedly pejorative term from the world of architecture and urban planning, where it has come to refer to an unhealthy preoccupation with sexy, monumental, and narrow-minded solutions—the kind of stuff that wows audiences at TED Conferences—to problems that are extremely complex, fluid, and contentious. These are the kinds of problems that, on careful examination, do not have to be defined in the singular and all-encompassing ways that "solutionists" have defined them.[11]

Solutionists see new ideas as culturally neutral. "What works in Palo Alto is assumed to work in Penang," Morozov observes.[12] But

The Trouble with Solutionism

Solutionism recasts the complexities of the human condition in terms of neatly defined problems with definite, computable solutions.

- Solutionism is *reductionistic*. It oversimplifies.
- Solutionism is an *abstraction*. It's divorced from reality.

solutions crafted for one context can rarely be abstracted for another without careful adjustments. The trouble with solutionism is not the solutions themselves so much as this inattention to the complexity of the human plight. It's reductionistic. Solutionists oversimplify the world's brokenness. "Solutionism presumes rather than investigates the problems that it is trying to solve, reaching 'for the answer before the questions have been fully asked.'"[13]

In a world awash with data, it's easy to think that if we mine the information for the right solutions, we'll solve all the world's problems. But we don't simply need more information or more solutions. We need God's revelation. Wisdom for leadership begins with the conviction that God speaks. God makes himself known through his world, Word, and works. Because the Father is sovereign over the world, and salvation through the Son is revealed in his Word, we have a better grid for understanding reality—in all its complexity and particularity. When a leader has heard from God, he can move beyond quick solutions to deep convictions that are felt in his heart and embodied in his life.

Knowing, Being, Doing: From Values to Conviction

As vulnerable as Silicon Valley's solutionism is to critique, we must admit modern evangelical Christianity isn't all that different. Methodological pragmatism focuses churches and missionary enterprises on "what works"—that is, programs and initiatives that yield immediate results—rather than on faithfulness to God's Word.[14] Consultants have told our church leadership team that to grow we should narrow our focus to a few key ministries—worship music, preaching, and families. It sounds like a slick pathway to success, but following their advice would mean shutting down our ministries to the poor or our focus on international missions. In reality, that "solution" skirts God's commands to look after orphans and widows (James 1:27) or go into the whole world to preach the gospel (Matt. 28:18–20).

Leaders typically express their wants and needs and those of their followers as *shared values*. They use values to measure and assess the goals and outcomes they're seeking to achieve.[15] Shared values are helpful for charting an organization's direction. "The clearer you are about your values, the easier it is for you and for everyone else to stay on the chosen path and commit to it."[16] This kind of guidance is especially needed in difficult and uncertain times. Shared values broker partnerships and unify teams.

But values aren't enough. Gene Wood and Daniel Harkavy remind us that one reason we hear so much about values today in the church is that Christian leadership has borrowed so heavily from the business model. Every business has values, but *no* business has convictions. R. Albert Mohler defines convictions as those "foundational beliefs that shape who we are and establish our beliefs about everything else."[17] A value is something to which you will commit, but conviction is a belief you'll sacrifice for. With values, you count the cost, but with convictions, no cost is too great. Values are negotiable, but convictions are nonnegotiable. We could adopt the Bible, the gospel, and excellence as values and find healthy direction for our church, but those values aren't equal. I'll die for the authority of God's Word. I'll take a bullet for the cross of Christ. But if our pursuit of excellence falters because the PowerPoint doesn't work on Sunday or the children's ministry runs out of goldfish crackers, I'm just going to get over it. A business's values may be high and lofty, but convictions are the sole domain of religion. Believers discover what is right and wrong from sacred revelation, and that is not subject to change.[18]

Sojourn Community Church's Midtown campus, where I pastor, is located in Shelby Park, one of Louisville's historic neighborhoods. The

Values versus Convictions

Values	*Convictions*
I will commit to.	I will sacrifice for.
I will contemplate the cost of.	No cost is too great for.
Are negotiable.	Are nonnegotiable.
Last for a season.	Last for a lifetime.
Can be changed by vote.	Cannot easily be changed.
Allow for external compliance.	Require internal ownership.

area has a rich history and a beautiful sixteen-acre park. But in recent decades, the average household income has fallen to less than twenty thousand dollars per year. Most houses are more than a hundred years old, and many need repair; some have been abandoned. Jobs are scarce, along with quality education and alternative activities for children.[19]

Church plants and mercy ministries are increasingly popular in inner-city contexts, but the difficulties often overwhelm many well-meaning Christians. Some churches have great hopes of change but lack wisdom and experience. It's easy to burn out and become disillusioned. Being in Shelby Park is both challenging and exciting. We thank God for locating us in this place. Sojourn's Pastor of Community Development, Nathan Ivey, tells the story this way:

> Early on we did a lot of listening. We started prayer walking and listening to God. We joined our neighborhood association, met business leaders, and interviewed government officials. We listened, and then we loved. We chose 30 needs we could address and commissioned our small groups into the neighborhood. We filled up hundreds of bags of trash, washed more cars and dogs than we can remember, cleaned gutters, raked leaves, and washed windows. The key was simple: Word-

and-deed ministry. We didn't have a budget, but we didn't need one. What we needed and what God provided was a desire to reach our neighborhood with the gospel. We've been faithful, and we've kept at it. Today, relationships that began eight years ago have led to conversions and ministries that now address basic needs, medical care, affordable housing, economic development, and leadership training.

What keeps us here? Pastor Nathan explains: "It began with the conviction that God commands us, the gospel compels us, and the Holy Spirit empowers us to go, show, and proclaim the love of God among the poor and vulnerable."

Convictional leaders have moved from values to deeply held convictions. And they go one crucial step farther. *Convictional leaders embody their beliefs.* They live them out. Leaders like Simon Sinek tell us leadership begins with knowing *why* we do what we do.[20] Leaders like Esther Lightcap Meek tell us leadership is all about character—*who we are.*[21] The time management experts will convince us that great leadership is about how much you can accomplish—*what we do.*[22] In truth, effective leadership embodies all three. Convictional leaders consider why they do what they do, they know the importance of character, and they are passionate about acting on their convictions. It's not enough to know the right answers. It's more than being the right kind of person. Conviction requires a threefold dynamic—*knowing, being,* and *doing.*[23]

When a Christian leader sits under God's Word and it cuts her to the heart, she is changed and moved to live out her belief. The prophet Jeremiah described it this way:

> But if I say, "I will not mention his word
> or speak anymore in his name,"
> his word is in my heart like a fire,
> a fire shut up in my bones.
> I am weary of holding it in;
> indeed, I cannot. (Jer. 20:9 NIV)

The truth God spoke to the prophet wasn't merely a value. Values don't burn inside our hearts. Truths believed and embodied are convictions.

Leadership Vision 1: The Convictional Leader

Convictional leaders embody their beliefs.

Convictional leadership requires . . .	*With . . .*	*With an effect upon . . .*
Knowing	Your head	Your outlook and intellect
Being	Your heart	Your attitude and emotions
Doing	Your hands	Your actions and relationships

Mohler says, "Convictions are not merely beliefs we hold; they are those beliefs that hold us in their grip."[24]

We may know what to say, but if it hasn't changed the way we live, then we're not convictional leaders. When we are captured by God's love, he moves us beyond merely *knowing* information. God changes our very *being* and empowers us for *doing* his mission. In Acts 1:8, Jesus tells his disciples, "But you will receive power when the Holy Spirit has come upon you, and you will be my witnesses in Jerusalem and in all Judea and Samaria, and to the end of the earth." The Holy Spirit changes who we are and moves us to action. He doesn't merely reveal more information about God. We come to know him, and he changes the way we live.

The Father's Sovereignty: From Information to Revelation

Sadly, Christian teaching can become nothing more than repetition of dry information. When that happens, leaders fall into the trap of presenting abstract concepts, disconnected from daily life: "If you husbands lead like Christ and she follows like the church, then your marriage will be a beautiful picture!" But how does this help the husband whose wife says, "Nope, I'm not in the mood, baby"? How does

Trinitarian Doctrine 1: Revelation

The Father's Sovereignty

The Son's Authority   The Spirit's Ministry

In his revelation, God speaks. He makes himself known through his world, Word, and works:*

- The Father's sovereignty over his *world*
- The Son's authority by his *Word*
- The Spirit's ministry, his particularizing *work*

* Adapted from John M. Frame, *Systematic Theology: An Introduction to Christian Belief* (Phillipsburg, NJ: P&R, 2013), 519ff.

this help the wife who grew up in an abusive household and struggles to trust any man? What does leading like Christ and following like the church even *mean* in real life? A conversation guide for couples and a list of sacrificial date night ideas may not sound particularly spiritual, but they help by making meaningful connections to daily life. We can have the right answers, but if those answers remain fluffy abstractions and not concrete practices, they have no power.

We don't need more information. We need to practice what we preach. God is inviting you out of the library where you have control over simple solutions. He wants you to come outside into the complexity and reality of his world and his Word. Convictional leaders hear from God and have power to live out what he says. So to understand conviction, we must begin with the doctrine of revelation.

When God speaks through his world, we call this *general revela-*

tion or *common grace*. General revelation is "the knowledge of God's existence, character, and moral law that comes through creation to all humanity."[25] David sang about this truth:

> The heavens declare the glory of God,
> and the sky above proclaims his handiwork. (Ps. 19:1)

But "general" revelation is a pretty boring name for it, because there's nothing general or common about how God speaks through his world.[26] Maybe we should call it awesome revelation—or even outrageous revelation! God speaks through the heavens above us and nature around us so that his presence is plain to us, even if we reject him (Rom. 1:19–21). God speaks through our consciences so that what God requires is written on our hearts (Rom. 2:14–15).

In fact, life in the world is intelligible to us because the Father speaks through what he has made. When Paul spoke to the Athenian philosophers, he explained it this way:

> The God who made the world and everything in it is the Lord of heaven and earth.... He himself gives everyone life and breath and everything else. From one man he made all the nations, that they should inhabit the whole earth; and he marked out their appointed times in history and the boundaries of their lands. God did this so that they would seek him and perhaps reach out for him and find him, though he is not far from any one of us. "For in him we live and move and have our being." As some of your own poets have said, "We are his offspring." (Acts 17:24–28 NIV)

We can learn about God's world and grow to know more about God through living in the world, because God has created a world where knowing is possible. God created us for a relationship with his world—"He made all the nations, that they should inhabit the whole earth" (Acts 17:26 NIV). He created us for a relationship with him—"that we would seek him and perhaps reach out for him and find him" (Acts 17:27 NIV). We have an epistemology—a doctrine of *knowing*—precisely because of our doctrines of creation, humanity, and *imago Dei*. Colin Gunton says, "There can be revelation because the world is so made that it may be known."[27] Every insight is under God's sovereign control—part of his incredible work of revelation. We are able to know because God has made us to know.

Sometimes, a sense of wonder and curiosity about the Father's world doesn't mark the lives of Christians. Even if someone is thirsty for the wisdom of general revelation, they aren't sure how to connect their curiosity with their Christianity. You might have a Christian medical student who is fascinated by the human cardiovascular system—and she wonders how her thirst for learning about capillaries and arteries can possibly connect with her faith. Another individual may love the structures and storylines of novels, but he feels a sense of shame because he is interested in something that seems so "secular." Is he making his passion for literature into an idol? No. Our passion to know more should never be a source of shame. We long to know because we've been created to know God and his world.

This is our Father's world. When God speaks in his world, he speaks as the King. God speaks as the one who is sovereign over history, culture, and leadership. Moreover, God—as Abraham Kuyper reminds us—delegates sovereignty in particular "spheres" such as the society, state, and church. But God rules it all. The determinative principle for our lives, our leadership, and our learning is "the Sovereignty of the Triune God over the whole Cosmos."[28] God is not just King over our spiritual lives. He is King of *every* sphere.

That truth alters a leader's posture toward so-called "secular" disciplines. Have you noticed how defensive Christian leaders can be? Have you noticed how we often choose sides before we understand an issue? The evangelical tribe I'm a part of has a tendency to be anxious and combative about anything we deem "secular."[29] We're worried that a naturalistic worldview has influenced our psychology and our politics and our music. But we're inconsistent. We don't have the same anxiety about the business principles that inform our leadership. How do we filter them? If we're honest, we don't even think about it most of the time. Don't misunderstand me. I'm not suggesting we take a defensive posture toward business principles. What I *am* suggesting is that we pay attention, with discernment, to everything that may help us lead. We must put into practice our belief that "this is our Father's world."

In Acts 17, Paul wasn't afraid to listen to (and even quote!) pagan philosophers like the Cretan Epimenides and the Cilician Stoic Aratus. Paul didn't quote the pagans uncritically; in fact, there's a good chance he was mocking the way that the philosophers of Athens appropriated these sources. But he knew what they had written, and he quoted them without apology. Paul's example should teach us to be attentive. Psychology, anthropology, biology, communications, and the world of business aren't off-limits. We shouldn't have a combative posture toward these other disciplines. As Donella Meadows states:

> In spite of what you majored in, or what the textbooks say, or what you think you're an expert at, follow a system wherever it leads. It will be sure to lead across traditional disciplinary lines. To understand that system, you will have to be able to learn from—while not being limited by—economists and chemists and psychologists and theologians. You will have to penetrate their jargons, integrate what they tell you, recognize what they can honestly see through their particular lenses, and discard the distortions that come from the narrowness and incompleteness of their lenses. They won't make it easy for you.[30]

Leaders in those fields know truth—not completely, not with an awareness of Christ as the one in whom all things hold together, but they have glimpsed some measure of truth. Wise leaders recognize and apply truth even when it comes from the lips of a pagan. As Gunton has said, "All truth is a species of revelation."[31] Read that again. Confidence should mark our posture toward learning, because everything there is to know belongs to our heavenly Dad. All truth is God's truth.

There is not one monolithic discipline of leadership. The streams of leadership in the world are many, moving, and changing. That's true for the political streams as well as for leadership in business.[32] But before we begin to explore leadership truth from those fields, we should confess God's sovereignty over them. God turns the king's heart like waters in his hand (Prov. 21:1). He holds all these streams. He's the Lord of government. He's sovereign over the businessman hustling sheep on the Ein Gedi plain, and he's sovereign over the businessman sculpting the latest skyscraper in Dubai. He's the Lord of trade.

Convictional leaders must pay attention—always listening for God's voice in the world. When we hear something that rings true about the Father's world in the voice of an economist or community leader, our ears should perk up. That truth was revealed by God's common grace. As Kuyper declared, "No single piece of our mental world is to be hermetically sealed off from the rest, and there is not a square inch in the whole domain of our human existence over which Christ, who is Sovereign over *all*, does not cry: 'Mine!'"[33] That's right. The Pulitzer is God's. Quantum mechanics is God's. There is not a square inch of knowledge that doesn't belong to God.

The Son's Authority: From Mastery to Mystery

It's humbling. We'll never know everything God could reveal to us. But it's also inspiring; a robust doctrine of revelation frees us from thinking we have to master all truth. Thank God we don't have to group and utilize all of the world's information. God wants to move us from the drudgery of mastering it all to the joy of mystery—the joy of discovery. This is the difference between studying a novel for a test and enjoying a novel with a friend. You don't have to memorize every player's stats to appreciate a good baseball game. You don't need to know astrophysics to gaze in wonder at the stars. And you don't have to master theology in order to know God and enjoy him. You only need to live in his world with listening ears.

Has your leadership journey become drudgery? Try reading about and exploring God's world outside the disciplines you typically study. Stray away from theology and ministry books for just a bit. Put down the commentaries for a day or two. Do you like film? Pick up a book on cinematography. Do you like football? Pick up Mark Schlabach's captivating biography of John Heisman.[34] Read about business or cultural anthropology. But don't be surprised if exploring the world raises questions that drive you back to the Bible and deeper into the mystery of leadership. It should.

Theology is the queen of the sciences because the Bible is our authority.[35] Where do we learn to live life in God's world? Where do we learn to love, trust, and obey God? We learn this in the Bible (Ps. 119:11, 104–5). Paul tells us, "All Scripture is breathed out by God and profitable for teaching, for reproof, for correction, and for training in righteousness, that the man of God may be complete, equipped for *every* good work" (2 Tim. 3:16–17). The Bible is true. The Bible is inerrant. The Bible is our rule. The Bible is sufficient to equip God's people for all of life.

The most important thing about the Bible is that it tells us the story of Jesus (Luke 24:27). Jesus is the Lord of the Bible. He gives the Bible its authority. The Bible is not primarily a book of doctrines, a manual of theological answers for life's big questions. As Geerhardus Vos stated, "The Bible is not a dogmatic handbook but a historical book full of dramatic interest."[36] When we say that the Bible is sufficient, we don't mean that it teaches us everything God would have us know. What we mean is that it is sufficient for revealing Christ, and Jesus's story gives us our worldview, our lens for explaining life in God's world. The Scriptures are sufficient because, in their unity and clarity, they give us the big picture that helps us understand the big questions we have about life.[37] The Son's Word helps us look at the Father's world and live in it with sobriety, sanity, and skill.

When Christians feel anxious about "secular" learning and have a hostile posture toward the world, there's a fallacy you'll sometimes hear. It goes like this: "God's Word is authoritative and sufficient. So, we don't need any truth from the culture. We just need the Bible." But that completely misunderstands what theologians mean when we say the Bible is authoritative and sufficient. As John Frame states, "Scripture contains all the divine words needed for any aspect of human life."[38] John Piper explains it this way:

> The sufficiency of Scripture does not mean that the Scripture is all we need to live obediently. To be obedient in the sciences we need to read science and study nature. To be obedient in economics we need to read economics and observe the world of business. To be obedient in sports

we need to know the rules of the game. To be obedient in marriage we need to know the personality of our spouse. To be obedient as a pilot we need to know how to fly a plane. In other words, the Bible does not tell us all we need to know in order to be obedient stewards of this world.[39]

The Bible was never meant to be a manual for surgeons or auto repair. The Bible is not a book of leadership methods that, when implemented properly, will change the world. To the overly fundamentalist religious leaders in his own time, Jesus said, "You search the Scriptures because you think that in them you have eternal life; and it is they that bear witness about me" (John 5:39). The Pharisees knew the Old Testament inside and out. They had all the information, but couldn't see what was right in front of them. Those religious leaders wanted to have the Bible as a book of quick religious solutions. They didn't want the more complex and difficult answer—living in the Father's world with Jesus as their lens.

Let's confess our sins together. We want quick-fix answers for all the world's problems. Father, forgive us. We've reduced Christianity to a privatized religion for elite fixers. Christ, have mercy. We've adopted a form of spirituality that is abstracted from embodied life in the real world.[40] God, have mercy on us.

Unlike the faithless Pharisees, we do acknowledge Jesus's authority, but we construct our theology with solutionist proof texts.[41] We want a 140-character, Tweet-able gospel. We acknowledge biblical authority, but then we make the Word a manual of methods. We reach for answers before questions have been fully asked. We've assumed that doctrine is flatly revealed in the Bible with little difference in meaning between a first-century and twenty-first-century context—supposing that theological truth is culturally neutral. This assumption impacts our understanding of theological education, Bible translation, and church planting. We're unaware of our cultural bias—thinking that what works in Tennessee will also work in Thailand.

We look to the *professor* leader with his big library and quick answers, and we think he's the definition of biblical conviction. In reality, he's a distortion. Our Christian solutionism is dangerous, because, like the Silicon Valley version, it's permeated with a misplaced eschatological hope. The buzz about the latest conference, book, and blog is that they'll help us "reach up to the heavens." But that's not the message of the Bible. It's the message of Babel (cf. Gen. 11:4–7). We somehow think that knowing the right answers will bring the kingdom. We believe that having the right information will bring salvation. But while solutionism may work in principle, it fails in practice. Ministry doesn't function as simply as we hoped, so we just get angry, frustrated, and overwhelmed. Like the Pharisees, we think that life is about mastering the Bible. Convictional leaders haven't mastered the Bible. The Bible has mastered them.

The Bible gives us the storyline of redemptive history—a worldview complex enough to provide an explanation for all of reality. The Bible tells us that God made mankind in his image to reflect his nature and cultivate his rule in the world. It tells us that Adam and Eve rebelled against God and that human nature since their time has been hostile toward God and his ways. The Bible's story explains the world's great achievements and humanity's great atrocities. As Richard Lints says, "The Bible, in its form and its content, records the dramatic story of God reaching into human history and redeeming a people for himself."[42] And the Bible promises us that God the Son one day will return to restore our broken world. It's a story that explains our longing for a better future.

We can think about the Bible's storyline in terms of four movements: creation, fall, redemption, and consummation. Timothy Paul Jones writes, "For believers in Jesus Christ, the same old story of God's work in human history is what continually reveals the truth about our world and us. It is through this story that God forms, reforms, and transforms our lives."[43]

Imagine if your church or Christian ministry read the Bible differently. What if we began to view the world with a nuanced and flexible perspective—one that takes into account the complexity of reality? The Son's Word provides us with a worldview that allows us to incorporate business and sociological principles into our leadership with discern-

God's Storyline*

- *Creation.* God created the cosmos and positioned Adam and Eve as corulers under him to rule and care for his world (Gen. 1:26–31). By establishing limitations on humanity's choices, God demonstrated that he remained the sovereign ruler and King of the universe (Gen. 2:15–16).
- *Fall.* Adam and Eve sinned and ceased to subject themselves willingly to God's reign. God exiled the first family from Eden and revealed his plan to redeem and reign over humanity through the offspring of Eve (Gen. 3:15–24). The story of Israel is the story of God's preservation of the people through whom he would bring this royal seed into the world.
- *Redemption.* Through Jesus the Messiah and King, God broke the power of the curse that resulted from the fall and of the condemnation that came through the law (Gal. 3:10–14). Through his suffering on the cross, Jesus endured God's wrath in the place of sinful humanity (Rom. 5:9–11). Through his resurrection on the third day, Jesus demonstrated his royal triumph over death—a triumph that, though already real and true, will not be fully realized or recognized until the end of time (1 Cor. 15:20–28).
- *Consummation.* In his own time and way, God will consummate the reign that Jesus Christ, the "King of kings" (Rev. 19:16), has already inaugurated. The city of God will descend to earth. God himself will dwell among his people and make all things new (Rev. 21:1–5).

* Timothy Paul Jones, *Family Ministry Field Guide: How Your Church Can Equip Parents to Make Disciples* (Indianapolis: Wesleyan, 2011), 72.

ment. It gives us the lens to see what is wheat and what is chaff. Let's think about leadership in light of the biblical storyline:

Where do we see evidence of God's *creation* in leadership? The world of leadership has God's creative fingerprints all over it. Historically, leadership has developed through two streams—community and commerce.[44] These are gifts we can trace back to the garden. When God said, "Let us make man in our image," he was creating the first man and woman for community (Gen. 1:26–27). When God placed the man in the garden to work and take care of it (Gen. 2:15), he made him a worker and gave him a vocation. Rick Langer observes, "Leading is normal human activity."[45] God ordained people to rule the created order. At times that includes leading other people to accomplish God's purposes. Where do we see evidence of the *fall* in leadership? Everywhere. People use their gifts of leadership to pursue money, power, and sex. That's why we have to lock up CEOs for insider trading. That's why politicians are always apologizing for scandals. And that's why pastors are constantly being fired or dividing churches. This is the corrupting world system John warned us against—the lust of the flesh, the lust of the eyes, and the pride of life (1 John 2:15–17). The gifts of leadership are given by God to enable us to be stewards. We must reject all forms of leadership that seek to exploit the creation and other people in it for personal gain.[46]

Where do we see evidence of *redemption* in leadership? For one thing, we should see that leadership itself is a grace. God makes leaders. God gives leadership. Further, we must see that God sends leaders with a purpose. He sends them to change or alter conditions that are not pleasing to him, whether that is, as Langer states, "slavery in Egypt or slothfulness in Crete (Ex. 3:7–9; Titus 1:5, 12–13)." That's why God sent Jesus. At the climax of the Bible's storyline, God entered into the broken human culture. He made paraplegics walk and made the blind to see. He met real human needs in their embodied expressions. He gave up his life as a bodily sacrifice for sins so the Father's purpose to justify for himself a people and the creation might be fulfilled.[47]

Where do we see evidence of *consummation* in leadership? Leadership has a goal. All great leadership shines a light ahead to God's ultimate purposes. We know this. Preachers are called to lift the eyes of their congregation toward their final calling and destiny. Leaders move their congregation toward substantial change today with hope for final transformation on the horizon.

The Spirit's Work: From "Finding Your Voice" to Hearing the Voice of God

Lack of clarity is a great downfall for a leader. A recent study shows that clear communication makes a leader 40 percent more effective. A leader is perceived to be more credible when he is clear about his most "deeply held beliefs—the values, standards, ethics, and ideals—that drive him."[48] In other words, before you can become a credible leader, you must find your voice. This requires knowing what you care most about, what defines you, and what makes you who you are.[49]

Christian leaders, before we can find our own voice, we need to hear the voice of God. So the first and most important leadership skill we need to learn is the skill of listening—listening for God's voice.

Listening

Listening is seeking to hear and understand God's voice in his world, Word, and works.

- *This does involve listening to our inner self.* We hear God speak through our consciences. We're embodied beings, so although his voice is dampened by our sin, we can even hear God speak in our longings and desires.
- *Beyond ourselves, we listen to God speak in nature,* in its beauty and its brokenness. Creation's glory echoes God's glory. We hear his greatness in the mountains' grandeur, and we taste his richness in a glass of wine. We hear God speak in the midst of loss and disability. The Father's world cries out for redemption. We hear his voice through the world's praises and laments.
- *We listen for God's truth in the world,* believing that he has revealed himself to all people by common grace. We can listen to the world of psychology, medicine, and sociology for evidence of his voice. God is speaking even there.
- *We listen for the Holy Spirit as he speaks through the church.* God's voice sharpens us when God's people confront our sin. We hear his voice encourage us as we listen to testimonies about how God is at work in people's lives. We're built up as we hear his wisdom sung in psalms, hymns, and spiritual songs.
- *We listen for the Holy Spirit as he prompts our hearts,* convicting us of our sin and our preconceived notions about life and leadership. We hear his voice in our inward groaning. He speaks for us even when we don't know what to pray for.
- *Most importantly, the Holy Spirit illumines our understanding of the Bible.* He gives us understanding and convicts us that what God says in his Word is true.[50]

We listen for God's voice in the world. We listen to our inner self. We hear God speak through our consciences. We're embodied beings, so although his voice is dampened by our sin, we can even hear God speak in our longings and desires. Beyond ourselves, we listen to God speak in nature, in its beauty and its brokenness. The glory of creation echoes God's glory. We hear his greatness in the mountains' grandeur, and we taste his richness in a great feast. We hear God speak in the midst of loss and disability. The Father's world cries out for redemption. We hear his voice speaking through the world's praises and laments. We believe that God has revealed himself to all people by common grace. We can listen to the world of government and business for truth about leadership, because God is speaking even there.

Most importantly, we listen for God's voice in his Word. The biblical storyline doesn't just provide us with a framework for understanding leadership in general. The story provides the lens for helping us live our personal leadership story as well. Redemptive history intersects with our personal history.

Listening for God's voice in his world is hard for us, because as leaders (and sinners) we like to hear ourselves talk. Listening requires our silence. We must quiet our expectations and try to hear others speak. We must quiet our hearts. I need to soothe the anxiety I feel when I'm trying to have quiet time but feel like I'm not getting enough done. We must listen well if we're going to hear God's voice in the noise.

Listening for God's voice in his Word is also hard, because the Bible judges our leadership. It exposes our arrogance, our greed, and our lust for power.[51] It shows us where we've reduced God's truth. It shows us where we've disconnected truth from reality and where we've failed to put it into practice. We need to stand under God's authoritative Word, and we need to receive the wounds it brings. Richard Lints puts it like this: "God's voice seems strange to us, different. It has a haunting ring to it. Its redemptive quality is paradoxically wrapped in clothes of judgment. The voice reveals God and it reveals us—only too painfully."[52]

Listening for God's voice is also hard because one of the consequences

of sin is that it has darkened our ability to understand (Rom. 1:21).
Abraham Kuyper dedicates an entire chapter of his *Principles of Sacred Theology* to the topic of "Science and Sin." He tells us that sin's effects aren't limited to the sphere of our choices and will. Sin also affects our ability to perceive. We all must admit that our background, context, and experience affect our perspective on life. Our interests govern our outlook. As Kuyper says, "Everybody preaches for his own parish."[53] Self-interest darkens a person's ability to hear what his spouse is really saying. A leader's experience and perspective may prevent her from seeing an issue from her coworker's point of view. In the same way, we struggle to hear God's voice in his world and Word because our expectations cloud our ability to hear. Hoping the Bible will say one thing, I am often disillusioned that it says something else. So I interpret it to mean something that was never intended. I listen but I'm not really listening.[54]

Listening is hard for us because we're bad at loving. We listen best to what we love the most. Lints says, "Our knowledge of God is impoverished to the extent that he is not always our first love."[55] Kuyper explains it this way: "A friend of children understands the child and the child life. A lover of animals understands the life of the animal. In order to study nature in its material operations, you must love her. Without this inclination and desire toward the object of your study, you do not advance an inch."[56]

Thankfully, the Bible gives hope to bad listeners and bad leaders. "Hope resides in the conviction that God has not left himself without a witness in our lives."[57] That witness is the Holy Spirit. Jesus tells us that the Father sends the Spirit in order to "bring to your remembrance all that I have said to you" (John 14:26). One of the first works of the Holy Spirit is to help us hear God's voice. He gives us understanding about what God has spoken.[58]

The Holy Spirit helps us hear God's voice because he warms our hearts toward God and helps us love him. He clarifies our convictions as our thoughts, words, and deeds are captivated and captured by his love.[59]

Convictional Leaders Model the Way

In November 2006, Sojourn moved into its first building. We called it the 930 Art Center. The renovated public school housed our church offices, gathering place, and children's ministry area. But we also saw the building as a community center. For our first few years there, the 930 operated a public gallery space for local artists and a music venue for local independent music artists. Our dreams and ambitions soared at the beginning. We wanted to break down the false divide between the secular and the sacred. We wanted to create natural connections between our church and our neighbors. We wanted to inspire curiosity about God's world and celebrate whatever was worth celebrating. We wanted to serve artists at various stages in their pursuits and meet their needs. Our mission statement described all this as "a shared space where people of various backgrounds and beliefs could come together for a shared vision of a more beautiful world." Sometimes these good desires found fulfillment. Sojourn's Director of Arts and Culture, Michael Winters, described it this way:

> I'd like to think that occasionally, as people tried to make sense of why a church would host something like a giant cardboard fighter jet kissing a goose, or a concert by rough-around-the-edges bands like Shellac, their curiosity turned into a little bit of awe. One time, I remember watching a guy across the room in the glow of concert lights. He had gone through addiction, a divorce, and a dissatisfied relationship with another church. The previous church was strict, serious, and ungracious. Now, he was new to our church. His eyes lit up in the glory of live rock and roll, wonderfully confused at how this could be happening in a church, a church he would soon call "his" church. I doubt he'd credit that show as the reason he committed to our church community, but I'm sure it played a part. It made a qualitative difference. On some nights, the mixture of song and light and laughter was really beautiful.[60]

But in April 2008, a little over two years into the space, our vision began to crash. An article in a local paper opened with these words: "They're young, involved and socially aware—and they think being gay is a sin."[61] It was true. We hold to traditional biblical views on marriage and sexuality. These views have led to no shortage of public scorn and mockery, including a series of articles in the local press seeking to embarrass and shame us. It was painful. We couldn't see the implications of standing firm on what we believe when it was happening. But the bad press eventually threatened the financial sustainability of the 930 arts-and-community-center ministry and led to its end.

Painfully, we learned that having convictions sometimes means losing friends and letting go of some dreams.

Convictional leaders work hard to align their actions with God's voice even when there are consequences. Leaders must practice what they preach, because followers do what they see. Only when leaders embody and live out their foundational beliefs—only when they model the way—do they have credibility and integrity. As leadership scholars James M. Kouzes and Barry Z. Posner explain it:

> Words and deeds must be consistent. . . . Through their daily actions, [leaders] demonstrate their deep commitment to their beliefs and those of the organization. . . . "Leading by example is more effective than leading by command. If people see that you work hard while preaching hard work, they are more likely to follow you." One of the best ways to prove that something is important is by doing it yourself and setting an example.[62]

Convictional leaders embody their foundational beliefs. God speaks. We hear from him, and we want to hear more. We ask questions of God's Word and his world to help us understand. We listen for the Spirit and then we join his work. We test out God's truth and discover how it works. We grow in skill and then call others to follow us as we follow Christ.

Living out your convictions *will* mean opposition. You can ask the prophet Jeremiah just how much the fire in his bones got him into trouble. But a leader's character is forged as he lives in the Father's world under the Son's Word and as he listens to the Spirit. It's Martin Luther's classic paradigm: true knowledge is born out of trials. Luther

Leadership Skill Set 1: Listening and Living
Embodying what you believe requires . . .

- *Listening.* Seek to hear God's voice in order to clarify your convictions.
- *Living it out.* Practice what you preach, because people do what people see.

said, "I myself . . . am deeply indebted to my papists that through the devil's raging they have beaten, oppressed, and distressed me so much. That is to say, they have made a fairly good theologian of me."[63] Luther knew that true conviction—true theology—is born out of obedience to God in the midst of life's fire. Conviction isn't born simply out of reading books. True conviction is born when you are facing sexual temptations. It's born when you are tempted as a leader to be greedy and arrogant. Convictions are most clear when continuing to take a stand means losing some friends or church members.[64]

I've been at Sojourn Community Church for seventeen years. As we've had an impact locally, we've also had a growing influence regionally and nationally. People sometimes ask me, "When are you going to move on?" I think what they mean by that is "When are you going to move on to the conference circuit or to work for a denominational entity or network?" But I believe the best thing I can do is stay grounded in a local community and model the mission.

I believe that everything God says in his world, in the Word, and through his people matters. Everything has a place. All of God's revelation is important. How do I show it's importance? I must live it out. I must model the way. It doesn't mean much if I teach catechism to my kids but act cantankerously toward my neighbors. The best way for me to teach my kids about grace is to model grace. I don't come to know that a leader has passion for the lost through his programs or sermons. I see his passion for the lost in his presence with them over dinner laughing and engaging. I see it in the way he boldly speaks gospel truth even when he knows it won't be received. Leaders who live out their convictions gain credibility. Both philosophers and leadership experts confirm this reality. Søren Kierkegaard says, "If a person does not become what he understands, he does not really understand it."[65] John Kotter says, "Behavior from important people in an organization . . . overwhelms all other forms of communication."[66]

Conviction is essential because only a convictional leader can be followed with confidence. Until you are living out your core convictions, it's unlikely many will be inspired to follow you or sacrifice to make your leadership vision a reality.[67]

How about you? What do you believe? What are the truths that burn inside you? A conviction is a belief about which you are thoroughly convinced. It's a truth about which you can say, "I've heard from God." You stand on that truth, and you're willing to die for it.[68] What nonne-

Chapter Summary

Leadership begins with *knowing where people need to go*. The first part of direction is having the integrity and credibility to lead with *conviction*.

Leadership Vision	Trinitarian Doctrine	Leadership Skills
Convictional leaders embody what they believe.	**Revelation:** God speaks. He makes himself known through his world, Word, and works.	Embodying what you believe requires . . . • *Listening.* Seek to hear God's voice in order to clarify your convictions. • *Living it out.* Practice what you preach, because people do what people see.

gotiable convictions do you bring to the organization you lead? What are you willing to be fired for? What would you die for?

Have you heard God's voice? Do you believe that God has spoken a word for you? Now is the time to trust him and put your belief into practice. Don't just say you believe it. Practice what you preach. Be a convictional leader. Live it out. Model the way.

Exercises

Here is a selection of ideas and activities to help you practice the leadership vision discussed in this chapter. Pick out one or two and incorporate them into your regular leadership rhythms.[69]

1. Choose a quiet place. Stretch. Breathe deep. Sit in a comfortable position, then release your anxieties and task list to the Lord. Ask him to open your heart to his Word. Read Psalm 19. What feelings do you notice in yourself? Attend to what the Lord is saying to you about his Word.

2. Get out of your office and take a walk outside. The lilies and birds spoke to Jesus about God's care (Matt. 6:26–31). How is God speaking to you? Write it down.

3. Call a chaplain and then prayer-walk through the halls of a local hospital. What is God saying to you through those who are suffering and serving? Is God inviting you to any act of obedience?

4. Ask the members of your ministry team to reflect on their most deeply held convictions and priorities. Then meet together and share what you've come up with. Talk about how to better align your leadership with your foundational beliefs.

5. One of the best indicators of our level of integrity is our calendar. If you lack clarity about what is most important, you will find yourself making compulsive decisions about your schedule. Fill out a time log every day for a month. Categorize what you spend your time on and record the amount you spend in key categories (e.g., work, family, personal development, hobbies). After the month is over, evaluate the way you use your time in light of your stated priorities.

Prayer

Our only Father, humble us Mary-like before the cross of your Son, our Lord, Jesus of Nazareth, so that through the Spirit we may be joined in the one body, the church, thus becoming your one mighty prayer for the world. Gracious God, whose grace terrorizes and sustains us, we pray for courage as we begin this course. Invade our lives, robbing us of fear and envy so we might begin to trust one another and in the process discover a bit of the truth. In this serious business grant us the joy and humor that comes from your presence. And for your sake, save us from being dull. Amen.[70]

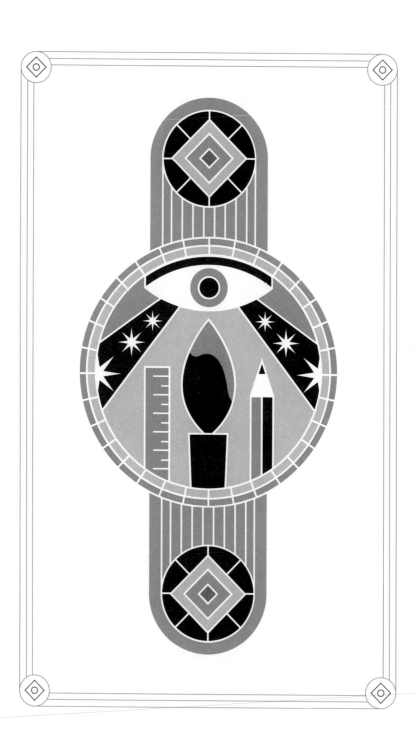

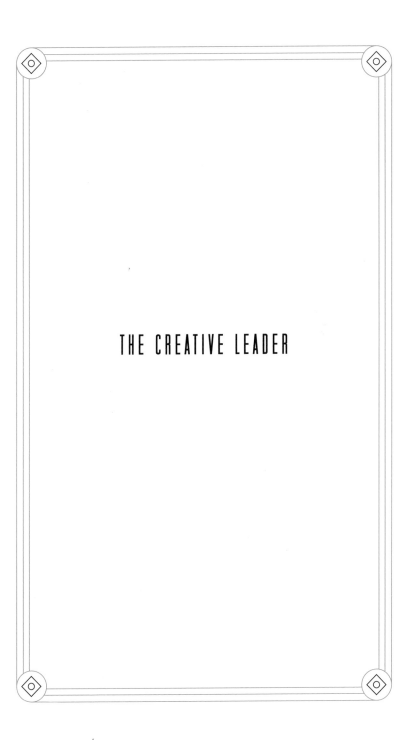

THE CREATIVE LEADER

There is much truth to the belief that creation everywhere displays to us vestiges of the Trinity. And because these vestiges are most clearly evident in "humanity," so that "human beings" may even be called "the image of the Trinity," "humanity" is driven from within to search out these vestiges.

Herman Bavinck, *God and Creation*

May I submit that if you deny your creativity, you suggest a deficiency in God's creation. The idea that only a gifted minority of human beings are creative is one of the most persistent and pernicious myths there is. It is totally false. Yet it dies with great difficulty.

Howard Hendricks, *Color Outside the Lines*

I have nothing to fear from other worldviews, because mine is bigger than all the others, containing their truths and filling in their blind spots. The Christian imagination is vaster than those that derive from narrow human frames of reference. The Christian imagination comprehends both the depths of human wretchedness and the heights of human greatness, the whole range of emotions from agony to joy, despair to ecstasy, the created universe in all of its order and its mystery. "All things are yours"! Because "you are Christ's"! Imagine that.

Gene Edward Veith Jr. and Matthew P. Ristuccia,
Imagination Redeemed

Unlike any other creature on this planet, human beings can learn and understand, without having experienced. They can think themselves into other people's places. . . . We do not need magic to transform the world, we carry all the power we need inside ourselves already: we have the power to imagine better.

J. K. Rowling, "The Fringe Benefits of Failure,
and the Importance of Imagination"

Eternal truths will be neither true nor eternal unless they have fresh meaning for every new social situation.

Franklin D. Roosevelt, convocation address,
University of Pennsylvania, September 1940

2

THE CREATIVE LEADER

IMAGINING THE WAY FORWARD

Summary: *You can be a person of deep conviction but still have no direction. In order to move forward, leaders need imagination to see the connections between their unchanging convictions and life in an ever-changing world. Creative leaders imagine the way forward. That's why we need God. God is the Creator. He has the best imagination. He created everything out of nothing at all. He sees the way forward through chaos and disorder like no one else. With God on our side, we see a brighter future for the communities where we lead, and we inspire others to join us as we pursue that God-given vision.*

What do you do when chaos breaks loose in a church board meeting? Are you tempted to quit or despair? Where do your emotions go when you're trying to navigate a budget crisis? How about when your small group ministry has gone sideways? In those moments of crisis, it's important to remember that the best things in life rise from the ashes of chaos and disorder.

Leaders see the dissonance between their convictions and reality. But the best leaders don't stop there. Even when they reach rock bottom, the best leaders are able to hold on to hope that beauty can rise. I recently heard Kevin Cawley, lead pastor of Redeemer Fellowship, Kansas City, say, "Creativity is born out of the gap between where things are and where they should be."[1] Creative leaders aren't delusional about the pain in their world, but they aren't stymied by it. They see trouble as opportunity. Creative leaders imagine the way forward. They see how their unchanging convictions can be worked out in an ever-changing world. Leadership scholar James MacGregor Burns says it this way: "At its simplest, creative leadership begins when a person imagines a state of affairs not presently existing."[2]

Leadership Vision 2: The Creative Leader
Creative leaders imagine the way forward.

When I think about imagination and creativity, I think about Steve Jobs, and I'm not alone. Avi Dan, a contributor to *Forbes*, writes, "To my mind, in the past 25 years no other company, not even Nike or Disney, has been as brilliantly and consistently creative as Apple."[3] In memorializing Jobs, Oracle founder and CEO, Larry Ellison, told *CBS This Morning* that Jobs was his "best friend for twenty-five years. He was brilliant. He was our Edison. He was our Picasso."[4]

Ellison's comparison of Jobs to Picasso is instructive. Picasso didn't do conventional art. Like Jobs, Picasso innovated and deviated from the norms of his day. Jobs was fond of the mantra "Good artists copy; great artists steal."[5] To copy is to do something exactly like somebody else. A good painter can copy, but that's not true creativity. Successful "stealing" is taking something and making it yours. "Stealing"—in the sense that Jobs was using the term—is when you take something and change it so much that it looks like it belongs to you.

Picasso and Jobs "stole" ideas in this good way—building on earlier and outside experiences to create radical innovations. Picasso blended influences from the ancient Iberian style and African style characters in order to create a new style of art—cubism. Jobs applied the very same creative process to revolutionize the field of computers. Long before his years at Apple, Jobs took a calligraphy course at Reed College because he enjoyed the beauty of art. "Reed College at that time offered perhaps the best calligraphy instruction in the country," Jobs told Stanford graduates in 2005:

> I learned about serif and san serif typefaces, about varying the amount of space between different letter combinations, about what makes great typography great. It was beautiful, historical, artistically subtle in a way that science can't capture, and I found it fascinating. . . . Ten years later, when we were designing the first Macintosh computer, it all came back to me. And we designed it all into the Mac. It was the first computer with beautiful typography.[6]

Jobs didn't walk passively through life. He was alert, making connections. He explains:

> Creativity is just connecting things. When you ask creative people how they did something, they feel a little guilty because they didn't really do it. They just saw something. It seemed obvious to them after a while. That's because they were able to connect experiences they've had and synthesize new things.[7]

Forbes contributor Carmine Gallo writes that when he was conducting his research for a book on the Apple Store retail model, he was surprised to learn that the inspiration for the Apple Store came directly from the Ritz-Carlton.

> Steve Jobs asked, "What can we learn from the hospitality industry and apply it to retail?" The next time you walk into an Apple Store,

you might want to notice the similarities. A "concierge" greets you at the door. You'll even find a bar at the back of the store—the Genius bar doesn't dispense alcohol like a hotel bar; it dispenses advice instead. A "good artist" would have copied another successful retail model. Steve Jobs, a "great artist," stole an idea from a completely different field.[8]

Leadership requires us to see beyond what's in front of us. In the spring of 2011, I sat on the front porch of our 930 Art Center building with a group of men after an elder meeting. I began to outline for them a creative vision for a sermon series on grace for the following fall. I talked to them about a new acrostic for the Reformed doctrines of grace—PROOF.[9] The premise of PROOF is that God's grace gives us a foundation on which to stand but, like strong drink, also makes us stagger in amazement. Jared Kennedy, our Pastor of Families at Sojourn Community Church, sat with us and took it in. A few weeks later, he left on a family trip to Disney World and began "stealing" PROOF:

On the classic *Pirates of the Caribbean* boat ride, the wax pirates are depicted in all of their buccaneer glory—drunk, burning villages, killing one another, stealing and carrying off women. It's not exactly the vision of manhood a pastor of families typically wants to put before his children. My young girls were a bit terrified. But there were young boys the same age celebrating these evil rum-guzzling scallywags. You can judge them *and* Disney if you want, but I saw something beautiful in it. In that moment, I sensed God say, "And that's how I've accepted you." I made an immediate connection to grace—grace enough to save a scallywag. I got up early the next morning and grabbed my journal. I wrote the words: "PROOF Pirates—grace enough to save a scallywag" at the top of the page and started doodling images to teach it below. We'd use a treasure map to teach about God's sovereign plan and a skeleton to teach about how God makes dead men walk. We'd talk about how Jesus is the anchor who keeps us forever. By that August sermon series, our children's ministry team hung a Jolly Roger in the children's hallway and put together a children's book / family devotional and a five-day curriculum.[10]

What's true about PROOF Pirates and Apple is that both Jared and Jobs are thieves. Their creation is not out of nothing. Jared stole PROOF from me. He stole the pirates from Walt Disney. Like Jobs with the Ritz-Carlton, Jared made connections and then inspired a team to build something that wasn't there before.

The Creative Process

The creative process is simple. Jobs teaches us that it begins with having *diverse experiences,* that is, getting out into and exploring the remarkable diversity of God's world. In order to be creative, I need the museum and I need the mountains. The choreographer Twyla Tharp teaches us, "Reading, conversation, environment, culture, heroes, mentors, nature—all are lottery tickets for creativity."[11] Tina Seelig, professor of creativity, innovation, and entrepreneurship at Stanford, says it simply: "Your knowledge provides the fuel for your imagination."[12] The next step, according to creative thinkers Eric Liu and Scott Noppe-Brandon, is *imagination.* They define imagination simply as "the capacity to conceive of *what is not*—something that, as far as we know, does not exist; or something that may exist but we simply cannot perceive."[13] Imagination is making connections between the experiences you've had and then seeing something that wasn't there before. J. K. Rowling says, "Imagination is . . . the uniquely human capacity to envision that which is not and therefore the fount of all invention and innovation."[14]

But imagination alone isn't creativity. Creativity is imagination applied.[15] Imagination is dreaming. It's a child picturing a tree with

What Is Imagination?

Imagination is the capacity people have to envision that which is not. It involves connecting experiences you've had in such a way that you see something that wasn't there before.

ostrich legs. Imagination is a pastor dreaming about a second service. For imagination to become creativity, it must be worked out. A child begins to create when she draws that tree with ostrich legs. Creativity involves that pastor creating the structures necessary to have that second service. Anne Kreamer writes, "Creativity requires both divergent thinking (the generation of fresh ideas) combined with convergent thinking (channeling those ideas into a practical solution)."[16] Imagination is MacGyver thinking up a way out of his latest jam. Creativity is grabbing the duct tape and disassembling a lighter.

Creativity

Creativity, simply put, is imagination applied.
The creative process involves . . .
Instruction → Integration → Improvisation

Creativity develops in three stages. We need basic *instruction* first. If someone's learning music, they first need to learn the keys, the notes, and the scales. Instruction in the basics gives a foundation for future learning. I teach my son about God's world and God's Word using a catechism. It gives him a basic language and worldview for future growth in biblical living.

The second stage is *integration*—making connections. With practice, a young musician moves beyond playing scales to reading music fluently. He doesn't have to stop and think anymore about where to put his fingers on the keys. We see this in biblical learning when a child begins to apply the truths he sees in the Scriptures or ask questions about how a Bible story relates to life.

The final stage of the creative process is *improvisation*. This should be our goal. Sometimes we want our kids to just obey what we've taught them. We want them to do what they're told. But if we only have that level of expectation for leaders, it just creates drones. A great musician has moved beyond competency. He doesn't just hit the right notes. He can play with style. I want something more for my kids too. I look forward to releasing them from our home to find their own way with the Holy Spirit.

Jazz and the Creative Process

"The popular misconception is that jazz players are untutored geniuses who play their instruments as if they are picking notes out of thin air. But studies of jazz have shown that the art is very complex—*the result of a relentless pursuit of learning and disciplined imagination*. It's that relentless pursuit and disciplined imagination, not simple genius, that allow jazz players to improvise—from the Latin *improvisus*, meaning 'not seen ahead of time'—and it's the improvisation that has become the defining hallmark of the art form." —Frank J. Barrett[*]

- *Instruction:* learning the basics. It's learning piano scales. Jazz players build a vocabulary of phrases and patterns by imitating, repeating, and memorizing the solos and phrases of the masters until they become part of their repertoire of "licks."[†]
- *Integration:* growing in experience and then making connections that weren't there before. It's like playing a song that you already know but playing it in a new arrangement or playing it for the first time with a friend. "After years of practicing and absorbing patterns, musicians recognize what phrases fit within different forms and the various options available within the constraints of different chords and songs. They study other players' thought and processes and learn to export materials from different contexts and vantage points, combining, extending, and varying the material, adding and changing notes, varying accents, and subtly shifting the contour of a memorized phrase."[‡]
- *Improvisation:* creating and finding my own way by putting newly imagined ideas into practice. It's like jamming with a jazz band and creating a new riff on the fly. "The goal of improvisation is to be mindful and creative, making up ideas on the spot that respond to what's happening in the moment."[§]

[*] Frank J. Barrett, *Yes to the Mess* (Boston: Harvard Business Review Press, 2012), 7.
[†] Ibid.
[‡] Ibid, 7–8.
[§] Ibid, 7.

The Myths of Creativity

Nowhere is there more confusion about leadership than in the area of creativity. Liu and Noppe-Brandon warn us that there are "paralyzingly prevalent" myths about creativity and imagination.[17]

The first is the myth of the *genius*. It says, "You either have it or you don't." This is for those of you who have read this far and are saying, "Yeah, but I'm not Steve Jobs." The myth of the creative genius implies, first, that some of us don't have an active imagination and, second, that whatever amount of imagination we may have is a fixed quantity and will never change. But if imagination is simply "the raw ability to conjure up a different reality,"[18] then those notions are demonstrably false. Imagination can be taught, instilled, and developed. Creativity *can* be cultivated. Tom and David Kelley tell us, "Creative confidence is like a muscle—it can be strengthened and nurtured through effort and experience."[19]

The second is the myth of the *artist*. It says, "Imagination is an unbounded mystery." This myth says that there is no real way to explain how imagination works. But that's an overly romantic notion. Liu and Noppe-Brandon observe that "people from all walks of life are habituated to saying that imagination is like intuition: a gut thing, beyond words and rational understanding."[20] Some go so far as to say that any constraints dampen creativity. It's not true. Though we may never know everything there is to know about imagination, we do know that the one who created our imaginations is a God of order. We may not be able to plumb the depths of creativity or explain every creative impulse, but anyone who has imagined a meal and then made a grocery list is framing and ordering their creativity. We can't reduce the creative process to an algorithm, but that doesn't mean we should throw up our hands.[21]

These myths blind us to our God-given creativity and to the joy of the creative process. According to Bruce Nussbaum, even some of the most talented people fail to recognize that what they do is indeed creative.

> They aren't seeing any bright light bulbs going off. They can't pinpoint any special moment when creativity "happened." I've heard of an en-

The Myths of Creativity

Subpoints adapted from *The Myths of Creativity*, by David Burkus:

The Genius: "You have it or you don't."

- "Creativity is merely a personality type." The myth says, "Creative types are born that way. You are creative or you aren't." But if creativity is simply the ability to make connections, it's a gift that every person can cultivate through disciplined work, preparation, and evaluation.
- "Creativity is for experts." The myth says that those with the deepest knowledge in a domain are most likely to have breakthrough ideas. In reality, a certain level of expertise leads to narrowed thinking and can even decrease creative output. The toughest problems are often solved by people at the edge of a domain, those with enough knowledge to contribute but enough ignorance to take innovative paths.

The Artist: "It's a mystery. It can't be bounded or understood."

- "Creativity requires complete originality." The myth says we come up with new ideas *ex nihilo*. But we're not God. If creativity is part of the *imago Dei*, creative leaders in every domain can learn—and "steal"—from a whole history of creative problem solving.
- "Creativity requires unbounded freedom." The myth says that creativity is dampened by constraints. In reality, order and boundaries fire creative energy. One example is the twelve-tone musical scale, which resulted in the greatest explosion of musical creativity in human history.

gineer working on an advanced jet engine—basically handcrafting a gigantic, complex, high-tech machine out of titanium, successfully boosting its efficiency by 20 percent—who failed to recognize that he's performing a creative activity. I've seen a student use a smartphone app technology to develop a whole new way for her Gen Y friends to experience art, and still not consider herself a creative person.[22]

Many who do see themselves as creative experience all kinds of anxiety about it. Studies have shown that people associate creative ideas with negative words like *agony, poison,* and even *vomit.*[23] It is especially true in the church. We're afraid that if we start being too creative theologically, we may all become heretics. The result is leaders who reject creative vision for predictability and conventionality and lose their joy along the way.

The biggest obstacle to creative leadership is a failure by the leader to recognize his or her own creativity. As Tharp tells us, "Creativity is not just for artists. It's for businesspeople looking for a new way to close a sale; it's for engineers trying to solve a problem; it's for parents who want their children to see the world in more than one way."[24] It's for ministers. Preachers need creativity to craft sermons week after week. Pastoral counselors need creativity to help others envision how Christ and his redemptive work connect to their struggles. It takes imagination to envision change for someone who has suffered through a lifetime of abuse. It takes creativity to help a man entrenched in sexual sin to see how his life could change.

Christian leaders need to put down the lies we've believed about creativity and put on the truth: We *are* creative. We create and imagine because we've been created in the image of the One from whom all creativity and imagination derives. A more robust doctrine of God the Creator will help us step into creative work with confidence and help us inspire others to embrace their God-given creativity as well.

The Greatest Creator

Far too often arguments about the age of the earth and modern science hijack our conversation about creation. But when God laid the foundations of the earth, the morning stars sang together and the angels shouted for joy (Job 38:4, 7). Christians believe that God is inherently outgoing and life-giving. God didn't need to create the world, but the Father, Son, and Spirit delighted to share their life, love, and joy.[25] One theologian writes, "Creation is a project—that is to say, it is made to go somewhere."[26] God was imagining the way forward. Just think about it:

God imagines. The triune God was there, before the beginning, abiding in love and dreaming the future into existence. We learn later, in Paul's letters, just how he delighted to share his inner life with us—the peace God gives when we pray far surpasses our limited understanding (Phil. 4:7); God delighted to fill us with his immeasurable love in Christ—to do more than we can ask or even imagine (Eph. 3:14–21); God's purposes for his people are beyond anything we would be able to draft or whiteboard (Rom. 11:33).[27] Before the foundations of the world, before the time came to fulfill his plans and dreams, God had pleasures and desires for us in Christ (Eph. 1:4–5).

God patiently hovers. He was full of desire, but God didn't rush it. The Bible tells us, "The earth was without form and void. . . . And the Spirit of God was *hovering* over the face of the waters" (Gen. 1:2). Troy Bronsink calls hovering "the posture of creative patience."[28] No sooner had creation begun than the Spirit slowed the process down to a crawl. God could have spun out the whole plan of redemption with one word, but he didn't. His pleasures and desires don't cook up in a microwave. The creation project took time. It unfolded bit-by-bit, day-by-day.[29] Part of the Holy Spirit's role in creation is to do the quiet detail work. Like a hovering dove or a nurturing mother, the Spirit hovers. He perfects and completes. He garnishes and beautifies.[30] Job 26:13 says, "By his breath [or Spirit] the skies became fair" (NIV). He gives ongoing life—sustaining the world God has made and making it fresh and fruitful (Pss. 33:6; 104:30; Isa. 32:15).

God acts. God didn't stop with a dream. He applied his imagination. God created every kind of place—the mountains, the rivers, the forests, the oceans. He created every kind of plant—trees, grass, bushes, the vegetables we eat, and the seaweed that grows under the ocean. He created every kind of animal—giraffes, butterflies, aardvarks, and stingrays. And he made you and me (Genesis 1–2). God spoke and his Word went out in the power of the Spirit. The Father creates through the Word (John 1:3). He accomplishes his creation work through the Son (Col. 1:15–16). That's how his dreams become a reality (Ps. 33:6; Heb. 11:3).

God holds it together. The New Testament tells us that God didn't merely make all things. He made them for a purpose. He made them for the Son. "All things were created through him and for him" (Col. 1:16). The Son gives the cosmos structure and coherence (Heb. 1:3).[31]

He gives shape and direction to the universe. He made all things. For his pleasure, they were created (Rev. 4:11). The heavens declare his greatness (Ps. 19:1), and history in its time will show his beauty (Eccles. 3:11).

God rests. God didn't need to stop. He was not exhausted by his creation work. But on the seventh day, God rested (Gen. 2:2–3; Ex. 20:8–11). And he taught that the rhythm of our work and creativity includes "stopping, setting down the brush, the drumsticks, the pen, the shovel, closing the laptop, finishing the sermon, and turning off the iPhone."[32] When God rested from creation, it didn't mean all his work was done. His redeeming and re-creating work continues (2 Cor. 5:17). But by modeling rest, God invites us to stop, receive what has been made as a gift of grace (Heb. 10:9–11), and see unfinished work as an opportunity to imagine and dream again another day.

In every stage, God's creation work is amazing. When we make things, we're like Steve Jobs and Picasso. We have to "steal." We use materials at hand. If you wanted to make a piece of artwork, you would take a blank piece of paper or a canvas. Then you would use acrylic, ink, watercolor, pencil, or maybe crayon to create something on that blank page. You might even cut out clippings from a magazine and use glue to paste them into a collage. But God didn't create that way. He didn't have any materials or supplies. God not only made everything; he alone creates *ex nihilo*. He made everything out of nothing at all. Catherine Vos sums it up nicely in *A Child's Story Bible*: "When a man builds a house, he must first have wood, nails, glass, and many other things. If he does not have something out of which to make it, he cannot build a house. But God made the world out of nothing at all."[33]

When we teach this to the kids in our children's ministry, we tell them to yell out something that they want to make, like a CAT! DOG! PIANO! RHINOCEROS! DUCK-BILLED PLATYPUS! After each ridiculous idea, we pause and look around to see if it has appeared. It never has. Only God can make something out of nothing. Do you realize that when God made a giraffe, there had never been one before? Not only did he make something from nothing with only his words, but

Trinitarian Doctrine 2: Creation

God made everything. His creation work is a purposeful project of love. God imagines and plans. The Spirit patiently hovers and garnishes the world with life. The Son accomplishes the Father's plan and holds all things together by the word of his power. And it is good. God is at rest with all he has made.

God imagines and plans. The triune God was there, before the beginning, abiding in love and dreaming the future into existence. Before the foundations of the world, before the time came to fulfill his plans and dreams, God had pleasures and desires for us in Christ (Eph. 1:4–5).

We imagine and plan. Our creativity begins with hopeful prayer, meditation, and brainstorms. Imagination means looking ahead beyond present reality and mapping out what is possible.

God patiently hovers. Part of the Holy Spirit's role in creation is to do the quiet detail work. He garnishes and beautifies. He gives ongoing life—sustaining the world God has made and making it fresh and fruitful (Pss. 33:6; 104:30; Isa. 32:15).

We patiently hover. Creative leaders call this an incubation period. We leave a margin between the time of sensing a problem and initiating a solution. Patience leaves room for awe and understanding. It gives time for nuance and detail.

God acts. God spoke and his Word went out in the power of the Spirit. The Father creates through the Word (John 1:3). He accomplishes his creation work through the Son (Col. 1:15–16). That's how his dreams become a reality (Ps. 33:6; Heb. 11:3).

We act. Creative leaders take risks. For us to become creative leaders, imagination must be cultivated. We must lay down our safety nets and step out. Because we sense God's presence, we can step out by faith to join him in his work.

God holds it together. God made all things with purpose. "All things were created through him and for him" (Col. 1:16). The Son gives the cosmos structure and coherence (Heb. 1:3). He gives shape and direction to the universe.

We reintegrate. We live in a time of great fragmentation. God invites us to entrust the materials we make, the time we invest, and the limited power and glory we hold to the larger whole of his purpose. He invites us to join ourselves to his creative project.

> *God rests.* In modeling rest, God invited us to stop, receive what has been made as a gift of grace (Heb. 10:9–11), and see unfinished work as an opportunity to imagine and dream again.

> *We rest.* The rhythm of our work and creativity includes stopping, finishing the sermon, and turning off the iPhone. God uses times of rest to teach us distance from and clarity of vision for our work.

also the things he makes are *completely* unique. There had never been a bear before God made the first bear. There had never been a human before God made the first human. God didn't need to have a wealth of experiences to make new connections. As Harold Best observes, "God is the first abstract artist."[34] God is the greatest creator. God imagines and plans. The Spirit patiently hovers and garnishes the world with life. The Son accomplishes the Father's plan and holds all things together by the word of his power. And it is good. God is at rest with all he has made. Within himself, he contains the fullness to fill all in all (Eph. 1:22–23). He has the best imagination. He even imagined the future. Just think—iPhones have been on his mind since before Methuselah. He dreamed it up. He made it happen.

In the Image of God

In early August 2010, Brandon Stanton arrived in New York City. He was a broke, out-of-work bond trader who had left Chicago earlier that summer to become a photographer. He'd set out on a photo tour of several American cities. He started in Pittsburgh and then moved on to Philadelphia. "My parents thought I was crazy," Stanton reports. "There were several awkward phone calls during this time. My mother didn't try to hide her disappointment. She saw bond trading as a very prestigious profession. Photography . . . seemed like a thinly veiled attempt to avoid employment."[35]

Stanton initially planned to stay in New York for a week and then catch a flight to the West Coast, but a beautiful vision kept him in the Big Apple. When his bus emerged from the Lincoln Tunnel and he entered the city for the first time, he was overcome by all the people. "That night, I created a photo album for my New York photos. I called it 'Humans of New York.'" The photo album grew into a blog and then a social media sensation. In just over one year, the *Humans of New York* Facebook page had over half a million fans. When St. Martin's Press turned the project into a photo book, it became an instant *New York Times* best seller.

Why are we so fascinated with profiles and faces? I think one Amazon reviewer captured the reason when she wrote, "This book is a gorgeous glimpse into the heart of humanity." Looking at portraits, or even just people watching, gives us a sense of what we have in common with all humanity. We see our family resemblance in every picture—two eyes, a nose, the varying yet familiar expressions of a human face. We are one. Yet we're so different.

Genesis 1:26 further explains our fascination with faces. God said, "Let us make man in our image, after our likeness." The verse uses two terms to describe God's own divine portraiture. These terms—*likeness* and *image*—give definition to two primary human relationships. First, the term *likeness* reveals the vertical relationship between God and all humanity.[36] We do hold something in common with all of mankind. We are all crafted in God's image. God made us to be a part of a vast family that reflects his glory. We have been imprinted with a divine role and a family resemblance.[37] Second, the term *image* reveals a horizontal relationship between humanity and the created order. We are God's representatives on earth. Like the faces on Mount Rushmore physically testify to the reign of American democracy across the Great Plains, our varied faces testify to the reign of God in the world. We were created to teach the world to love him, enjoy him, and submit to his rule.[38] Sometimes poorly but many times beautifully, we live out the creation mandate by creating culture across the world.[39]

Resembling God—being his image to the world and in the world—

includes at least five dimensions that help to shatter the lies we're tempted to believe about creativity.

First, we are relational beings. Because God is a Trinity and he has lived in community eternally, he has created us to live in community as well. There is no such thing as a lone artist, a lone businessman, or a lone ministry leader. Michael Horton describes it this way: "Father, Son, and Holy Spirit live in unceasing devotion to each other, reaching outward beyond the Godhead to create a community of creatures serving as a giant analogy of the Godhead's relationship."[40]

Even the so-called lone artist isn't completely alone—if he has a belly button. His conception of art is rooted in a tradition of human expression, whether he knows or acknowledges it or not. He is connected to some kind of family and history. Since we're made as relational beings, it pays to believe that creativity can be experienced best with others.

Second, we are emotional beings. We live emotional lives, because God experiences emotion. He is the God who sees the great wickedness of the human race and experiences regret and a troubled heart (Gen. 6:5–6). Our Savior is the one who wept at a friend's funeral (John 11:35). He is the mighty warrior who delights in his people and rejoices over them with singing (Zeph. 3:17). When we experience a full range of emotions, we are imaging our Creator. When our creativity reflects disgust, anger, delight, pain, peace, and joy, we look like our God. Creativity involves making connections—what I called integration, above—and often the first connection we make is an emotional one. This isn't an ability that some people have and some people don't. The truth is that we *can* make these connections because, like God, we all feel.[41]

Third, we have longings and desire. Think about how you long for more. You want a healthier body, so you change your diet or adapt your exercise routine. You long for things to be done more efficiently, so you rework your schedule and rewrite job descriptions at the office. You long for a better relationship with your spouse, so you plan date nights and daydream about how to pursue her. In Adam's song about

Eve, we see strong desire (for companionship and sexual fulfillment, Gen. 2:23–25) present in the garden long before Satan subverted it. But because our desires are fallen, many leaders are afraid to talk about them. A leader may be unhappy with a staff member's performance, but if his emotions are high, he may have a difficult time expressing exactly what he expects or how the staff member can improve. If desire is an implication of being made in God's image, we need to grow in our skill of recognizing, expressing, and asking for what we want. Desire matters. God made us with desire so that all people would desire him and worship him (1 Chron. 16:23–25; Ps. 37:3). What we all ultimately long for is God, though in our sin, that desire is distorted and deflected. As a Christian leader, you want God. God knows this, and it's why he tells us to express our desires and ask for anything (Matt. 18:19; John 14:14; 16:24). We should ask like little children who aren't afraid (Matt. 7:7–12). And if we can be that open about our desires with God, we shouldn't be afraid to be open about our desires with one another.

At the beginning of this chapter, I explained that creativity is often born out of the gap that exists between where things are and where things should be. Embrace the emotions you have about what's broken around you. Embrace the desires you have to bring order to the pain and chaos. Step into the relationships God has given you. You don't have to be a genius to bring your feelings, wants, and community to bear on the obstacles you face. These first three implications of being God's image— the truth that God has made us to relate, feel, and desire—destroy the myth that only a genius can be creative. These three realities, which are common to mankind, lead to the creative impulse. We're created for relationships so we naturally make connections. We're all emotional creatures, so very often the first connection we make—whether joy, fear, anger, or disgust—is an emotional one. And we all have desires. We see something right with the world, and we want more of it. We see something wrong with the world, and we want to find a way to make it right. It doesn't take a genius to relate, feel, or want. You just have to be human. We should be able to sit with other leaders and say, "Hey team, what are you feeling? What are we going for? What do we really desire?" You'll find the freedom to do this when you see these abilities are rooted in God's design. You're made in God's likeness, and he created you—yes, even you—to image forth creativity.

Fourth, we can think and reason. We can plan and will. God made everything, and because God made everything, he owns everything. Because God owns everything, he is also the King of everything. He rules everything—all creation. On the fourth day, God created the sun, the moon, and the stars (Gen. 1:14–19). They show God's rule over his creation by marking off the seasons, the days, and the years. These markers order our world. They pattern our time. God rules over the world he made by guiding and directing it to do everything that he planned. He didn't create the world wondering what might happen. God works out everything according to what he wants (Eph. 1:11). And no one can stop God from doing what he wants, because nothing is outside his control. He controls both grasshoppers and hurricanes.[42]

Because we see God's greatness in bringing order and pattern to the world, we shouldn't be surprised when we desire to bring order and pattern out of chaos as well. This isn't a capacity that only type-A organizers have. In fact, seeing connections between reasoned thinking and imagination should destroy the myth that creativity is just some mysterious "thing." In reality, creativity can't exist at all without some level of order. Andy Crouch tells us:

> Creativity cannot exist without order—a structure within which creation can happen. On a cosmic level the extraordinary profusion of species could never survive if the world were an undifferentiated soup of elements. This is true of human creativity too. Without the darkened box of a theater, films would lose their compelling power. Without the lines and spaces that make up written English, this book would be a soup of letters. Creativity requires cosmos—it requires an ordered environment.[43]

Genesis presents God himself as both Creator and ruler of the universe. Crouch continues, "Creators are those who make something new; rulers are those who maintain order and separation."[44] In reality, creativity cannot exist without order—a structure within which creating can happen. New connections that are made must be organized and implemented in order for newly imagined ideas to become a reality. So God hasn't only given us the ability to relate, feel, and desire; he has also given us the ability to think and plan. Our sinful tendency is either to hold so tightly to structure that we stifle growth or not to hold it at all, so chaos reigns. But one of God's greatest gifts to the world is the gift of ordered creativity and fruitful space—not a structure that boxes us in (or that boxes God in—God forbid!) but a plan and structure that nurtures life and freedom.[45]

Finally, we value. We evaluate worth. We attach moral value and aesthetic value to all kinds of things. Harold Best says: "I don't know anyone who doesn't love or value art, or who isn't somehow drawn to the aesthetic quality of something: a finely wrought tool, a beautifully sutured incision, a quilt, or a Chevrolet. The love of quality—whether or not beauty is consciously thought of—is universal."[46]

When we evaluate, we pass judgment. We say, "This is good," "This is better," or "This is bad." We do this not because we're judgmental. It's because we're made in the image of the Judge. We're made in the image of the one who made all things and then took a step back and said, "It's good. It's good. It's very good." Wise leadership is impossible without discernment, that is, without the ability to evaluate what is right or wrong and what is good or better. It shouldn't surprise us that some of the most skillful creatives in the Bible—Bezalel, who crafted the tabernacle (Ex. 31:3; 35:31), and Solomon, the king and scientist and sage (1 Kings 4:29; 2 Chron. 9:23)—were said to be filled with a Spirit of wisdom and discernment. This ability comes from God, who is himself the only wise God (Rom. 16:27) and grants wisdom to the foolish.

When creativity is grounded in our ability to think and evaluate, we are set free from seeing it as a mystery that can't be taught. Creativity is the skillful application of God-given imagination. It *can* be learned, honed, and grown.

We can be creative leaders because we've been made in God's likeness. We image forth the Creator. And because we're made in his

Implications of Being Made in God's Image

- We are *relational*. God made us for community, because he exists eternally in community.
- We have *emotions*. God made us to feel, because he experiences emotions and feels deeply.
- We have *desires*. God made us with longings, because he has desires for the world.
- We *think*. God made us to think and organize, because he is a God of order and not disorder.
- We *value*. God made us to assign value, because he is the Judge of all things.

image, we have imagination. We can see the way forward through the chaos and disorder. We can envision a more beautiful life for the people under our care. With God on our side, we see a brighter future for the communities where we lead, and we can inspire others to join us as we pursue that God-given vision.

Imagine the Way Forward

In the previous chapter, I argued that strong leaders take the time to listen to God's voice and clearly define their convictions. Often convictional leadership and creative leadership are pitted against one another. Convictional leaders can stagnate. Information overload leaves them paralyzed so they never implement creative ideas. Creative leaders are on the other end of the spectrum. They can tend toward novelty—the constant pursuit of fads.

We need leaders who combine both conviction and imagination. Convictional leaders have a strong belief that something *must* be. Before any of those *musts* get accomplished, we need to dream. When we combine our conviction of what *must* be with a dream of what *could* be, we get vision. Andy Stanley says, "Vision is a clear mental picture of what could be, fueled with the conviction that it should be."[47] Kouzes and Posner tell us:

Every organization, every social movement, begins with a dream. . . . Leaders *envision the future by imagining exciting and ennobling possibilities.* . . . Much as an architect draws a blueprint or an engineer builds a model, you need to have a clear vision of what the results should look like before starting any project.

They go on to quote Rupessh Roy: "You need to have clear goals and a vision to make a positive difference; and you have to be able to share that vision with others and get them to believe in it."[48]

When we encounter trials and tribulations in ministry, it would be easy to despair. But a creative leader can dream about how those challenges of suffering are really opportunities for glory. Kouzes and Posner put it this way: "If you are going to be an exemplary leader, you have to be able to imagine a positive future."[49] In fact, they say, "it's this quality of focusing on the future that most differentiates people who are seen as leaders from those who are not."[50] Leaders know where people need to go. They envision the way forward. They are able to imagine in advance what it will look like to work out their convictions in a particular place. With a clear vision in mind, they inspire others to join and follow their lead.

Leadership Skill Set 2: Dreaming and Persuading
Imagining the way forward requires . . .

- *Dreaming.* Make creative connections between where you are and what God wants.
- *Persuading.* Be winsome. Be a poet. Help your people dream.

Nick Bogardus leads Cross of Christ Church in Irvine, California. One could argue that no place in America has produced more church movements in the past fifty years than Nick's context—Orange County. Calvary Chapel, Vineyard, Saddleback, TBN, Campus Crusade, and the

Crystal Cathedral were all birthed there. Not only is Orange County a very churched culture, but it also has exported a lot of theology and practice to American evangelicalism at large. It might be tempting as a new church plant to simply copy the most "relevant" strategies from the church down the street. How does Nick cultivate a creative vision for his unique context? Here is what he told us:

> I'm not a great preacher. In many ways, I'm still trying to find my voice. I love digging into the biblical text, but sometimes I have a hard time.... I watched an interview with Rick Rubin on the BBC about six months ago. Rubin is arguably the best music producer of the last 50 years, having produced groundbreaking records with the likes of the Beastie Boys, Red Hot Chili Peppers and Johnny Cash. It inspired me to try identifying patterns in his work. I found a playlist of his greatest hits and started listening. I noticed many of the songs, especially the hip-hop hits, began with a declarative that grabbed your attention—think "No sleep 'til Brooklyn!" or "I'm going back to Cali." As I distill the theology of a sermon, I try to turn it into a similar phrase that I could start a sermon with and even use like a chorus in a song.... While I'm still learning, simply being curious has helped me create in a way that shows people the gospel isn't just true but good.

The church needs leaders like Nick who make space to dream and then work creatively like poets. If we are going to see our convictions carry weight in a world that is increasingly skeptical of our faith, we need to develop winsomeness and poetic skill. Tharp says, "If art is the bridge between what you see in your mind and what the world sees, then skill is how you build that bridge."[51] Ministry leaders are in the business of bridge building. Often when pastors want to teach about theology, their preaching turns into a lecture. And it's boring. Honestly, that's a really sad thing, because the Bible isn't boring. It stirs the heart. We say, "Pray." But Lamentations says, "Pour out your heart like water" (2:19). We say, "God is sovereign." But Jesus says, "God knows and cares for the sparrow" (cf. Matt. 6:26; 10:29). We say, "Jesus saves." But the Psalm says, "Light dawns for the righteous" (Ps. 97:11 RSV). *The Dictionary of Biblical Imagery* reminds us:

Because of the predominantly theological and devotional purposes to which Christians put the Bible, it is almost impossible not to slip into the error of looking upon the Bible as a theological outline with proof texts attached. Yet the Bible is much more a book of images and motifs than of abstractions and propositions. . . . The Bible is a book that *images* the truth.[52]

People think not merely in syllogisms but also in stories. We need to engage the people we lead logically, but we need to persuade and inspire as well.[53] We have young preachers in our community who bring strong biblical conviction to the pulpit, and I encourage it, but I exhort them to be poets as well. Preach but paint the picture.

Movie producer Brian Godawa describes how, after first coming to the faith, he tended to reduce other Christians to their doctrinal commitments, "judging their status before God based on my creedal scorecard. 'Well, you did okay, eight out of ten doctrines correct, but those two wrong ones set you back on the "hierarchy of doctrinal knowledge." I guess I will tolerate you.'"[54] He continues:

I noticed in myself a tendency toward reducing everything to logical debate. I became argumentative. Encounters with unbelievers and even believers would seem to always end in cognitive dispute. . . . I would engage in rigorous debate with the unenlightened and proceed to destroy unbelieving worldviews like they were going out of style. It was like genocide of unbelief. "So, you're a naturalist? Well, if you believe everything has a natural cause, then your own thoughts are caused by nature, which means your truth claim of naturalism is self-refuting." WHAM! "So, you're a relativist? Well, if you believe there are no absolutes, then that is an absolute, and your relativism is self-refuting." WHAM! . . . I felt like the Muhammad Ali of apologetics. . . . But I eventually learned that winning an argument is not always the same as persuasion; you can win the battle of debate but lose the war for a soul.[55]

When our hearts are increasingly warmed by the gospel, our witness sounds less and less like the work of a lawyer and more like the songs of a poet. Maybe you're thinking, "I'm not a poet. I'm also not a movie producer." You're right.

But let me tell you something else that is true. You are creative. This is important.

No leadership will thrive without creativity. Engineers need creativity. Businessmen need creativity. Children's ministry needs creativity. Counseling needs creativity. Preaching needs creativity.

"The weakness of the Pharisee in the days of old," warned A. W. Tozer, "was his lack of imagination. . . . He saw the text with its carefully guarded theological definition and he saw nothing beyond."[56] Religion is built on fear and control. When we're afraid, we build closed systems and standards to control others. Without creativity, Christian leaders become copycats who follow like drones after the latest ministry trend. Without creativity, preachers speak only in propositions and principles.

Where are fear and control going to get you in your parenting? Nowhere. I need to be filled with the life-giving, creative Spirit to parent my kids well. I need to know what God's Word says about parenting. Then I need to know my kids. Then, through the stories I tell them and the adventures we have together, I need to inspire them to make those creative connections between what should be and what is in their lives. I pray that my parenting looks more like Jesus speaking parables and less like a recitation of tax law.

John Hodgman is a self-professed agnostic and prolific humorist who writes for *The Daily Show*. In a recent podcast interview, he described creativity this way:

> It's not that you have to create a new idea. You have to learn to be receptive to new ideas when they come. This is the whole concept of the *genius loci*—the genius of a place. [It's the idea that] creativity was a spirit that came to you. And that's what it feels like when it's really working. You really feel like you're getting dictation from somewhere else. It's the closest to thing to a religious experience that I've ever had, because it truly feels like it's coming from some other place.[57]

Christian leader, here is an invitation for you. Because you are in communion with God, you have more than a divine muse. You have

God himself. He made you in his image. Be receptive to his voice, and then offer your life to God. As you offer your gifts, Christ perfects them.

Ironically, I hit a massive creative wall while doing edits of this chapter. I worked through the Trinitarian implications of creativity, but I didn't know how to communicate it. I sat down with another pastor and shared my struggle. He challenged me to rest in my giftedness. He told me to stop trying to be smart. He told me to stop trying to be so creative but rest in the creative gifts God has given me. I came back

Cumulative Chapter Summary

Leadership begins with *knowing where people need to go*. When you combine *conviction* and *creativity*, you have vision to see the way forward.

Leadership Vision	Trinitarian Doctrine	Leadership Skills
Convictional leaders embody what they believe.	**Revelation:** God speaks. He makes himself known through his world, Word, and works.	Embodying what you believe requires . . . • *Listening.* Seek to hear God's voice in order to clarify your convictions. • *Living it out.* Practice what you preach, because people do what people see.
Creative leaders imagine the way forward.	**Creation:** God made everything. His creation work is a purposeful project of love.	Imagining the way forward requires . . . • *Dreaming.* Make creative connections between where you are and what God wants. • *Persuading.* Be winsome. Be a poet. Help your people dream.

to revising the chapter and felt empowered to offer what I have. Brené Brown tells us, "Vulnerability is the core of shame and fear and our struggle for worthiness, but it's also the birthplace of joy, creativity, belonging, and love."[58]

Lay down your anxiety and your fear, and play a little more. Step into a fully human creative life—one that makes real connections between the truth God has spoken to you to and the real world you inhabit every day. I know you can see the gap between where your church is right now and what God wants for your community. Start making creative connections and lead your people. Help them dream about how you will get from here to there. Dream for yourself and then start talking about those dreams with your people. Step into poetic inspiration with confidence, because, after all, you are made in the Creator's image. You *are* creative. You won't be stepping out alone. The same Spirit who hovered over the waters hovers over your heart and your church (Gen. 1:2). He created you in his image, and he goes with you (Josh. 1:9; Matt. 28:20). Start imagining. Start dreaming. Start inspiring. Start living faithfully the script God has given you. Start creating.

Exercises

Read through this selection of ideas and activities to help you practice creative leadership. Pick out one or two and incorporate them into your regular leadership rhythms.[59]

1. As you read magazines and newspapers or search the web, save articles or photos that touch your heart. Paste them in your journal to help fire your imagination and guide your prayer life.

2. A few times this week set aside thirty minutes before bedtime to journal about your daydreams. Write bits and pieces of what you dreamed about for your family, ministry, church, and neighborhood.

3. Journal about your desires. What do you see in your life right now that is not working well, and what do you want to do about it? What are you passionate about, and what ideas get you excited? Where in your life do you see God at work currently? What is God calling you to step into?

4. Sketch out God's long view. Clear a desk or table. Grab some crayons or colored pencils and paper. Read Jeremiah 29:4–14. Draw out what is happening in this passage. Draw your own neighborhood or city as a modern context for Jeremiah's promise. Don't worry about being an artist. Just have fun sketching it out.

5. Set aside a day simply to dream and think about a vision with your team. Talk to your team members and find out their hopes, dreams, and aspirations for the future of your organization or ministry. Identify the biggest blocking issues that are keeping the vision from being achieved. Brainstorm and imagine creative ways to move the organization forward.

6. Gather the team again. Share metaphors, symbols, examples, stories, pictures, and words that represent the vision of what you're trying to become. Focus on biblical images and images from the life story of your church. Save these and pick them up at a later date to remind your team about the vision or to share the vision with others.

Prayer

I acknowledge, O Lord, with thanksgiving, that thou hast created this thy image in me, so that, remembering thee, I may think of thee, may love thee. But this image is so effaced and worn away by my faults, it is so obscured by the smoke of my sins, that it cannot do what it was made to do, unless thou renew and reform it. I am not trying, O Lord, to penetrate thy loftiness, for I cannot begin to match my understanding with it, but I desire in some measure to understand thy truth, which my heart believes and loves. For I do not seek to understand in order to believe but I believe in order to understand. For this too I believe, that "unless I believe, I shall not understand."[60]

Part 2

MISSIONAL ORGANIZATION

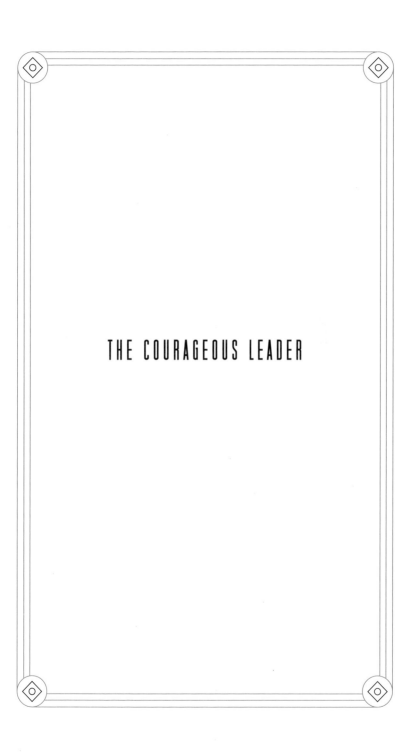

THE COURAGEOUS LEADER

Why does this Trinitarian understanding of God matter in general? It matters profoundly in the matter of mission that we represent who God really is. He is not a generalized Unitarian mysterious God we cannot know. He is the God and Father of our Lord Jesus Christ, made known through Jesus historically and by the Spirit experientially. And he draws his redeemed people into participation in his life and love to continue his mission on earth.

Ross Hastings, *Missional God, Missional Church*

What is risk? I define risk very simply as an action that exposes you to the possibility of loss or injury. If you take a risk you can lose money, you can lose face, you can lose your health or even your life. And what's worse, if you take the risk, you may endanger other people and not just yourself. Their lives may be at stake. Will a wise and loving person, then, ever take a risk? Is it wise to expose yourself to loss? Is it loving to endanger others? Is losing life the same as wasting it?

John Piper, *Don't Waste Your Life*

So much of what we hear today about courage is inflated and empty rhetoric that camouflages personal fears about one's likability, ratings, and ability to maintain a level of comfort and status. We need more people who are willing to demonstrate what it looks like to risk and endure failure, disappointment, and regret—people willing to feel their own hurt instead of working it out on other people, people willing to own their stories, live their values, and keep showing up.

Brené Brown, *Rising Strong*

More failure comes from an excess of caution than from bold experimentation with new ideas. . . . "The frontiers of the kingdom of God were never advanced by men and women of caution."

J. Oswald Sanders, *Spiritual Leadership*, quoting the wife of Archbishop Howard Mowll

I have a certain way of being in this world, and I shall not, I shall not be moved.

Maya Angelou, Twitter post, April 29, 2014

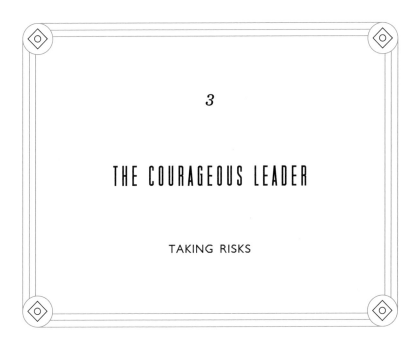

3

THE COURAGEOUS LEADER

TAKING RISKS

Summary: *Courageous leaders expose themselves to uncertainty and risk. Courage is for the broken, vulnerable, and weak. It comes from the invulnerable God who made himself vulnerable for us. God's mission teaches us courage. The Father loved the world and sent the Son. The Father and Son send the Spirit. The Spirit forms the church and calls her to participate in his mission to the world. Courageous Christians join God's mission with a threefold motivation: God commands us; the gospel compels us; and the Spirit moves us. God fills us with his Spirit, and he empowers us to move forward with courageous love. God wants us to join his mission to the hard places. He calls us to leave behind what hinders and follow our Lord where he leads.*

In June 2010, the curators of TEDxHouston asked Brené Brown to open their first event.[1] TEDxHouston is one of many independently organized events modeled after TED—a nonprofit addressing the fields of technology, entertainment, and design. TEDx organizers bring together "the world's most fascinating thinkers and doers" and challenge them to give the talk of their life in eighteen minutes or less. When Brown asked organizers what they wanted her to talk about, they answered, "Be awesome. Have fun. Do your thing." That surprised her, because Brown is a shame-and-vulnerability researcher. Talking about shame, Brown says, "makes most organizers a little nervous and compels a few to get somewhat prescriptive about the content of the talk."[2] Brown made a decision to trust her research. On the night before the talk, she looked at her husband and said, "I think I'm going to experiment tomorrow. I think I'm going to *be* really vulnerable while I'm talking about vulnerability." Her husband said, "I think that's a terrible idea." Nevertheless, Brown put herself out there. She talked about her own breakdown and spiritual awakening. She even talked about having to go to therapy. Then as she drove home, Brown thought, "I'll never do that again." She describes the next morning:

> I woke up with one of the worst vulnerability hangovers of my life. You know that feeling when you wake up and everything feels fine until the memory of laying yourself open washes over you and you want to hide under the covers? *What did I do? Five hundred people officially think I'm crazy and it totally sucks. . . . I must leave town.*[3]

Sometime later, Chris Anderson from TED called Brown and asked if the talk could be posted on the TEDx website. Brown was mortified. She said, "I'm flattered, but no thank you." Anderson said, "I think December 23rd would be great." Soon Brown's talk, "The Power of Vulnerability," appeared. The video has more than twenty million views. At the time of writing, it was one of the top five most viewed TED talks in the world.

In her talk, Brown embodies what she believes. Courageous leadership is vulnerable. It takes risks. Courage isn't armoring up and mitigating uncertainty. Courage is

- waking up and going for a run after a cancer report,
- trying to get pregnant after a second miscarriage,

- pressing back into relationships after a messy divorce,
- stepping into work after getting fired or missing a promotion.

When we think about people who do things that are truly brave, it's easy to see how vulnerability underpins all acts of courage. That's how vulnerability emerged in Brené Brown's ground-theory data. Courageous leaders expose themselves emotionally to uncertainty and risk. Brown says, "As adults, we realize that to live with courage, purpose, and connection . . . we must again be vulnerable. We must take off the armor, put down the weapons, show up, and let ourselves be seen."[4]

Leadership Vision 3: The Courageous Leader
Courageous leaders take risks.

What Brené Brown discovered in her research was already revealed to us in God's Word. When God bears his strong arm (Isa. 53:1), he shows us his strength through suffering, affliction, and being crushed (Isa. 53:3–5). God lets himself be known. He has shown up without armor, and he keeps showing up again and again. As pastor and leader Dick Keyes writes, "[When we think of a] unique and revolutionary hero . . . [we must look] to Jesus Christ, who was willing to endure being spat on and scorned for the sake of those whom he had come to save (and being spat on was only the beginning)."[5] Courage is for the broken, vulnerable, and weak. It comes from the invulnerable God who made himself vulnerable for us.

God's Insane Vulnerability

The more time we spend in a churched culture, the easier it is to forget how those outside of Christianity view our risk-taking missionary enterprise.[6] In Nik Ripken's book *The Insanity of God*, he tells of his family's journey from the hills of Kentucky to war-torn Somalia. The Ripkens have faced their son's death, the realities of war, and overwhelming evil. Nik says:

> From the world's point of view the cross of Jesus will always be a stumbling block. From the world's point of view God does not come and die, God comes to control and destroy. From the world's point of view, if we were God, we would act from a position of power, not from a stance of love and humility. Today, as throughout all of history, a God who "so loves the world that he gave his only begotten son" is an act of insanity.[7]

This Trinitarian act of "insanity" is the root of our courage and missionary passion.

As Christians, we believe the Father, Son, and Holy Spirit have lived with one another eternally as distinct persons. The persons of the Trinity don't merely exist together. God reveals himself to us in the ways the persons of the Trinity *work* together. Systematic theologians call this *Trinitarian economics*. When God works, there are particular *roles* the three members of the Trinity carry out in the way each relates to the world. In creation, the Father speaks through the Word, and the Spirit hovers and sustains the creation. In redemption, the Father plans, the Son accomplishes that plan on the cross, and the Spirit applies that salvation to our lives.

What's amazing and insane about the Trinitarian economy is that God is constantly stepping out and giving everything away. Can you imagine an economic system like that? It's the promise of utopia, but in reality people have never made it work. Greed and selfishness infect every human government, but God's governance overflows with love. As Ross Hastings describes it, "To be Trinitarian means first to understand the fundamental loving relationality of God and the power of that relationality. It is the power of love."[8] God's eternal love is so deep it overflows like rivers of rushing water.

God didn't need to create the world. His eternal love was enough. But the love was so deep that the Father, Son, and Spirit delighted to share it. Love spilled out in the work of creation.

God didn't need to redeem the world either. But the Father's love was so deep that he sent his only, unique Son. Often the church thinks about missions simply as something we're commanded to do. We think about mission as if it began with the Great Commission in Matthew 28. The truth is that God was on mission before it was an activity for Christians or a line item in the church budget. As Paul Stevens says, "Mission is God's own going forth. . . . He is Sender, Sent, and Sending."[9] The Lord of the Scriptures made himself vulnerable. Before he ever sent us, eternal Love moved into our neighborhood.[10]

Each member of the Trinity moves out with missionary vulnerability.[11] The Father sent the Son (John 3:17; 5:36; 6:57; Gal. 4:6; 1 John 4:9); the Father and Son send the Holy Spirit (John 14:26; 15:26; Acts 2:33); and the Father, the Son, and the Holy Spirit send the church into the world (Matt. 28:19–20; John 17:18; 20:21; Acts 1:8; 13:2–3).[12] God's mission is *from* the Father, *through* the Son, and *by* the Holy Spirit.[13] This is God's missionary grammar. We see it on full display in Ephesians 1:3–14:[14]

Mission is *from* the Father. God the Father loves his children. His missionary plan involves choosing children from broken families and bringing them into his own perfect home. The Father showers his kids with blessings and love. Paul couldn't be clearer. The God and Father of our Lord Jesus Christ "blessed us in Christ with every spiritual blessing in the heavenly places, even as he chose us in him before the foundation of the world. . . . In love he predestined us for adoption as sons through Jesus Christ, according to the purpose of his will . . . with which he has blessed us in the Beloved" (Eph. 1:3–6).

Mission is *through* the Son. Jesus is a loving Bridegroom who accomplished everything necessary to win the heart of his beloved bride. He joins himself to us even though we bring nothing but debt and dirt into the marriage. "In him we have redemption through his blood, the forgiveness of our trespasses, according to the riches of his grace, which he lavished upon us" (Eph. 1:7–8).

Mission is *by* the Holy Spirit. His presence definitively seals God's chosen people and guarantees their perseverance. "In him [Christ] you also, when you heard the word of truth, the gospel of your salvation, and believed in him, were sealed with the promised Holy Spirit" (Eph. 1:13). The Spirit stays with us through everyday pain, struggles, and hardship. He intercedes for us in our weakness (Rom. 8:23–27). He calls, guides, and empowers the church community to be an embodied witness to the gospel—a tangible expression of God's missionary vulnerability.[15]

The distinctive roles of the Trinitarian members highlight particular aspects of God's mission, and the unity of the persons "results in a coherent and mutual divine mission in the church, in the world, and in creation."[16] This is why Jesus can say to Philip, "Whoever has seen me has seen the Father" (John 14:9). When we look at Jesus's vulnerable, self-giving, and courageously cruciform life, we see God as he is through and through.

We usually think of courage as the will to risk and lose reputation, career, or life for the sake of something we believe in. As Keyes says, "Our courage is in proportion to how much we risk losing, and how great the risk is of losing it."[17] God's courage goes the full distance even though for him it is not a matter of risk. When the Father sent the Son and the Son agreed to go, Christ's impending death was a certainty. His separation from the Father was inevitable.[18] But love overflowed and Jesus resolutely "set his face" to go (Luke 9:51). It may look like insanity, but this courage isn't self-destructive. It's the freedom to respond to life's highest priorities. Martin Luther King Jr. once said, "If a man has not discovered something that he will die for, he isn't fit to live."[19] King's words are extreme, but they are backed up by his courageous life.

Christian leaders should find their reason to live and die in response to God's missionary work. But as Stephen Seamands writes, ministers faced with challenges often ask the wrong questions:

> Confronted with an absence of passion for mission, we often ask, "What must we do to dispel our apathy and rekindle our passion for renewed mission involvement?" We issue calls to prayer and devise strategies to motivate. . . . Of course, good may come out of

Trinitarian Doctrine 3: Mission

The Father's Plan
Mission is *from* the Father

The Son's Victory
Mission is *through* the Son

The Spirit's Power
Mission is *by* the Holy Spirit

God's mission is his eternal plan to move out in love to rescue desperate, needy, and rebellious children through the life and work of Jesus. The Father sent the Son to reconcile the world to himself. The Son sends the Spirit into our hearts. The Spirit forms and fuels the church to carry out God's mission in the world.

"Mission has its origin in the heart of God. God is the fountain of sending love. This is the deepest source of mission." —David Bosch*

* David J. Bosch, *Transforming Mission: Paradigm Shifts in Theology of Mission* (Maryknoll, NY: Orbis, 1991), 392.

our efforts, but our approach is wrongheaded because it's based on the faulty assumption that mission is primarily about what we do for God.

If, however, we begin with the assumption that the Father, Son and Holy Spirit are already passionately engaged in mission to the world, the question gets reframed. . . . It becomes "What's hindering us from joining the mission in which the Father, Son and Holy Spirit are already engaged?"[20]

This broken world, our own sin, and the Devil guarantee we'll have challenges. In the midst of those challenges, God invites us to share his life. God invites us to go *with* him on mission. Specifically, God invites us to ask three sets of questions:

- Father, what are you doing in the world? Am I eager to join you?
- Jesus, what are you doing in me? Am I experiencing renewal?
- Spirit, what are you calling me to do? Am I willing to step out and take a risk?

We must respond to Jesus's call: "As the Father has sent me, even so I am sending you" (John 20:21). Answering these questions gives us three motivations for courageous missionary leadership. Our mission is *unto* the Father, *about* the Son, and *by* the Holy Spirit. God commands us. The gospel compels us. The Spirit moves us. The remainder of this chapter unpacks these three motivations for missionary courage.

God Commands Us

God is on mission, and we are under orders to be courageous and join him. We see this from the very beginning of the Bible. God created Adam and Eve and then commanded them to go out on a courageous mission—be fruitful and multiply and fill the earth (Gen. 1:28). Instead of being joyful, God-honoring, courageous cocreators, people rejected God's love. The fall ruined a courageous humanity and darkened our hearts. That's where God's mission and our new co-mission with him enter the story. God looked down on fallen humanity, and he felt compassion for us. His love spilled over. The Father sent the Son into the world (John 1:1–14; 3:16) to seek and to save lost people like you and me (Luke 19:10). Jesus came to serve and give his life on the cross as our ransom (Mark 10:45). He fulfilled all of the prophecies about a coming Savior, and he won victory over sin and death. God is on mission to win us. As Zach Bradley says, "The rushing river of *missio Dei* . . . rolls from Eden to New Jerusalem, and we are caught in its currents."[21]

Now, the Father calls and commands us to join his mission (Matt. 28:18–20; John 20:19–23; Acts 1:8). He demands that we do so, and his commands come with authority—"*all* authority in heaven and on earth" (Matt. 28:18). Being sent under the authority of God's Word should give us confidence. The Great Commission is not fulfilled easily, but its completion is as certain as the suffering and difficulty fulfilling it entails. When God's people obey his command, he's faithful to do a multiplying work. We see this happen throughout the early church:

But the word of God increased and multiplied. (Acts 12:24)

So the word of the Lord continued to increase and prevail mightily. (Acts 19:20)

In the whole world [the gospel] is bearing fruit and increasing. (Col. 1:6)

We are called to join God under his Word as he works in the world. People under God's Word can see where God is taking us. We know God is at work to form the world anew. He's bringing every tribe, tongue, and nation (Rev. 7:9–11). So we are not afraid to take initiative and join him.

Obeying God's original creation mandate has always meant taking risks. God is incorruptible and sovereign. He doesn't risk, but we *must* risk in order to obey God's commands and join him in his work. It takes courage to write, teach, design, and build (see the table in chap. 2, p. 75, under "Trinitarian Doctrine 2: Creation").

It takes even more courage to join God's Great Commission. In our modern age, a naturalistic worldview and functional deism—the belief that God made the world but remains distant from our everyday lives—blinds our eyes from seeing God at work around us. The reality of God using us to fulfill his commands doesn't make the old prophecies any less true.[22] His Word still does a multiplying work today (Matt. 24:14; Mark 13:10).

We need to ask and imagine, "Where is God at work?" This should be our regular practice. Jesus modeled prayerful dependence on the Father for us. When he healed the man at the pool of Bethesda, there were many others—blind, lame, paralyzed—who needed healing (John 5:2–3). Jesus didn't let human need dictate his agenda; he healed just one. At the same time, Jesus didn't allow the religious establishment to direct him; otherwise, he would have healed no one because the miracle occurred on the Sabbath. What motivated Jesus to approach this one man and ask, "Do you want to be healed?" (John 5:6). Jesus tells us that he acted under the Father's authority: "My Father is working until now, and I am working. . . . Truly, truly, I say to you, the Son can do nothing of his own accord, but only what he sees the Father doing. For whatever the Father does, that the Son does likewise" (John 5:17, 19).

Courageously joining God follows conviction and creativity. Before we act, we need a deep conviction that God is at work. Before we have the power to do anything, a picture of doing it must capture our imaginations. If you can't imagine yourself crossing the finish line, you will never train for a marathon. If you can't imagine graduating from college, you won't grind it out through final exams semester after semester.

Alan Hirsch describes how, in the early stages of an organization, courageous vision is in the driver's seat. As a church grows, however, programming and administration can sideline mission. Bureaucracy sneaks into the driver's seat. Calling becomes strategy. Roles become tasks. Teams become organizational charts. Celebration becomes performance reviews and pay scales. Certainty and routine breed complacency.[23] Institutionalism thrives on mitigating risk. Leaders fear failure, and they try, in effect, to send themselves—attempting to sustain a movement on their own.[24] This may work for a while, but eventually the organization will collapse. Leaders of these organizations have taken their eyes off the Father. As Oswald Chambers says, "We slander God by our very eagerness to work for Him without knowing Him."[25]

Churches need courageous leaders to seek God and declare where he's at work. As Henry Blackaby wrote, "We don't choose what we will do for God; He invites us to join Him where He wants to involve us."[26] We need prophetic voices, which call the people back to God and his mission.[27] We need prayerful leaders who regularly ask, "What is our part to play in God's unfolding rescue plan? Are we eager to join him?"

The Gospel Compels Us

The trouble with seeking God and joining him is that leaders have issues. Leaders who want to do great things for God encourage me. But beneath the surface other issues often are at work. In a narcissistic culture, our courageous risk taking is prone to be driven by sinful motives. Jeremiah 17:9 tells us,

Courageous Leadership versus Conforming Leadership*

Courageous Leadership	Conforming Leadership
Leaders are pioneering influencers.	*Leaders* are static bureaucrats with position.
Followers embody a way of life,	*Followers* represent a codified belief system,
. . . share the vision and mission,	. . . work for a centralized organization.
. . . and change the future.	. . . and preserve the past.
The church is mobile and dynamic,	*The church* is static and fixed,
. . . a decentralized network of relationships.	. . . governed by policies and procedures.
Leadership appeals to the common person . . .	*Leadership* tends to become elitist/exclusive.
. . . is transformational (spiritual authority).	. . . is transactional (institutional authority).

* Adapted from Alan Hirsch, *The Forgotten Ways: Reactivating the Missional Church*, 5th ed. (Grand Rapids, MI: Brazos, 2009), 196. Brazos Press is a division of Baker Publishing Group. Used by permission.

> The heart is deceitful above all things,
>   and desperately sick;
>   who can understand it?

Psychologists agree: what looks like heroic action on the surface can actually be driven by our "selfish gene" or by our subconscious psychological drives.[28] Some things appear to be admirable but are done for all the wrong reasons. Even goals that appear noble and righteous can be driven by comparison and competition. The philanthropist who crusades for social justice may be exposed as a greedy miser when his bank records come to light. The megachurch pastor with a shining

Leadership Skill Set 3: Seeking and Joining

Following God by taking risks requires . . .

- *Seeking.* Look for where God is working.
- *Joining.* Speak up, step out, and act. God is inviting you to join him in his work.

"As God's obedient child, you are in a love relationship with Him. In His timing, He will show you where He is working so you can join Him. Don't be in a hurry to be constantly engaged in activities for God. He may spend years preparing your character or developing your love relationship with Him before He gives you a large assignment. Don't get discouraged if the task or 'call' does not come immediately. Remain faithful in what He has told you to do, no matter how small or seemingly insignificant it may appear. God knows what He is doing. Focus on deepening your communion with God, and out of that fellowship will inevitably flow effective service for God." —Henry Blackaby

*Seven Realities of Experiencing God**

1. God is always at work around you.
2. God pursues a continuing love relationship with you that is real and personal.
3. God invites you to become involved with Him in His work.
4. God speaks by the Holy Spirit through the Bible, prayer, circumstances, and the church to reveal Himself, His purposes, and His ways.
5. God's invitation for you to work with Him always leads you to a crisis of belief that requires faith in action.
6. You must make major adjustments in your life to join God in what He is doing.
7. You come to know God by experience as you obey Him, and He accomplishes His work through you.

* Henry Blackaby, Richard Blackaby, and Claude King, *Experiencing God: Knowing and Doing the Will of God*, rev. ed. (Nashville: B&H, 2008), 51–64, esp. 63.

ministry may be exposed as arrogant and power hungry. Keyes reminds us, "Centuries ago, Augustine observed that Romans, with great self-discipline, would put aside many vices such as lust or greed all in order to indulge one vice—the love of praise."[29] To me, this just sounds like the temptation to count Twitter followers or be preoccupied with buildings, budgets, and how many butts you can shove into the pews. If you want to get really personal, it's like the temptation to watch my book sales obsessively.[30]

We mistake audacity for courage. Courageous leaders *are* vulnerable. They take risks, but they are sober, because true courage is self-sacrificial. Courage isn't about counting followers. It's not about twenty million TED talk views. High-functioning anxiety can look like courage, but it's actually a hindrance to the courageous life. Any audacious dope can build a platform. Courage is about the greater risks—moving forward with character and integrity. It takes courage to lead, die, and be forgotten.[31]

History is littered with organizations, governments, and churches that held deep convictions and ideals but are now dead and forgotten. It's possible to connect your convictions to creative strategies but still fall apart. One bad implementation or corrupted character can derail the best vision.

We have huge obstacles to courage rooted deep in our hearts. Since Adam and Eve, we've been overwhelmed by fear, shame, and guilt. Let's go back to the garden to understand where these primal emotions came from.

THREE OBSTACLES TO COURAGE

Fear. Adam was God's son. Our first parents were made in God's likeness (Gen. 1:26). They were God's beloved children. Their original identity was grounded in an intimate relationship—one that God kept with loyal love. God loved and cared for Adam perfectly. He provided Adam with everything he needed.[32] But it wasn't long before a spiritual battle began for Adam's soul. When Satan came into the garden, he questioned God's intimate love: "Did God actually say, 'You shall not eat of any tree in the garden'?" (Gen. 3:1). The snake questioned God's motivation with the subtle "actually." And by broadening the prohibition to say, "not eat of any," he painted a picture of God as one to be dreaded—stricter than he really is. Satan raised doubts in the woman's mind about God's love and care. The woman took the bait. Even though she lived in a utopian home with a perfectly available and consistent Father, Eve failed to trust. Soon, Adam and Eve were hiding in fear (Gen. 3:8–10).

You can be the same way. You're avoiding a thorny issue at a board meeting because the timing isn't right. You say to yourself, "I'm not sure how much more time I have here anyway." Maybe you've thought about transitioning your small group ministry, but you're not confident that God will bless the change, so you've just done nothing instead. Do you find it easier to sit behind your desk and hide, watching the Twitter show, than to get your work done? You don't feel safe where you are. You fear failure. Maybe you even fear abandonment, but you're missing opportunities all the time. Fear is ruling over you.

Shame. When Satan slithered into the garden, he didn't just call God's trustworthiness into question. He tempted Eve to think life apart from God is better than life lived with him. "You will be like God," he said (Gen. 3:5). Satan wanted the woman to believe that if she took what God prohibited, her eyes would be opened. He promised a new awareness about life—"You will be like God, knowing good and evil." He promised her a self-determining will and autonomy. She'd decide for herself what was good and evil. Eve took Satan's bait. By evaluating the forbidden fruit as "good" (compare the refrain "God saw that it was good" in Genesis 1), she usurped God's role in determining what is best. Her assessment that the fruit was "desirable" (Gen. 3:6 NIV) uses the same word found in the prohibition against covetousness in the Ten Commandments (Ex. 20:17). Eve supposed the tree's fruit would get her wisdom, insight, and success without God's help. That's the height of pride.

But Eve's confidence and self-assertion didn't get her what she wanted. It didn't set her free. When they ate the fruit, our first parents immediately fell into deep shame. Though their eyes were opened, they were rewarded only with seeing their nakedness. Shame is what we feel when we refuse to root our identity in what God says. Shame says, "I am not enough. I *am* bad. I don't matter."[33] We feel exposed, because our independence from God always results in emptiness. Merely affirming ourselves and putting up a front can't remedy it. That's because real shame isn't just about *what we've done*. As Christian counselor Mike Wilkerson points out, "it's about *who we are* in relation to God."[34] We must own our sinful independence and admit that God's point of view is better than our mask. The identity he gives us is truer than the identities we try to create for ourselves. Unless we submit to his story, we're hiding behind fig leaves (Gen. 3:15).

Guilt. God had given Adam his creation mandate (Gen 1:28–30). He had given Adam an opportunity to explore and take initiative as the first scientist and under-shepherd over all creation. Adam classified every animal and named every one (Gen. 2:19–20). God had also given Adam a warning, to protect him. "And the LORD God commanded the man, saying, 'You may surely eat of every tree of the garden, but of the tree of the knowledge of good and evil you shall not eat, for in the day that you eat of it you shall surely die'" (Gen. 2:16–17). Satan tempted Eve to presume that God wouldn't follow through on punishing her disobedience. "You will not surely die," he hissed (Gen. 3:4). The snake wanted Eve to believe that sin had no consequences. Satan spoke only about what she would gain and avoided mentioning what she would lose in the process.

We may be tempted to believe the same thing. After all, the man and woman did not immediately die physically. Their eyes were indeed opened (Gen. 3:7), and they obtained knowledge belonging to God as the Serpent had promised (Gen. 3:22). But though the man and woman did not die immediately upon eating the fruit, the expectation and assignment to death were soon enough. Their expulsion from the garden shows us they'd died spiritually. Although they became like God in one way, they were cut off from eternal life—the one feature of divinity that God had shared with them before. They were burdened with guilt (Gen. 3:7). Adam couldn't bear it, so they shifted blame (Gen. 3:12). Guilt put him in a straightjacket so they could no longer move forward on mission.

The Primal Effects of Sin

Fear	Shame	Guilt
Adam and Eve hid (Gen. 3:8–10).	They made coverings (Gen. 3:7).	They shifted blame (Gen. 3:12).
Sin produces fear of *where* I am (my situation or place).	Sin brings shame about *who* I am (my identity).	Sin causes guilt over *what* I've done (my sinful actions).

The greatest challenges leaders face are the demons within. We all have a dark side. We sleep with our own worst enemy on the nights when we sleep alone. The primal effects of sin in our soul box us in, keeping us from living a courageous life with God:

- Some leaders are driven by irrational fear that their situation and work is not adequate. They are driven to work harder and longer to prevent their fears from becoming a reality. Fearful leaders can feel a need to control every circumstance and event. They can have a tendency toward perfectionism and compulsive overeating, spending, or exercising.[35]
- Some leaders feel an exaggerated need for approval, acceptance, and being appreciated. Their desperation for praise flows from a deep sense of shame.[36]
- Some leaders struggle with a deep sense of guilt. Even if they can't quite explain it, they have a drive to make a significant mark with their lives. This kind of ambition can be a form of self-atonement.[37]

WHO CAN DELIVER US?

Who can deliver us from this body of leadership death? Thanks be to God who rescues us through Jesus Christ our Lord (Rom. 7:24–25).

Jesus faced our fear. When Jesus had been fasting for forty days in the wilderness, the Devil confronted him in the midst of his hunger:

"If you are the Son of God, command these stones to become loaves of bread" (Matt. 4:3; cf. Luke 4:3). Satan challenged the Savior to act apart from faithful dependence upon God and all God ordains for his provision. Jesus quoted Deuteronomy 8:3 in response:

Man shall not live by bread alone,
but by every word that comes from the mouth of God. (Matt. 4:4)

In the original context of Deuteronomy, Moses reminded Israel that during their time in the desert, God was testing them. He allowed them to be hungry and gave them manna so they might learn that people don't merely need bread but need God's constant, sustaining word. Sometimes we quote those words as if Jesus was talking about having good theology, that is, knowing the right Bible verses for each and every situation. But Jesus (like Moses before him) was talking about a deep trust in God's goodness. Our lives are sustained by God's every word—his constant care.

Throughout the Bible we are told to "fear not" over a hundred times. In Christ's resurrection, we see that our greatest fear has been banished permanently (1 Cor. 15:55–57). John tells us, "There is no fear in love, but perfect love casts out fear" (1 John 4:18). Through Christ, God has transferred us from the kingdom of fear into the kingdom of the Son he loves (Col. 1:13).

Jesus bore our shame. In that desert after his baptism, the Devil offered Jesus comfort in the place of suffering: "All these I will give you, if you will fall down and worship me" (Matt. 4:9; cf. Luke 4:6–7). To give in to this temptation, Jesus would have had to put on a mask. That would have required a redefinition of Jesus's identity. Satan wanted Jesus to take up his sovereign authority while sidestepping the cross. But Jesus knew who he was. He embraced the paradox of being God and man. He embraced his role as both sovereign King and suffering servant. He accepted the identity given to him by the Father (Luke 3:22).

When he went to the cross, King Jesus bore our sin and shame, and he shared his righteous identity with us. First Peter 2:24 says, "He himself bore our sins in his body on the tree, *that* we might die to sin and live to righteousness." The only way to resolve our shame is to own it and to see that Jesus was exposed for it.

Owning our identity as sinners and Jesus's exposure in our place is the only pathway to owning our identity as saints. It's only the person in Christ who can claim God's promise, "The old has passed away; behold, the new has come" (2 Cor. 5:17). As Ed Welch says, "This is the gospel: God touches us. . . . This is what the universe itself is waiting for. It is an unbalanced transaction that displaces our shame and replaces it with holiness."[38] In this way, the gospel invites us into something that's even more freeing than vulnerability alone. The Bible doesn't simply push down shame. It invites us to both own it and replace it. The gospel gives us a new courage that embraces the gift and the terror—of being known.[39]

Jesus took our guilt. One more time the Serpent tempted Jesus: "Throw yourself down" (Matt. 4:6; Luke 4:9). The essence of this temptation is that of presuming on God and displaying before others one's special favor with him. In other words, Satan tested Jesus with entitlement. Jesus responded once again with Scripture. This time, he quoted Deuteronomy 6:16. Jesus feared God the Father and refused to put him to the test. To do this would be an act of unbelief masquerading as extraordinary faith. Demanding evidence of God's care through miraculous protection was wrong. The appropriate attitude is fearing God and keeping his commandments (Deut. 6:17).

Jesus's perfect obedience is amazing. In the face of every temptation, he feared God and obeyed his voice (Heb. 4:15). Jesus's sinlessness seems so distant because we are guilty (Rom. 3:23). Our guilt may express itself in unrestrained excess or hot-tempered anger. It can look like quiet bitterness or a straightjacket of laziness. However it looks, the root sin is a willful rebellion against the ways of God.

But Jesus took our guilt. He canceled the charge of our legal debt that stood against us and condemned us. He has taken it away. He nailed it to the cross (Col. 2:14). He paid the debt we owed for our sin, and he imputes to us his perfect obedience (Rom. 3:19–26). Now we can obey God without presumption—with a heart that's motivated by gratitude.

When Sojourn Community Church started, we borrowed Tim Keller's motto: "In the city, for the city." But something strange happened as we planted campuses and had children. We saw a steady stream of people moving away from our inner-city campus to our other campuses in the suburbs. In place of "*In* the city, *for* the city," the new motto seemingly became "*In* the subdivision *for* the school system." Folks in their twenties would come to the inner-city campus. Then they would relocate to a suburban one by the time their oldest child entered kindergarten. I was angry (and maybe a little entitled), because I felt like we were drifting from my vision. I was ashamed. I'd championed a multisite system to leverage suburban resources for the downtrodden inner city. But now it seemed we were just contributing to more "white flight." I was afraid, and I began to ask, "Is our inner-city campus even sustainable?" Not only were key leaders leaving, but the transition of so many families to our suburban locations created a massive divide and financial strain. I stopped asking, "How are we going to thrive?" and I began to ask, "How are we going to survive?"

I started dreaming up schemes for how to handle this. I thought, "Something *has* to change!" I wanted to bombard the church with new programs and propaganda: "*We will* be *in* the city, *for* the city." I wanted to attract the wealthy to make up for relocated giving. I wanted to make our campus more attractive for middle-class families. I wanted the spiraling to stop. But then I met Ruth. She was sitting on the back row alone. As I greeted her, she was eager to share just how thankful she was for Sojourn, and she wanted immediately to explain why her husband wasn't there. You see, they hadn't paid their rent in five years. They were afraid that if they both left home at the same time, landlords would come and lock them out. "What brings you here?" I asked. She told me a story about how she'd been alienated, judged, and condemned by a previous church. Then she said, "I come here because I can be poor here."

In that moment, I was reminded of my own poverty while growing up down the street from a barrio in California with my single mom on welfare. God gave me this reminder to help me refocus. The poor are not a problem. The poor are a gift. God wasn't calling us to retool and cater to those who were leaving. He was calling us to love the poor. As Larry Crabb says, "It is our weakness, not our competence, that moves others; our sorrows, not our blessings, that break down the barriers of fear and shame that keep us apart; our admitted failures, not our paraded successes, that bind us together in hope."[40] In that moment of shared vulnerability with Ruth, a fresh courage emerged in me. I had a new desire to lay down my old, compulsive, corporate-church vision. I wanted to put aside fear, shame, and guilt and join God where he was already at work right in front of me.

Typically, I wake up in the morning feeling like an orphan. I've been chosen, loved, called, and empowered by God (Rom. 8:15; Gal. 4:6), but I'm riddled with anxiety, overwhelmed by shame, and weighed down with guilt. Fear, shame, and guilt constrain God's mission in my life. I need a fresh sensitivity to what God has done for me and what he is doing in me. To get up and move forward with courage, I need to get happy—to cheer up—and remember I am a child of the King. I am forgiven, accepted, loved. I am his. I am no longer my own. God is my Father. Christ is my brother. The Spirit is my guide.

Imagine I invited you over for lunch but when you came, my kids started begging you for their basic needs: "Could you give us something to eat? Can you help me buy a pair of shoes?" That would be wrong. I provide for them as their father. They don't need to act like beggars. Sadly, that's what many Christian leaders do when ministry gets uncomfortable. We complain and murmur and act like orphans. We need to remember that God supplies our every need (Phil. 4:19). He tells us to cry out to him, because he gives good gifts to those who ask (Matt. 7:11). A courageous leader—a man or woman who stands sure in his or her adoption—has faith to believe God is who he says he is and we are who God says we are as well.

Jesus says, "My yoke is easy, and my burden is light" (Matt. 11:30).

Are You Living as an Orphan or a Child of God?*

Serge, a mission agency committed to radical, courageous mission, has a checklist they've developed that I find to be a helpful diagnostic. In this checklist they ask, "Are you living as an orphan or a child of God?" Read through the characteristics of an *orphan* in the left column, think about the tendencies you recognize in yourself, and underline words or phrases that most apply to you. In the right hand column are the *child of God* counterparts to each orphan characteristic. Make these truths a matter of daily meditation. Use them as goals to pray toward.

The Orphan	The Child of God
"I will not leave you as orphans." (John 14:18)	*"You have received the Spirit of adoption as sons, by whom we cry, 'Abba! Father!'" (Rom. 8:15)*
Feels alone. Lacks a vital daily intimacy with God. Is full of self-concern.	Has a growing assurance that "God is really my loving heavenly Father."
Is anxious over felt needs: relationships, money, health. "I'm all alone and nobody cares. I'm not a happy camper."	Trusts the Father and has a growing confidence in his loving care. Is being freed up from worry.
Lives on a succeed/fail basis. Needs to "look good" and "be right." Is performance-oriented.	Is learning to live in daily, conscious, partnership with God. Is not fearful.
Feels condemned, guilty, and unworthy before God and others.	Feels loved, forgiven, and totally accepted because Christ's merit really clothes him or her.
Has little faith in God, lots of fear, lots of faith in himself: "I've got to fix it."	Has a daily working trust in God's sovereign plan for his or her life as loving, wise, and best. Believes God is good.

* Adapted from *Sonship*, 3rd ed. (Greensboro, NC: New Growth, 2013), 22–24.

Jack Miller put it like this: "If you are assured that whatever he asks of you, he also gives you the resources for, and that you have his love with you, no fight is too big to take on."[41] Adoption is the root of courage. Remember it daily. Our ministry load is often heavy, but we experience rest and joy in the labor, knowing the outcome ultimately depends on Christ, not on us.[42]

The Spirit Moves Us

Often we are told that being in the center of God's will is the safest place in the world. It's a lie. If you've lived on the mission field or spent some time studying the prophets, you know that it's just not true. Frankly, Christian ministry more often looks like what Paul described:

> Five times I received at the hands of the Jews the forty lashes less one. Three times I was beaten with rods. Once I was stoned. Three times I was shipwrecked; a night and a day I was adrift at sea; on frequent journeys, in danger from rivers, danger from robbers, danger from my own people, danger from Gentiles, danger in the city, danger in the wilderness, danger at sea, danger from false brothers; in toil and hardship, through many a sleepless night, in hunger and thirst, often without food, in cold and exposure. And, apart from other things, there is the daily pressure on me of my anxiety for all the churches. (2 Cor. 11:24–28)

Paul was barreling forward toward conflict with fearless, shameless, and guiltless freedom. He was present and engaged with people in the work. His life with God was vulnerable and unpredictable. It was wild and untamed. This is being fully alive. This is being on mission with God in a fallen world.

James McGregor Burns says, "What activates and fires [leadership initiative] is conflict."[43] Our Savior told us to "do good to those who hate you" (Luke 6:27). But he also warned us, "I have not come to bring peace, but a sword" (Matt. 10:34). Jesus had enough foresight to see the conflict his mission of love would inspire (Matt. 10:21–22).[44]

This can be surprising for a church leader who is first starting out. Many leaders enter ministry a bit high on idealism, but then quickly

discover how challenges arise even from within the church. As pastor
Eugene Peterson jests:

> In sixty-three years I've worshipped and worked in . . . eleven Christian
> congregations. . . . I was pastor to one of these companies for thirty
> years and thought I could beat the odds and organize something more
> along the lines of Eden, or better yet New Jerusalem. But sinners kept
> breaking and entering and insisting on baptism, defeating all my uto-
> pian fantasies.[45]

From a human perspective, following the God you can't see *is* risky.
Staying on mission in a broken-down world requires the kind of leader
who senses where God is at work in the midst of brokenness and pain
yet still steps out in faith. In the first chapter, I cited John Piper's
definition of leadership: *knowing where people need to go and taking
the initiative to get them there in God's way and by God's power.* One of
our pastors recently shared his struggles at home in front of a group of
forty men at an elder meeting. A few weeks later, he opened up to me
about his sharer's regret. His vulnerability was necessary. A courageous
life of obedience sometimes leaves a leader scared to death and about
to throw up, but leaders are often most courageous and strong in the
Spirit when they feel weak and wrong.

Courageous leaders stand in the gap and stay on mission even when
suffering and opposition come. Leadership researchers James M.
Kouzes and Barry Z. Posner describe courage this way:

> What gets people through the tough times, the scary times—the times
> when they don't think they can even get up in the morning or take an-
> other step—is a sense of meaning and purpose. The motivation to deal
> with the challenges and uncertainties of life and work *comes from the
> inside*, not from something that others hold out in front of you as some
> kind of carrot.[46]

By God's grace, what is on the inside of the Christian is the Holy
Spirit of God. God's Spirit propels us forward on mission. We need him
to take God's grand mission and empower us to make it concrete in our
context (Acts 1:8). We can face the daily challenges of life and ministry

without fear, because God has given us the Spirit of power, love, and a sober mind (2 Tim. 1:7). We have more than bootstrap perseverance. We have God himself. The third person of the Trinity is the vital connection between our lives and God's purposes.

In the Bible, we see that the Holy Spirit takes our fear and insecurity and he grants us *power*. Think about Joshua. Even before his mentor Moses died, Joshua heard him tell the people, "Be strong and courageous. Do not fear or be in dread of them, for it is the LORD your God who goes with you. He will not leave you or forsake you" (Deut. 31:6). After Moses's death, God spoke to Joshua directly: "Have I not commanded you? Be strong and courageous. Do not be frightened, and do not be dismayed, for the LORD your God is with you wherever you go" (Josh. 1:9). God warned Joshua about discouragement because he knew Joshua would be tempted. God takes leaders who are fearful and weak, and he gives them strength. Joshua had courage to face the giants and dividing walls of Jericho because God was with him. We've been commissioned under the authority of the new Joshua. Our powerful God came for us and now goes with us (Matt. 1:23; 28:20).

In the Bible, we see that when the Holy Spirit shows up, he takes our selfish ambition and grants us *sobriety* and *love*. Think about Peter. He was audacious. He often spoke before he thought. During Jesus's earthly ministry, Peter got in the way more often than he provided any leadership or help. He was always ready to jump ahead and pull his sword. He was the first one out of the boat (Mark 14:29), but he was also the first one to sink (Mark 14:30). He denied Christ three times (Mark 14:66–71). He begged Jesus not to die (Mark 8:32–33). What happened to Peter? Later in life he wrote, "But in your hearts honor Christ the Lord as holy, always being prepared to make a defense to anyone who asks you for a reason for the hope that is in you; yet do it with gentleness and respect" (1 Pet. 3:15). Gentleness and respect? You can hardly believe this is the same guy! God transformed Peter from brash and impulsive to wise and sober.

God's presence moves us outside of ourselves into the mess of ministry. The Spirit moves us to action. That's what we see in the early church. In Acts 2, the Holy Spirit showed up and redirected the apostles' attention away from themselves to God's greater purposes. They were moved from the solitude of the upper room to public worship—public boasting in God. Hastings explains:

> It is the church intoxicated with God, actively participating in the life of God, the church in worship that is the missional church. The church of Acts 2 was just such a church. Evangelism was effected through the church at worship. The three thousand converts were attracted first by the disciples' "declaring the wonders of God" (Acts 2:11) in their own tongues. The church was accused of being drunk. When the church is accused of being drunk with worship, intoxicated with God, it is most missional.[47]

On the day of Pentecost, we hear Peter and the others speak out. In the very next chapter, while bystanders marvel at the healing of the lame beggar, Peter asks, "Men of Israel, why do you wonder at this, or why do you stare at us, as though by our own power or piety we have made him walk?" Listen to Peter worship. "The God of Abraham, the God of Isaac, and the God of Jacob, the God of our fathers, glorified his servant Jesus" (Acts 3:12–13). Peter is transformed. He is doing the things that got Jesus killed, things which a couple of months earlier he was begging Jesus not to do. The Spirit is pointing Peter away from himself to the Savior, and that gesture moves the church on mission. Throughout the book of Acts, it happens again and again. The Spirit creates a new community with an identity, which borders on insanity (Acts 4:32–35), but as crazy and countercultural as it is, the Lord just keeps adding to their number.

When challenges arise, the Holy Spirit gives the church wisdom. He empowers leaders to guide the community (deacons in Acts 6; the Jerusalem Council in Acts 15; the Ephesian elders in Acts 20:28). The Holy Spirit gifts the church to move out in active ministry (Rom. 12:14–26). The challenges keep coming. In fact, they get worse. Jesus promised they'd face all kinds of opposition in the form of insults, slander, persecution, and all kinds of evil (Matt. 5:10–12), but the Spirit keeps leading the church out into the world. As they go, he unmasks principalities and powers through their ministry of suffering service (Ephesians 6).[48]

The Holy Spirit is still at work in the church today, moving leaders beyond themselves and beyond their egocentric goals. The Spirit spurs you on. He takes abstract ideas and makes them concrete realities. For example, I've said over and over again in this chapter, "God is love." But do you believe that? Do you know it? Has this truth settled deep within your soul? The Bible tells us, "God's love has been poured into our hearts through the Holy Spirit who has been given to us" (Rom. 5:5). The Spirit is with you, and he's able to give you an overwhelming sense of God's love for you. Paul writes, "The Spirit himself bears witness with our spirit that we are children of God" (Rom. 8:16).

The Holy Spirit gives leaders the courage to ask, "What if health and sustainability are more important than growth and production?" "What if we valued the most beautiful way to do something as the best way?"[49] That's true courage. Courage is choosing what is enduring over what is expedient; health over growth; depth over style.

What does it mean to be filled with the Spirit? Though it's a spatial metaphor, being filled with the Holy Spirit is not really about space—like filling up a cup with water. The metaphor describes a personal relationship with the Holy Spirit characterized by surrender and abandonment.[50] The Holy Spirit leads us to act. Courageous leaders go out first. They are the first up the mountain. They are the first to address the issue. The first person to jump in the pool takes the biggest risk.[51] As Stephen Seamands says, "Following the Triune God on mission will involve taking risks, moving out of our comfort zone, and stepping out in faith toward unfamiliar places where God is leading us."[52]

Do you want to live a Spirit-filled life? Be on the lookout for where God is at work; then move forward. Exercise just a mustard seed of courage. I'm convinced that courage is so potent that it only takes a little to move mountains (Matt. 17:20). We don't need pounds of it, but tablespoons, to fill us up.[53]

Three Motivations for Joining God's Mission

God Commands Us
Mission is *unto* the Father

The Gospel Compels Us
Mission is *about* the Son

The Spirit Moves Us
Mission is *by* the Holy Spirit

Courageous leaders must ask . . .

- Father, what are you doing in the world? Am I eager to join you?
- Jesus, what are you doing in me? Am I experiencing renewal?
- Spirit, what are you calling me to do? Am I willing to step out and take a risk?

The Paradox of Courage

When we think about boldness and courage, we often think about heroes. That's the way courage is personified in literature and movies, but Jesus's humility teaches us that courage is more subtle. Michael Crawford, lead pastor of Freedom Church in Baltimore, Maryland, described it to me this way:

> There's a ho-hum-ness about courage. It's somewhat habitual. I think courage is sometimes cloaked in such humility that it's unrecognizable. There's a woman in our church whose husband was shot and killed three years ago in Afghanistan. She's just humbly serving and if you didn't know her name and her circumstances, you'd think she's an ordinary person. Because I know her story, I think it's courageous for her to show up. I think it's courageous for her to wake up. I think it's courageous for her to continue to raise her kids. Those aren't things most people ever write a movie about. Courage is normal. There's a demand for it in the everyday pieces of life.

Jesus identified with everyday people in their mundane situations. He did it courageously. He confronted his disciples' pride to welcome little children (Matt. 19:13–15). He took time out to gently speak to Martha about her busyness (Luke 10:38–42). He picked up a towel to wash his friends' dirty feet (John 13:1–17). Jesus's humility, lowliness, suffering, and service provide the pattern for our mission. God calls us into embodied, everyday mission, like that of Jesus.

Courage is in the little things:

- It is an artist, midway deep into a project, not knowing how it will turn out.
- It is walking back into the kitchen with tears to tell your spouse you are sorry.
- It is standing in front of people who need a leader when you're trembling inside.

After commissioning his disciples in John 20:21, Jesus breathed on them and said, "Receive the Holy Spirit" (20:22). Jesus's breathing is deeply meaningful. Out of an overflowing heart of love, God had breathed out creation. Out of an overflowing heart of love, he had breathed life into humanity. Now, out of an overflowing heart of love, Jesus breathed life into his church. In the Gospel of Matthew we read of Jesus commissioning his disciples with these words:

> And Jesus came and said to them, "All authority in heaven and on earth has been given to me. Go therefore and make disciples of all nations, baptizing them in the name of the Father and of the Son and of the Holy Spirit, teaching them to observe all that I have commanded you. And behold, I am with you always, to the end of the age." (Matt. 28:18–20)

This promise is certain—"I am with you *always*, to the *end* of the age"! We go out, but we go *with* God. His continuing presence transforms our everyday life into a missionary adventure.

Courage is in the little things, and courage is in the big-vision ventures as well. Jack Miller was a pastor and seminary professor in the Philadelphia area. He struggled with failure and was on the brink of losing his faith when he took a sabbatical to Spain. While he was there, he traced God's missionary promises through the whole Bible. He saw the depth of God's love for the lost, the Spirit poured out into the church, and the kingdom of God advancing. Miller was reinvigorated for mission and started doing crazy things. He came home from Spain and started preaching in the streets. When gang members, drug addicts, bikers, and other street folks stopped to listen, he invited them into his house. Some stayed for months. Many became Christians. At least two became his sons-in-law. He started a new church to welcome these converts, and he continued going out on the street to share the gospel.

The church grew, but Jack was still thinking about those missionary promises and the power of the Spirit. So when Ugandan refugees showed up at his church, he brought seminary students to Uganda to shovel trash from the streets of Kampala and preach in the markets. Next he went to Ireland. Then back to Spain. One by one, people started joining Jack and his wife, Rose Marie, on their mission to bring the gospel to the world. Soon Jack and his friends had to form a missionary group to manage all that was happening—that's how World Harvest Mission started. It's now called Serge, and the group has nearly three hundred missionaries worldwide.[54]

Jack came to see that the gospel he shared with the lost would also empower the church to reach the lost. He came to understand that receiving and being full of the Holy Spirit is what leads us with courage into the world.

Courageous leaders come in all sizes, from the hall of faith in Hebrews 11 to the everyday courage of leading a family. Big vision without daily faithfulness is shallow and empty. Doing the small things without having the faith to dream puts God in a box. But living in the paradox of courage—daily faithfulness combined with bold imagination—is what God's mission looks like.

On Sundays, I typically preach for four services at our Midtown campus. One Sunday before the last evening service, I took a seat in the balcony and watched the church flowing in. I had been preaching on John 7. In that passage, the beloved disciple recounts how Jesus stood before the people on the last and great day of the Festival of Tab-

Cumulative Chapter Summary

Leadership begins with *knowing where people need to go*. When you combine *conviction* and *creativity*, you have vision to see the way forward.

Leadership Vision	Trinitarian Doctrine	Leadership Skills
Convictional leaders embody what they believe.	**Revelation:** God speaks. He makes himself known through his world, Word, and works.	Embodying what you believe requires . . . • *Listening.* Seek to hear God's voice in order to clarify your convictions. • *Living it out.* Practice what you preach, because people do what people see.
Creative leaders imagine the way forward.	**Creation:** God made everything. His creation work is a purposeful project of love.	Imagining the way forward requires . . . • *Dreaming.* Make creative connections between where you are and what God wants. • *Persuading.* Be winsome. Be a poet. Help your people dream.

But it's not enough to have direction. Moving forward requires *courage*. We must take initiative.

Courageous leaders take risks.	**Mission:** God moves out in love to rescue his children. The Father's mission plan is accomplished through the work of the Son and by the agency of the Holy Spirit.	Taking risks requires . . . • *Seeking.* Look for where God is working. Opportunities are invitations. • *Joining.* Speak up, step out, and act. God is inviting you to join him in his work.

ernacles. Jesus, proclaimed, "If anyone thirsts, let him come to me and drink. Whoever believes in me, as the Scripture has said, 'Out of his heart will flow rivers of living water'" (John 7:37–39). Jesus was speaking about the Holy Spirit. While I sat in the balcony watching people file into the auditorium, I heard the Spirit speak. He whispered, "Do you believe what you've been preaching all day? Do you believe that the very men and women in this church tonight are filled with the Holy Spirit? Do you believe they are ready to do courageous and amazing things in this city and beyond?" I was shaken, repentant, and filled with courage.

What would it look like if rivers of Holy Spirit courage were unleashed in every member of your church? Tap into God's goodness. Hear God's command to go. Get up tomorrow and get secure in your adoption. Be prayerfully sensitive to where God is at work. Seek him. Look for opportunities, but don't stop there. Join God in his work. Step up to the challenges you see. Join the mission. You haven't been given a spirit of fear. So let the rivers of Trinitarian love flow out through you to others.

Exercises

Below is a selection of ideas and activities to help you practice courageous leadership. Pick out one or two and incorporate them into your regular leadership rhythms.[55]

1. Journal about the challenges you are facing. They may be theological challenges ("I'm not sure what I believe about this"), operational challenges ("I don't know how to do this"; "I'm not sure how this works"), or relational challenges. Is your temptation to complain about these challenges or see them as opportunities? If your tendency is to complain, confess your sin to God.

2. Talk to your team members and find out the biggest challenges they are facing. Are they theological challenges, operational challenges, or relational challenges? Spend some time exploring these together to understand them more fully.

3. Read a missionary biography. Pray and ask the Spirit to bring to your mind specific opportunities to join him where he's working. What did the Holy Spirit bring to mind? Write it down.

4. Make a list of the people who you are praying will respond to God. Beside each name list one intentional way you can pursue him or her in the next month.

5. Write an account of how God has been at work in your life in the past six months. Ask the Holy Spirit to make you sensitive and open to an opportunity to share your experience with a seeking friend.

6. Journal about potential opportunities you see to change your regular ministry skill set. Where do you see God at work in your church community? Neighborhood? City or region? What can you do to join God in that work? Do it. Take a risk. Get out of your comfort zone.

7. Ask the people you lead (church members, ministry volunteers, leaders) for their ideas about how you and your organization can join something God is already at work doing in your community. Write it down and follow up.

Prayer

Lord Jesus, after giving your life on the cross, you entered the glory of the Father. Allow all people to share in your risen life. In you, Jesus, God made a new covenant with us. You are with us always, until the end of time. Jesus, you appeared to your disciples after your passion. Strengthen our faith by your presence in our midst. Jesus, you promised the Holy Spirit to the apostles. May the Spirit of consolation renew our faithfulness to you. Jesus, you sent your apostles to proclaim good news to the ends of the earth. May the Holy Spirit make us witnesses to your love. Amen.[56]

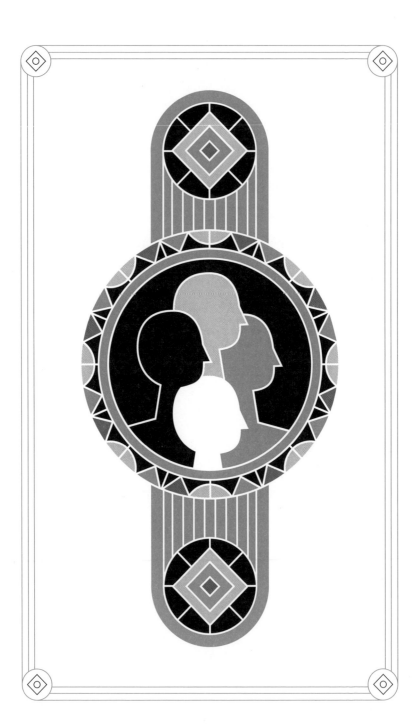

THE COLLABORATIVE LEADER

We were made in the image of the triune God. We find our identity through relationships. Just as there is both unity and plurality in God, so communal identity should not suppress individual identity and individual identity should not neglect communal identity. Through our union with Christ by faith, Christians are being remade in the image of the triune God. The church should be a community of unity without uniformity and diversity without division.

Tim Chester, *Delighting in the Trinity*

Organizational health is so simple and accessible that many leaders have a hard time seeing it as a real opportunity for meaningful advantage. After all, it doesn't require great intelligence or sophistication, just uncommon levels of discipline, courage, persistence, and common sense.

Patrick Lencioni, *The Advantage*

The truth is you can't do it alone. Leaders alone don't make anything great. Leadership is a shared responsibility. You need others, and they need you. You're all in this together. To build and sustain that sense of oneness, exemplary leaders are sensitive to the needs of others. They ask questions. They listen. They provide support. They develop skills. They ask for help. They align people in a common cause. They make people feel like anything is possible. They connect people to their need to be in charge of their own lives. They enable others to be even better than they already are.

James M. Kouzes and Barry Z. Posner, *The Truth about Leadership*

Much Christian leadership is exercised by people who do not know how to develop healthy, intimate relationships and have opted for power and control instead. Many Christian empire builders have been people unable to give and receive love.

Henri Nouwen, *In the Name of Jesus*

People are people. And people are problems. But—and this is a very big but—people who are practiced in collaboration will do better than those who insist on their individuality.

Twyla Tharp, *The Collaborative Habit*

4

THE COLLABORATIVE LEADER

EMPOWERING THE TEAM

Summary: *God's story of redemption is rooted in community. It begins with the Trinity—the perfect covenant community. Within the Godhead, collaboration is conducted in perfect unity, diversity, and harmony. But human collaboration is marked by flesh and sin. To lead together, people must grow in unity and ever-increasing maturity. Collaborative leadership requires organizational clarity—authority, responsibility, and accountability. To thrive, it also requires a personal vision—adaptability, autonomy, and ambiguity.*

One of the best compliments I have ever received was from another pastor who said, "The best part about Sojourn isn't Daniel Montgomery . . . it's the team. It's Robert Cheong, Mike Cosper, Kevin Jamison, Michael Winters . . ." The visiting pastor went on to say how our leadership team had impacted him. The compliment wasn't generated by marveling at our effectiveness or our timely results. Rather the pastor had seen and sensed a healthy mosaic forming in our leadership.

But teamwork and collaboration have not always been so obvious in our community. I can still recall nineteen-year-old Mike Cosper, who would one day become an elder and key leader of Sojourn, pulling me aside as a representative of our core group to share a long list of problems with my leadership, our church-planting timeline, and Sojourn's vision and theology. I responded with honesty, "Dude, I don't know what I am doing, but I do need to know if you have my back?" My honesty and vulnerability led to Mike's vulnerability. He confessed that he had been a part of the grumbling. Our breakdown together a few months into the church plant was actually a breakthrough. We resolved then and there to have one another's backs.

Fifteen years later, Sojourn has evolved from a fledgling core group of thirty to a federation of organizations—four campuses with four lead preaching pastors and a church-planting network of a few dozen churches. I wish I could say we don't struggle with collaboration like we once did. I feel more mature and stronger as a leader than ever before, and yet in some ways I feel more fragile and more vulnerable. As a team, we still practice confession and submission with humbling regularity. Often, I find myself asking, "Is it worth it? Are all the meetings, personalities, planning, and complexity worth it?"

On my worst days, I'd rather go it alone. Sometimes teams are as much a source of frustration as they are an opportunity for faith. But the triune God, who lives eternally in relationship, created us for relationships. He wants collaborative leaders who empower the team.

The God Who Collaborates

In the Bible, there are two basic kinds of relationship—contract relationships and covenant relationships.[1] A for-profit business—like a coffee shop—typifies the *contract* relationship. A barista at your local coffee place provides you with an Americano, and you leave a few dollars in return. In a contract negotiation, an arrival at a mutually satisfactory agreement is important. Like buying a car, it's important to settle on a price before you take it off the lot. Contracts have obligations and conditions that *require* performance. The terms must be fulfilled. If I go into business with you and I break one of the terms of our contract, our business relationship is over. And even when all of the terms are kept, some contracts—like the fading ink on a receipt—last for only a specified period of time. Because the parties in a contract are consumers, I may choose to break my contract on purpose if it no longer benefits me. If the coffee shop down the street offers a better brew or a quieter reading room, I may walk away. As Tim Keller puts it, "Throughout history there have always been consumer relationships. In a consumer relationship (*a thing-oriented relationship*), it could be said that the individual's needs are more important than the relationship."[2]

Sociologists "argue that in contemporary Western society the marketplace has become so dominant that the consumer model increasingly characterizes most relationships."[3] We've made the world into a market.

Today, we stay connected to people only as long as they are meeting our particular needs at an acceptable cost to us. When we cease to make a profit—that is, when the relationship appears to require more love and affirmation from us than we are getting back—then we "cut our losses" and drop the relationship. This has also been called "commodification," a process by which social relationships are reduced to economic exchange relationships.[4]

People can easily become projects to be managed rather than persons to be encouraged. Even in ministry, we can slip into evaluating leaders and the value of those we lead by standards of efficiency, production, and replacement cost—money, attendance, and performance alone—rather than by faithfulness and true fruitfulness.

We weren't created to lead and love this way. Collaborative leaders live life with God and others under the rule of loyal love. God made us for community, because the Trinity has lived in community eternally.

Theologians have long talked about how the persons of the Trinity communicate with one another and make agreements with each other (Gen. 22:16; Isa. 45:23; Jer. 22:5; Heb. 6:13). As Michael Horton says, "God's very existence is covenantal: Father, Son, and Holy Spirit live in unceasing devotion to each other."[5] This truth has implications for us. God created us for community because the Trinity has lived an eternally *covenantal* life.

Covenantal Collaboration

In the Bible, a covenant either creates a family relationship—like the marriage covenant (Prov. 2:17; Mal. 2:14; Eph. 5:21–33)—or it confirms a family relationship that has already been established—like a couple renewing their vows. In Genesis 14:13, powerful kings of the desert (including Abraham) formed a covenant alliance to help each other in case of attack by enemies. They weren't related, but they would protect one another *like family*. After years of trying to outwit each other, Laban and Jacob made an agreement to do no more harm. They were related, but now they covenanted together to treat one another that way—*like family* (Gen. 31:44). When Joshua led Israel into the land of Canaan, he attacked the Canaanites who lived there. The Gibeonites tricked him into making a covenant (Josh. 9:6). This peace treaty between two unrelated nations ensured they would live *like family*. Jonathan and David were friends, and their friendship was formally solemnized by agreements of covenant loyalty (1 Sam. 18:3; 23:18). When David came into his kingdom, he kept his promise to Jonathan by treating his descendant *like family* (2 Samuel 9).

The Trinity is an eternal family. The Godhead created covenants to establish family unions. God made them to picture his own internal life—the committed love between Father and Son. When God calls people to *participate* in his mission to the world, he is also calling them into a covenant *partnership*.[6] We see this in the series of covenants God made with his people. In each one—at creation, with Noah, with Abraham, with Moses, with David, and in his new covenant—God sets apart a particular people as his beloved children and invites them to collaborate *like family*.

Trinitarian Doctrine 4: Covenant

A covenant is an agreement that either creates or confirms a family relationship. The Trinitarian family members—Father, Son, and Holy Spirit—make agreements with one another. God also makes promises to his people, and he keeps these agreements with loyalty and love.

Major Covenants between God and Mankind in the Bible

- The covenant with creation (Genesis 1–3)
- The covenant with Noah (Genesis 6–9)
- The covenant with Abraham (Genesis 12, 15, 17)
- The covenant at Sinai (Ex. 19:3b–8; 20–24)
- The covenant with David (2 Samuel 7; Psalm 89)
- The new covenant (Jeremiah 31–34; Ezek. 33:29–39:29)

The biblical concepts of covenant and family can feel foreign to us, because most of us have grown up in a culture where family is falling apart. Our society devalues community and family commitment, prizing individualism instead. The world bombards us with false messages, like "The lone individual is the blazing center of the universe." Every generation has been accused of being narcissistic and self-preoccupied. Baby boomers were called the "me generation." Generation X was characterized by the phrase "Enough about you . . . let's talk about me." And *Time* recently dubbed the Y generation the "me, me, me generation."[7] But this is not a generational thing. It's a fallen human thing. Sin separates what God joins together. We are prone to self-interest and given to think "me first." Working with others is hard. Unity is fragile. Collaboration? Why bother? You only live once, so grab all you can for yourself.

The Bible stands in stark contrast to modern individualism. The biblical story is one of collaboration.[8] It begins with the Trinity—the Father, Son, and Holy Spirit collaborating together in perfect harmony for all eternity. Then, in Genesis 1–2, God creates humanity in his image. He makes them male and female to populate the whole earth

Modern Individualism versus Biblical Collaboration*

	Modern World View (individualism)	Biblical World View (collaboration)
Basis	Contractual	Covenantal
View of self	Autonomous (self-reflective)	Interdependent (social, relational)
View of relationships	Exchange (contractual)	Communal (covenantal)
Source of moral authority	Relativistic (self-constructed)	Transcendent (established by God)
Reason for church involvement	Needs-related	Relational give and take
Highest virtue	Self-esteem	Love
Approach to conflict resolution	Communication (negotiation)	Moral approach (reintegration or reconciliation)
Life purpose	Self-fulfillment	Self-transcendence (love)
Foundation of forgiveness	Generating self-forgiveness	Receiving forgiveness
Primary motivation to forgive	Personal health (functional coping)	Glory to God and communal harmony

* Taken from *Conformed to His Image* by Kenneth Boa. Copyright © 2001 by Kenneth Boa. Used by permission of Zondervan www.zondervan.com.

with little teams we call marriages and families. God is a relational being, and he creates us as relational beings to represent him to the whole creation. Living in community is part of God's Trinitarian identity, and it is part of our identity as well. Pastor Brad House describes the phenomena of community this way:

No one really debates the need for people to exist within community. It is not merely a Christian understanding; it is a human understanding. But belonging in and of itself will never be enough. Hanging the need for community on belonging is like hanging the need for water on thirst. The need for both is deeper. Thirst is a symptom of a deeper design—that your body was created to require water to survive. While we can technically survive without community, we don't function properly without it. The deeper need for community is embedded in the very fabric of who we are; it is part of our design.[9]

Collaboration isn't a lofty ideal. Collaboration is God's pattern of leadership, the pattern he models himself. God could have accomplished his entire redemptive plan by himself, but he decided to *partner* with people. He calls us into community—into his family. He collaborates with us to accomplish his mission. The Father, Son, and Holy Spirit live together as a committed family and are "reaching outward beyond the Godhead to create a community of creatures serving as a giant analogy of the Godhead's relationship."[10] Because our covenant God exists eternally in community, we're created for community. Because God eternally collaborates, we must collaborate. Leaders can be alone, but they can't lead God's way and lead alone.

Collaborative leaders empower the team. They enable others to pursue a common mission. We will look at this from three angles—the message, ministry, and mystery of collaboration.

Leadership Vision 4: The Collaborative Leader
Collaborative leaders empower the team.

The Message of Collaboration

When I started out as a church planter, older pastors would lean in and tell me, "You can't have friends in the church." As the church grew, this same counsel came to me again and again, often unsolicited. Eventually, as Sojourn grew larger, I got to know pastors of large churches, and I quickly noticed they were alone. They lived a friendless, lonely life. Counselors seemed to be their only friends, and even then, at an hourly rate.

Something is terribly wrong with the modern-day pastor. The average tenure of a pastor in his church is three to four years.[11] He's often discouraged, depressed, and disconnected. He is disconnected from other ministry leaders and disconnected from the people he leads. Pastors need community with one another and with their church. They need to share their experience and expertise with others for greater impact. They need to collaborate on the mission with other staff and key leaders. Pastors need to break out of isolation, both in their practical ministry philosophy and in their theology of leadership. They need a bigger doctrine; one that helps the church work together. Pastors need the God who collaborates.

Jesus wasn't like the modern pastor. Jesus had friends (John 15:15). Sure, Peter was arrogant. Yes, Judas stabbed him in the back. Simon was a zealot (that's code language for potential terrorist,[12] Matt. 10:4). James and John were delusional at times (Matt. 20:21; Mark 10:37; Luke 9:54). But Jesus always had friends. A life without friends isn't life in the image of God. We need the joy, life, and pain of community.

From the very beginning Sojourn has needed covenantal collaboration. We live in a culture that celebrates what is cool, casual, and comfortable, but our diversity challenged us to grow in vulnerability and tested fidelity. Our church plant was the combination of three distinct tribes:

- Nathan Quillo had led a growing and evangelistic youth group at another church, but he was fired for fruitfulness after the kids in the group were smoking and skateboarding in the parking lot. The displaced leaders of the group began meeting in homes with about thirty people. Sometimes Nathan would teach and they'd sing. Often they'd just share life and pray together.

- The second tribe was made up of theologically outspoken seminary students. They viewed Sojourn as a great experiment for their Reformed, elder-led, and missional "church plant or die" idealism.
- Then another group of kids merged with us. Loy Thurman was reaching kids for Christ from the hardcore and "straight-edge" scene around Bardstown Road. They wore black and did evangelism in mosh pits. They weren't exactly your typical college-aged Christians.

We were all over the map theologically, culturally, and practically. We even had competing visions of what Sojourn should be. We were a motley crew to say the least. But in our diversity, God brought unity and eventually maturity.

That's what God desires for our teams. He wants churches to reflect his beauty—unity and diversity working together toward growing maturity.

UNITY

When Paul began to plead with the Ephesian church to work together in unity, he began by appealing to their common identity and common calling. Paul wrote, "There is one body and one Spirit—just as you were called to one hope that belongs to your call—one Lord, one faith, one baptism, one God and Father of all, who is over all and through all and in all" (Eph. 4:4–6).

In Ephesus, the church was made up of Jews and Gentiles. At Sojourn, our team was a group of hardcore renegades, and I was their occasionally fearless leader. John Edmund Kaiser says, "Unity is more than a warm fuzzy feeling. It's a source of power for effective mission to the world."[13] Where does a church find unity? Ephesians tells us the church is called as one body, and Christ is our head. There may be many expressions, many personalities and backgrounds, and even differing local communities of faith, but we are *one* universal church in Christ Jesus.

In *Sticky Teams*, Larry Osborne reminds us that a unified and healthy leadership team doesn't happen spontaneously. Unity must be a leadership priority. Think of how often a divided board has resulted in a church blowing up. Unity makes an organization healthy and gives it spiritual power.[14] The author of Hebrews warns us, "See to it that . . . no 'root of bitterness' springs up and causes trouble, and by it many become defiled" (12:15). Leaders must create environments conducive to unity and remove the divisions, turf battles, and bitterness, which sabotage the Spirit's work.

So what kind of unity are we fighting for? Osborne identifies three irreducible minimums: (1) doctrinal unity, (2) relational unity, and (3) philosophical unity.[15]

- *Doctrinal unity* is agreement on the essential matters—the deep convictions a local church has covenanted together to contend for. We must have unity around the most important things—things the church has found important enough to write into its common confession or statement of faith. Maintaining doctrinal unity requires clear preaching and teaching, and faithful discipleship and training.
- *Relational unity* is mutual respect and friendship. This doesn't mean everyone has to be "besties," but it does mean we get along well enough to avoid miscommunication, stereotyping, and personality conflicts. These block the way when it's time to tackle tough issues. Maintaining relational unity takes bold love. Collaborative leaders will have awkward conversations and have the courage to make decisions in the midst of conflict.
- *Philosophical unity* is a basic agreement about our priorities and methods of ministry. This area is usually the hardest to develop. Most church fights aren't over theology; they're over priorities and methods. Maintaining philosophical unity requires clear vision and organizational clarity.

Where do we find the strength to fight for this kind of deep unity? We find it in remembering that Christ is the Head of the body (Col. 1:18). Throughout the history of the church, God calls together a diversity of people. He unites them around a common identity, one that is rooted in who he is and what he has done for them. The Father calls us as a community and then the Son sends us out together in pursuit of a common mission.

DIVERSITY

Paul goes on to say, "But grace was given to each one of us according to the measure of Christ's gift. . . . And he gave the apostles, the prophets, the evangelists, the shepherds and teachers, to equip the saints for the work of ministry, for building up the body of Christ" (Eph. 4:7, 11–12). "Diversity of agenda is deadly," says Kaiser; "diversity of background is helpful, and diversity of role is essential."[16] Leaders must celebrate our diverse gifting. God gifts a diverse people to grow a dynamic mission. He's given us different sounds and stories. He weaves us together as a symphony. When we work together for unity, our diversity reflects his beauty. We work for racial reconciliation out of a desire to love our neighbor *and* because of a conviction that God has designed the church to display his beauty through diversity. When we work together for unity, our economic diversity displays his beauty as well. When those who grew up middle class draw near to the poor, it can be overwhelming. But we believe in holistic discipleship that addresses both the physical and spiritual state of the poor. As Randy Nabors has said, it takes more than community development: "Every poor community needs a great church."[17] Holistic discipleship takes the church in all of its diversity. Paul teaches us that we have "gifts that differ according to the grace given to us" (Rom. 12:6). If there is a woman who is being unjustly divorced, she needs the church. She needs people with gifts of mercy to weep with. She needs people with strength to give structure to her life. She needs counselors and she needs the preaching of the Word to inspire her to move forward.

MATURITY

God's church displays a *unity* of calling and a *diversity* of gifts. We can learn to use these gifts to build one another up as the church grows to *maturity* in love. Paul puts the goal this way: "To equip the saints for the work of ministry, for building up the body of Christ, until we all attain to the unity of the faith and of the knowledge of the Son of God, to mature manhood, to the measure of the stature of the fullness of Christ" (Eph. 4:12–13).

A vision of unity in diversity is beautiful, but we fail to achieve it because we're broken. Immaturity and sin keep us from working together well. But if we have a deep conviction that God has put the church together as a community, we'll keep working together. We'll pursue maturity (Heb. 6:1–2)—we'll pursue it personally, we'll pursue it for our team, and we'll pursue it as a team.

For the first five or six years of Sojourn, we had a lone evening service. We were against buildings, against morning services, against asking our people for money, and against saving cash (because you are supposed to give it away, right?). Then we grew and got older. Suddenly we needed a space for our kids during services. After telling our people for years about the evils of buildings, we came to the church in repentance. We said, "Hey, actually we do need a building, and we need you to give money, like, now." The church forgave us, and they gave generously. We got the building and launched a morning service. Then Sojourn grew from three hundred to seven hundred on Sunday in just a few months. We had to mature, and we had to acknowledge our immaturity along the way. The expectation of healthy collaboration is maturity manifesting as growth and change.

The Father calls the church to grow up in maturity and love. As challenges escalate, the need for mature collaboration escalates.[18] Pursuing a mature team requires pursuing maturity ourselves. The collaborative leader needs to ask, "Am I ready to change?" Collaboration can only happen if we're humble enough to seek change. Leaders are called to be the chief repenters in our communities. A community's growth toward maturity begins with the leader's own growth. We must continue to change or we will die. I tell my church if I thought I'd be the same pastor a year from now, I'd quit. Moreover, if I didn't have the hope my congregation would be different in a year, I'd also quit. Collaboration calls for continual change. To stop growing is to stop living. Our hope is not in the way things are but rather in the God who began a good work in us and who will be faithful to complete it (Phil. 1:6). We have hope because God finishes what he starts (2 Cor. 9:10; Col. 1:28). My hope for my marriage, my children, my coworkers, our church, and

The Message of Collaboration

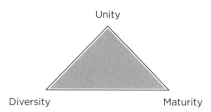

Unity

Diversity   Maturity

The message of collaboration involves the Father's call to *unity*, the Son sending us on mission with a *diversity* of gifts, and the Spirit sanctifying us into harmony and *maturity* in love.

- **Unity:** *Leaders stand united with a common confession.* "There is one body and one Spirit—just as you were called to one hope that belongs to your call—one Lord, one faith, one baptism, one God and Father of all, who is over all and through all and in all" (Eph. 4:4–6).
- **Diversity:** *Leaders celebrate diverse giftings.* "But grace was given to each one of us according to the measure of Christ's gift. . . . And he gave the apostles, the prophets, the evangelists, the shepherds and teachers, to equip the saints for the work of ministry, for building up the body of Christ" (Eph. 4:7, 11–12).
- **Maturity:** *Leaders grow.* ". . . until we all attain to the unity of the faith and of the knowledge of the Son of God, to mature manhood, to the measure of the stature of the fullness of Christ" (Eph. 4:13).

our neighbors is that I will be different and they will be different a year from now. Perfect Trinitarian harmony is idealistic, but we find hope by trusting that God grows us.

The Ministry of Collaboration

It's possible to have a strong theology of covenants—a strong theology of collaboration—but still be an organizational mess. It's true that the church is a people, not a building. It's a family, more than the sum of its organizational parts. But in some communities, the local church has literally fallen apart. Leaders have neglected the ministry of collaboration altogether. It's sad, because mission has no momentum unless the team shares it and organizes around it. A key question for us as leaders must be, "Has my mission-vision gone from *me* to *we* practically?"

For the first seven years, Sojourn was a self-contained, single-site church. In 2009, Lifespring Community Church, a church plant in a Louisville suburb, approached us about merging. By that autumn, Lifespring dissolved and nearly a hundred of our members joined the newly formed East campus. We became a multisite church. Initially, our new site functioned primarily as an additional off-site service. After six years, this is no longer the case. At the time of writing, Sojourn is a multisite church with four locations and four lead pastors. We've been forced to collaborate. The multisite model allows us to best steward the gifts, talents, passions, and experiences of the team God has given us. At Sojourn, we have diverse, gifted leaders in songwriting, church planting, and preaching who are both local church pastors and *movement* leaders, whose skills can be utilized for greater impact. Collaboration across multiple campuses divides the effort and multiplies the effect.[19]

But it hasn't been easy. We went from one young church, nine years old, to birthing three additional campuses in a few short years. The strain and difficulty have been both expected and shocking. Like a married couple adjusting to new children, we are experiencing the complexity of a growing family. Communication between two people is difficult. Communication in a growing church is harder still. Communication channels within our multisite family often feel like an intricate, complicated highway system. Simply put, it's really hard to know what's going on and to keep everyone on the same page. There is beauty in complexity, though. As Paul David Tripp says, relationships are a mess worth making.[20] One key to doing ministry collaboration is having clarity about how we are organized. Specifically, we need clarity about three things—authority, responsibility, and accountability.

AUTHORITY

Someone has to be in charge. John Maxwell calls this the law of the edge, "The difference between two equally talented teams is leadership."[21] Osborne says, "In a church, [that] leader sets the agenda, general tone, and direction for ministry. When a tough problem or exciting opportunity comes along, everyone [looks to that person] for direction."[22] Biblically speaking, Christ has given leaders to the church to equip the members. Just as the Father has the originating and authoritative role among the persons of the Trinity, the church needs primary leaders who serve as the first among equals (1 Tim. 5:17).

In Luke 7, a Roman centurion sends messengers to Jesus, because his servant, whom he values highly, is sick and about to die (7:2–3). Jesus goes immediately, but when he is not far from the house, the centurion sends another message: "I did not presume to come to you. But say the word, and let my servant be healed" (7:7). The solider has faith in Jesus's authority because he is a man both under authority *and* with authority: "I say to one, 'Go,' and he goes, and to another, 'Come,' and he comes, and to my servant, 'Do this,' and he does it" (Matt. 8:9; Luke 7:8). Jesus commends him: "With no one in Israel have I found such faith" (Matt. 8:10; cf. Luke 7:9). The centurion sees the connection between Jesus's authority and his own leadership. Primary leaders have power to determine issues and control jurisdiction. They are both in control and under control.

Leadership with authority can either advance the mission or be abused and the mission can be hindered. Solomon tells us:

When the righteous increase, the people rejoice,
> but when the wicked rule, the people groan. (Prov. 29:2)

By justice a king gives a country stability,
> but those who are greedy for bribes tear it down. (Prov. 29:4 NIV)

Being in authority and under authority means Christian leaders must manage the tension of being both first and equal. Sometimes there is greater authority and a larger power distance between leader and follower. For example, we are commanded to submit to governing authorities (Rom. 13:1–7). Children are commanded to obey their parents (Eph. 6:1–3). And people are to obey and submit to their overseers (Heb. 13:17). At other times, we're called to recognize our equality under God's authority. In Christ, there is no male or female, slave or free (Gal. 3:26–29).[23]

RESPONSIBILITY

Everyone on the team must have responsibilities. Leaders have duties, obligations, and tasks they are required and expected to do, and they should task team members in keeping with their particular gifting and calling.

The apostle Paul gave us the image of many parts working together within one body (1 Corinthians 12). Some parts look more glorious than others, but all are indispensible. Throughout the New Testament, we see God bringing together particular people for the sake of gospel ministry. Leaders must believe God has put together their team of leaders for such a time as this. Each member of the team has received gifts from God, and those gifts can be used to build up the team as a whole. Every member of the team has a place where he or she will add the most value.[24] The key is finding it. We've all experienced being part of a team where people are in the wrong role. Maxwell asks:

> What happens to a team when one or more of its members constantly play out of position? First, morale erodes because the team isn't playing up to its capability. Then people become resentful. The people working in an area of weakness resent that their best is untapped. And other people on the team who know that they could better fill a mismatched position on the team resent that their skills are being overlooked. Before long, people become unwilling to work as a team.[25]

Leaders of a maturing church must have the discernment to give responsibilities according to each team member's particular gifting and in keeping with the overall mission of the organization. Don't rush this, because it takes time to understand how each team member is wired.

A prideful person will take on too much responsibility. A coward takes on too little. Successful people find the right place for *themselves*. A successful leader finds the right place for *others*.

Giving and Developing Responsibilities

Consider this list of questions, which can help you develop gifted people and root them in places where they will best contribute to the overall mission of your organization.

Ask yourself . . .

- Am I trying to do everything myself?
- Do I expect others to do what I do, whether it fits their abilities or not?
- Am I developing people or an assembly line?
- Do I release people to reach their potential?
- Can I release responsibilities to people who demonstrate the capacity to handle them?
- Can I convey my organization's purpose so that team members understand how their role is important?
- What do I project would happen to staff morale if people were allowed to work within their particular calling and gifting?
- Do I believe a person working in his or her gifting will neglect other duties? Why or why not?
- Who is joining our team? What kinds of team members are coming aboard? How am I developing the team? Am I training them for a solid future?
- Who is leaving our team? What kinds of members are leaving our team and why?

ACCOUNTABILITY

Once responsibilities are given, it's essential that each team member be held accountable. For the mission to move forward, peers must give an account to one another.[26] They need to hold one another accountable to high, agreed-upon standards.

Consider Paul's relationship with John Mark. At the outset of Paul's second missionary journey, he decided to leave Mark behind (Acts 15:38–40). John Mark had deserted him on the previous mission (Acts

Accountability Questions

Try using these questions to begin incorporating accountability into your regular team rhythms:*

- Do I give others a reason to question my character?
- Do I know my responsibilities and perform them with excellence?
- Am I dedicated to the team's success? Am I trustworthy?
- Can people count on me for consistency no matter how a situation develops?
- Do my actions bring the team together?

* John Maxwell, *The 17 Indisputable Laws of Teamwork* (Nashville: Thomas Nelson, 2001), 131.

13:13), so Paul held the young man accountable. He was willing to confront a difficult issue even though it meant conflict and disassociation from his partner, Barnabas. They parted ways, but it didn't end their relationship. Years later, Paul called for Mark, and asked for his help (2 Tim. 4:11). Mark had grown and changed. A setback isn't the end of a leadership story.

Paul is a model for us. Moral failure or poor performance requires strong accountability (Gal. 2:11–19). This may mean practicing church discipline (Matt. 18:15–18)[27] or letting a staff member go, but the Christian leader always keeps theological and relational restoration in view. Leadership like this is meant not to weed out the weak but to help us grow.

Some teams have no real leader. Think back to school projects. The nerd did all the work and the jock did the presentation. No one collaborated. The responsibilities were unclear, and there was no accountability. We subconsciously learn that the only way to do things right is to do them ourselves. And sometimes we never grow out of this thinking.

God's way is different. The gospel message forms us as a community and sends us with order, not chaos. The best structure for organizing

The Ministry of Collaboration

Authority

Responsibility   Accountability

There is beauty in complexity when we're organized around God's mission. The mechanics of collaboration involves three things—authority, responsibility, and accountability.

- **Authority:** *Leaders have power to determine issues and control jurisdiction.* The church needs primary leaders who serve as the first among equals within a plurality. The team rises and falls with humble, strong leadership under God's authority.
- **Responsibility:** *Leaders have duties, obligations, and tasks they are required and expected to do.* Leaders should be tasked and should task others in keeping with their gifting and calling.
- **Accountability:** *Leaders must submit to regular review of their actions.* They must give an account. Accountability should be personal. It's best if it happens in community and if it's ingrained into the culture of an organization through regular rhythms of review.

around the mission involves all three of these factors—authority, responsibility, *and* accountability. People don't trust authority, because they've so often seen it abused. But if we only have responsibilities, that results in bureaucracy, and people begin to beg for authority. Add authority to responsibility without accountability and you can easily get a dictator. There we are back at abuse again. Put all three ingredients together and you get a structure that is organized and ready for mission. The leader in accountable community is set up to lead and function as God intended—faithfully equipping and building up Christ's body (Eph. 4:12).

Authority, Responsibility, and Accountability*

- *Responsibility + Accountability + ~~Authority~~ = Bureaucratic Leadership.* In a bureaucracy, there is no power to bring necessary change. A bureaucracy is safe in the short term, but it's ineffective, and it lacks power. Over the long haul, the organization stagnates, because it can't change.
- *Responsibility + ~~Accountability~~ + Authority = Authoritarian Leadership.* Under authoritarian leadership, there is no accountability. This kind of leadership may be effective and powerful in the short term, but it's not safe. Over time, the organization implodes as a result of poor decisions or abuse of power.
- *~~Responsibility~~ + Accountability + Authority = Reactionary or Impulsive Leadership.* An impulsive leader or leadership team may have power, but they lack any clear goals or responsibilities. Over the long haul, impulsive leaders just fall apart, and their organizations deteriorate as a result of mission drift.

* Adapted from John Edmund Kaiser, *Winning on Purpose: How to Organize Congregations to Succeed in Their Mission* (Nashville: Abingdon, 2006), 70–72.

We want teams fueled by the mission of collaboration—*unity* and *diversity* working together in growing *maturity*. We want teams that minister together with organizational clarity—clear *authority, responsibility*, and *accountability*. Those values require a continued investment.

The Mystery of Collaboration

Collaborative leaders enable the team to pursue a common mission. Pursuing a mature and united team means *empowering* them to go forward even when the mission gets messy. The mystery of collaboration is having this personal vision of empowering others. James MacGregor Burns describes it this way: "Instead of exercising power over people, transforming leaders champion and inspire followers."[28] The first virtue needed to be a leader is humility. Humility recognizes leadership as a gift that can't be assumed or earned. Any authority we have is a gift from God (John 19:11; Rom. 13:1). Rick Langer reminds us:

> Human authority is always delegated authority. God appoints people for particular roles in accordance with his sovereign timing. Think of how Esther was given "for such a time as this" (Est. 4:14). Think of how God turned Nebuchadnezzar's heart toward his purposes (Dan. 4:25, 32, 36). "He brings down one; he exalts another" (Ps. 75:7b). "The king's heart is a stream of water in the hand of the LORD; he turns it wherever he will" (Prov. 21:1 ESV). Leadership serves divine purposes—by intention or by accident.[29]

Humility makes us leaders who serve the mission, not ourselves. Humility shapes our leadership in service to those on mission with us. The way we treat those who follow us shows the One who leads us. We should have the attitude within ourselves we see in Christ Jesus. He didn't consider equality with God as something to be held onto, but he emptied himself and took the form of a servant. He did this in obedience and submission to his Father's mission (Phil. 2:5–11). Submitting to his Father's will didn't keep Jesus from leading. In fact, being an excellent follower leads to more influence than we would otherwise have.

Leadership Skill Set 4: Serving and Supporting

Empowering the team requires . . .

- *Serving.* Be humble. Value others as more important than yourself.
- *Supporting.* Give your team what they need to grow through ministry challenges.

How do we humbly empower our teams? We provide them with the support they need to grow through ministry challenges. To feel supported and grow, team members need three fundamental things:

autonomy, self-directing freedom to exist and act separately from the organization; *ambiguity,* an environment that is messy enough for team members to wrestle with and discern their purpose through suffering; and *adaptability,* freedom and space to make new things and bring all members' imaginations to bear on their work. Let's take each of these elements in turn.

AUTONOMY

First, to feel empowered, leaders need self-directing freedom. They need autonomy. Autonomy is about knowing one's own call and place within the organization.

Overemphasizing an organization's needs can result in a strict hierarchy and oppressive dictatorial rule. One mark of a cult is that followers lose their own identity as they're swept up into the personality and vision of the cult leader.[30] Churches often fall into this trap. An insecure leader will only keep others around who are weak enough to stay in his shadow and never challenge the vision. Insecure leaders can't tolerate autonomy. Strong leaders under an insecure leader will tire of tyranny.

On the other hand, overemphasizing an individual's needs can result in permissive democracy and a lack of productivity. Collaborative efforts sometimes *seem* more productive than they are, because of the way our minds experience them. It's easy to feel productive when we're part of a group—listening to others' ideas, contributing, and giving feedback. For most of us, it beats staring at a blank screen.[31] But very often with group work, little actually gets done.

Having autonomy requires keeping the organization's needs and the individual's needs in balance. To find that balance, individual team members need confidence that they are making unique contributions to the organization as a whole. Christ's vision for the church is that of a body where every member makes an individual contribution as a unique part of the whole (1 Cor. 12:12–31). Clearly defined gift-based responsibilities give team members the personal ownership and security they need.

Organizations flourish when leaders' gifts and callings are recognized, and they are empowered with the freedom necessary to act on their own. Healthy organizations give leaders breathing room to become passionate champions for their own particular ministry area and role.[32] In such organizations, leaders are loyal, faithful, and committed members, and yet they still have freedom to be themselves. As David Benner says, "[We must] cultivate the safety for both of you to be your own unique persons . . . to be important threads of [your own] sacred otherness."[33]

AMBIGUITY

Second, to be empowered, team members need to embrace ambiguity. It's an unavoidable reality. God is not the author of chaos, but he uses suffering and a lack of clarity in our fallen world to make his purposes prevail and lead us to maturity.

The military trains soldiers to function within VUCA environments. That military-acronym-turned-corporate-buzzword stands for volatile, uncertain, complex, and ambiguous. The authors of *The Practice of Adaptive Leadership* call it living in the disequilibrium. They tell us, "Disequilibrium can catalyze everything from conflict, frustration, and panic to confusion, disorientation, and fear of losing something dear."[34] Volatility and disequilibrium shouldn't surprise us. As Thomas Merton wrote, "Once again I dimly realize the enormous proportions of the ambiguities in myself. I cannot expect to resolve them. Nor should I be surprised at the ambiguities in others."[35] This fallen world is filled with tension, paradoxes, suffering, complicated organizational charts, and messy relationships.

In a world that fits the VUCA standard, we need teams that are more than competent. We need teams that can be flexible enough to adapt and change when the unexpected happens. We need teams that gain from disorder.[36]

In the midst of a VUCA environment, a military leader needs total domain awareness (TDA, if you need another military acronym). He needs to know where his battalion is in relation to the whole—air support, the next battalion, the enemy, and the troop's place in the overall battle plan. Total domain awareness gives the leader the ability to react on the fly to the unexpected and turn difficult circumstances into strengths. It's easy to get sucked into only seeing your own messy circumstances and not see how your part relates to the whole. We have a finite perspective. We live in a VUCA world, but God lives in a TDA world. He is more aware of the part each of the pieces plays than we will ever be.

Collaborative leaders must embrace ambiguity. We need to give the people we lead permission for things to be messy and even for things to fail. Ambiguity is a reality and necessity because we are not God. The advantage of failing, being attacked, being oppressed, or even just being stressed is that this forces leaders to rely on him (2 Cor. 12:9). Weakness is our greatest strength. It leads us to increasing dependence on the Spirit.

ADAPTABILITY

Finally, collaborative leaders need creative adaptability. Reality is always changing, so we must adapt to solve the problems that change brings. Sadly, most people resist change. The truth is that we're delusional—denying that change has taken place or that problems have arisen. Even when problems are acknowledged, leaders chase after nostalgia or novelty instead of embracing creative solutions. It's true in churches that are plagued by boring songs, colorless sermons, drab sanctuaries, and bad art. It's true in churches that abandon good traditions rather than adapt them to new contexts.

Here is the sobering reality. Leaders must adapt or they will watch their organizations die. As Ichak Adizes tells us: "To manage an organization is to continuously solve problems. An organization is without problems only when there is no change. This happens only when the organization is dead. To solve problems and have no new and more complex ones emerge is equivalent to dying."[37]

At Sojourn, we want to empower leaders to innovate, contextualize, and make decisions. For example, we strongly believe a multisite

Five Questions for Empowering Creative Freedom in an Organization*

1. Are people who make mistakes or experiment with new ways of doing things being marginalized?
2. When strategic decisions need to be made, are the perspectives of frontline people considered?
3. When something bad happens (a member leaves the church, a new ministry initiative fails), is the news acknowledged and is the event debriefed for its lessons, instead of used as a moment for punishment?
4. Are communication and interaction nurtured across all formal and informal boundaries?
5. Do people have a healthy view of the latest strategic plan as "our current best guess" rather than a sacred infallible text?

* Adapted from Ronald Heifetz, Alexander Grashow, and Marty Linsky, *The Practice of Adaptive Leadership: Tools and Tactics for Changing Your Organization and the World* (Boston, MA: Harvard Business Press, 2009), 106.

church is not a franchise. Each congregation should take on the character of its neighborhood. Sojourn's Midtown campus is filled with the urban poor, young professionals, and other urbanites. Our East campus is dominated with young families and white-collar workers. Speaking to an upwardly mobile middle class is different from speaking to downtrodden, poorer people. The Jeffersontown and New Albany campuses have their own unique challenges and opportunities. We strive not for "brand" conformity but for relentless and passionate adaptability. Everything from the Sunday message to the worship music to group life needs to be adapted to the unique context and congregation.

Collaborative leaders foster a culture where people enjoy autonomy, thrive in ambiguity, and innovate solutions to new challenges. Team members need creative freedom to make new things and think up new ideas. We want men and women to flourish as creative, adaptive individuals—to bring their own imaginations to bear on their work. This means we give them more than a list of tasks. We empower them to be adaptive.

The Mystery of Collaboration

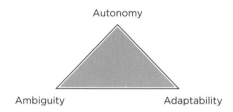

Autonomy

Ambiguity   Adaptability

Empower your team with the support they need to grow as leaders through ministry challenges.

- **Autonomy:** *Leaders exist and act separately from the organization.* They must have self-directing freedom.
- **Ambiguity:** *Leaders experience volatility, uncertainty, and complexity.* They must embrace the inscrutability of leadership because God is unsearchable.
- **Adaptability:** *Leaders make new things and think of new ideas.* They bring their own imagination to bear on their work.

Ultimately being a leader who empowers others involves letting God in the room. It means letting go of control and giving your team the autonomy and creative freedom to enter the mess and truly collaborate. As Jack White told *GQ*:

If you get something cooking, you [could] just stay with it and keep doing it. That's easy. To really let God in the room and let the natural things that happen when people collaborate and work together occur— that's when you're doing your best. You're producing, you're creating. It's because you relinquish control. . . . I think people get in the mindset that when you are the director of the movie, when you're the producer of the album, you're in total control, and you boss everybody around, and you become a control freak and tell people and nitpick and micromanage. That's not what happens. You really just sort of build a room and you just press record, and you just let people do what they do best.

Just let it happen. Anybody can go in there and get on an ego trip and bark orders at people and stuff, but it's so stupid. There's no joy in that. There's no beauty in that. Sometimes you get some funny stories out of it, but you're not going to accomplish much.[38]

God Is in the Complexity

Immediately after I converted, I started a Young Life Bible study. I hungered to learn more about God and to share my faith with my friends. It grew. Soon twenty-five or so faithful believers, new believers, and unbelievers came to that study. But after a year I still hadn't connected to a local church. So I went to my Young Life leader and said, "I can't do this." Before I could lead others, I needed men in my life to teach me discipline and listen to me confess my sin. Eventually God put a community like that in my life. I started working at a Christian bookstore. I'd go to the owner with my questions and he'd *never* answer them. Instead, he taught me how to study. He'd just point me to a book. I'd ask, "What about the holiness of God?" He'd say, "Go pick up A. W. Tozer. Go pick up R. C. Sproul." I didn't know it at the time, but that bookstore owner discipled me. He taught me to wrestle with ideas. He invited me into his home. I ate dinner with his family. Seeing them eat dinner together was huge for someone who grew up without a dad. I saw Christianity lived out in the man's life. Living in community with him changed me.

Sometimes I wonder why it isn't still that simple. When I was a kid, it was easy to make friends; the streetlights coming on at dinnertime was the greatest boundary to our community. When you get a job, get married, and have kids, relationships become increasingly more complicated. In a growing church, relational complications are compounded. Most leaders have trouble keeping track of all the hats—director, counselor, teacher, family member, coach, and the list goes on. I just gave you nine different categories for thinking through all of these relationships. Is the mess even worth making?

The truth is that I need community just as much as I did when I started out as a Christian. Kouzes and Posner remind us, "A grand

Cumulative Chapter Summary

Leadership begins with *knowing where people need to go*. When you combine *conviction* and *creativity*, you have vision to see the way forward.

Leadership Vision	Trinitarian Doctrine	Leadership Skills
Convictional leaders embody what they believe.	**Revelation:** God speaks. He makes himself known through his world, Word, and works.	Embodying what you believe requires . . . • *Listening*. Seek to hear God's voice in order to clarify your convictions. • *Living it out*. Practice what you preach, because people do what people see.
Creative leaders imagine the way forward.	**Creation:** God made everything. His creation work is a purposeful project of love.	Imagining the way forward requires . . . • *Dreaming*. Make creative connections between where you are and what God wants. • *Persuading*. Be winsome. Be a poet. Help your people dream.

But it's not enough to have direction. Moving forward requires *courage* and *collaboration*. We must take initiative, and we must work in God's way—as part of a team.

Courageous leaders take risks.	**Mission:** God moves out in love to rescue his children. The Father's mission plan is accomplished through the work of the Son and by the agency of the Holy Spirit.	Taking risks requires . . . • *Seeking*. Look for where God is working. Opportunities are invitations. • *Joining*. Speak up, step out, and act. God is inviting you to join him in his work.

Collaborative leaders empower the team.	Covenant: an agreement that either creates or confirms a family relationship. God makes promises both to himself and to his people, and he keeps these agreements with loyalty and love.	Empowering the team requires . . . • *Serving.* Be humble. Value others as more important than yourself. • *Supporting.* Give your team what they need to grow through ministry challenges.

dream doesn't become a significant reality through the actions of a single person." It requires a team with members that trust one another and can lean on each other when times get tough. "Leaders foster collaboration by building trust and facilitating relationships."[39] Christian leaders can step into the challenges of teamwork with even greater confidence because we see that God is on our team. He lives in the midst of all our relational complexity. The Father has given us a message of collaboration. The Son organizes his church as a body for ministry. The Spirit empowers us to work together, grow, and adapt to the challenges ahead.

Exercises

Read through this selection of ideas and activities to help you practice collaborative leadership. Pick out one or two and incorporate them into your regular leadership rhythms.[40]

1. Explicitly say to your team members, "I trust you," and tell them why. *Saying it* matters; and obviously, you'd better mean it.

2. Arrange a team discussion on the topic of authority and submission. Ask people to share their positive or negative experiences of submission with each other. How does understanding these experiences inform your understanding of Ephesians 5:21, "submitting to one another out of reverence for Christ"?

3. Arrange a team discussion about spiritual gifts. Ask team members, one by one, to identify the parts of their jobs or volunteer roles they most enjoy. Ask them to identify the particular parts of their roles where they feel most gifted. Don't try to identify others' gifts before they share. Listen, listen, and listen some more.

4. Ask those who know you to give you their take on what your particular gifting is. Plan a way of using your gifting to benefit the team in the next month.

5. Put the interests of your organization and your team ahead of your own. Every morning for the next two weeks, ask a team member, "What can I do for you today?" Then do it. Talk to God about what this is like for you. What do you see about yourself?

6. Sign on to set up or take down an event. This part of event planning is the least sought after. What is it like for you to do a simple task that doesn't require your skill or expertise?

7. Think about those on your team who are eager to learn new skills (theological, relational, operational). Take time right now to schedule a coaching time with them. Put it in your calendar.

Prayer

All praise to you Father of our Lord, Jesus Christ, who Spirits your church into being, making us members one of another. It is a great mystery that we are your body. But we praise you for it, for otherwise we would be so alone—condemned to live alone, to die alone. But you have given us one another in all shapes and sizes. We do not fit together all that well, but we pray that the puzzles of our lives may please you and entertain you, so that in the end we add up to be your kingdom. Help us to live with the confidence of that kingdom, in the light of your Son's resurrection, so that when all is said and done, this may be said: "They were a strange lot, but look how they loved one another." Amen.[41]

Part 3

SOULFUL COMMUNION

THE CONTEMPLATIVE LEADER

There was no more glorious mystery brought to light in and by Jesus Christ than that of the holy Trinity, or the subsistence of the three persons in the unity of the same divine nature. . . . And this revelation is made unto us, not that our minds might be possessed with the notions of it, but that we may know aright how to place our trust in him, how to obey him and live unto him, how to obtain and exercise communion with him, until we come to the enjoyment of him.

John Owen, *Pneumatologia*

The whole dance, or drama, or pattern of this three-Personal life is to be played out in each one of us; or (putting it the other way round) each one of us has got to enter that pattern, take his place in the dance. . . . Good things as well as bad, you know, are caught by a kind of infection. If you want to get warm you must stand near the fire; if you want to be wet you must get into the water. If you want joy, power, peace, eternal life, you must get close to, or even into, the thing that has them. . . . If you are close to it, the spray will wet you: if you are not, you will remain dry.

C. S. Lewis, *Mere Christianity*

We are relational beings because we are created in the image of a re-lational God. . . .

. . . God exists in a relationship of love. God designed us to enjoy giving and receiving. God designed us to be *for* another. God designed us to receive *from* another. We even receive our understanding of our self in relationship with another. This is what it means to be a rela-tional being. Because we bear God's relational likeness, we can com-mune with God. We also have the capability of connecting with each other in mutually self-flourishing ways.

Richard Plass and James Cofield, *The Relational Soul*

Let us set off at once and lose and intoxicate ourselves in the very heart of God.

Jean-Pierre De Caussade, *Present Moment*

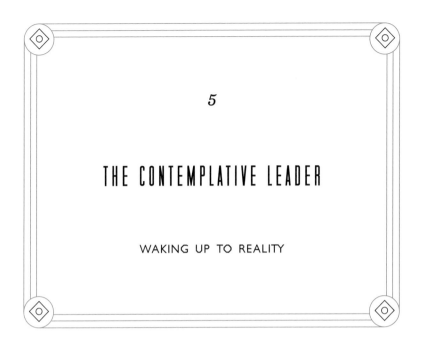

5

THE CONTEMPLATIVE LEADER

WAKING UP TO REALITY

Summary: *The American church settles for a subhuman life, because it refuses to rest. Compulsive leaders all eventually crash, but God is different. God lives in eternal rest and perpetual joy, and we're invited to share in it. Our union with Christ gives us access into the intra-Trinitarian life. We experience the Father's love through the work of the Son and the fellowship of the Holy Spirit. Because they've experienced communion, contemplative leaders are able to give their transformed presence to others. To have communion with others, we first must commune with God. We must abide in God in order to encourage those we lead.*

It's easy to settle for a subhuman life. Despite all our efforts, achievements, and success, many of us discover each night that our hearts don't rest. You might think that busyness is just a modern problem,[1] but King Solomon reminds us that we are facing an ancient struggle:

"What has a man from all the toil and striving of heart with which he toils beneath the sun? For all his days are full of sorrow, and his work is a vexation. Even in the night his heart does not rest" (Eccles. 2:22–23).

This isn't a problem only for busy and important people. It's a problem for everyone:

- A sixth grader wakes up at 5:00 a.m. to get to swim practice. She goes to school all day then rushes to piano lessons in the afternoon. Straining under her parents' Ivy League expectations, she stares at homework until 9:00 p.m.
- A college student, pumping Red Bull into his bloodstream, takes honors classes and volunteers at the soup kitchen to build his résumé. He works out twice a day and attends every social event to avoid being single and alone.
- Young married couples are pulling fifty to sixty hours per week each at work. Since they have no children, they also feel it's their Christian duty to lead a small group, serve in children's ministry, sit on the church finance committee, and participate in neighborhood cleanups. They're exhausted and feel guilty about their exhaustion. They think, "Maybe we'll slow down when we have kids."
- A new mom is bitter with the sudden life change. Just a few months ago, she was up-to-date on the latest fashion, up late for girls' night out, and spending an hour every morning pouring over the Scriptures and her women's Bible study. Now she's up for the 2:00 a.m. feeding and diaper change. She can't even get quiet time on the toilet.
- The fifty-year-old businessman can't keep up with this new generation. He sees younger men willing to work twice as long for half as much. It threatens his livelihood and his identity. In spite of a failing body and his doctor's warnings, he works round the clock. He doesn't want a heart attack, but he doesn't know how to slow down.

I could go on, but I hope you see the point. This is the North American church. The examples I've shared are not exceptional case studies but the common experience of people in our churches, from pastors to preschoolers. We are all going somewhere. We're all running late. We're all too stressed out to see what's happening.

Step back for a moment and consider what our busy lives communicate to our neighbors. Children are busier.[2] People are unhappier.[3] Pastors are quitting.[4] Thirty-five hundred churches close their doors each year.[5] Louder than any sermon, our lives are shouting:

- We don't trust God.
- We don't know how to stop working.
- We don't know how to enjoy life.

We settle for less than we're made for. We settle for less than Jesus paid for. We refuse to stop. We refuse God's rest. We aren't meant to live this way. It's a compulsive, subhuman life.

The Compulsive Cycle

I've lived it. In 2010, I had completed nearly ten years of ministry. We were in the midst of a capital campaign to renovate a new building. Externally, things looked great. But I was burned out and dying inside. It all climaxed in Florida. We did beach things. My kids buried me in the sand. We ate out at seafood places. But I was a zombie. The one or two days of slowing down and settling at the start of a needed vacation never ended. Reality felt distant. My wife Mandy can always tell when I'm tired. On this trip, even my in-laws noticed: "What's wrong with Daniel? Is he not feeling well? He doesn't seem his usual self." Reading the Bible was dull. My prayers felt parched. I was afraid. Is this how pastors die spiritually? Where is God? Is this my life?

I called a pastor friend. I explained my state. How did this happen? It all felt so sudden, but it wasn't. This was half a decade in the making. I reaped what I had sown. Soon, with the help of others, I could articulate exactly what happened.

Christian leaders often find themselves in that place—emotionally, physically, and spiritually exhausted. A few years back, Rich Plass and Jim Cofield, from Crosspoint Ministries, listed seven signs of burnout for the *Sojourn Network* website. I was exhibiting most of them.

Why do we burn out? Sometimes there are external factors (e.g., a severe illness in the family; overwhelming financial pressure because of

Seven Signs of Burnout*

1. Inner restlessness with an underlying sense of anxiety that leads to a defensive, angry spirit.
2. Deep emotional weariness leading to obsessive or scattered thoughts.
3. Waning relational intimacy and a growing fantasy world—particularly sexual fantasies.
4. Numbness of soul. People become tedious to us, and we have no internal energy to give attention to their needs.
5. Feelings of boredom, melancholy, and depression in response to a growing hopelessness.
6. Pretending. Living according to a false self-image rather than having our identity rooted in God.
7. Random spiritual practices or disciplines that have been crowded out by life's demands. A spiritual life that has a serious lack of enthusiasm and love for Christ.

* Jim Cofield and Rich Plass, "Seven Signs of Burnout," *Sojourn Network*, February 26, 2013, http://www.sojournnetwork.com/news/seven-signs-burnout.

a job loss), but sometimes our souls are at risk because of the compulsions driving us from within.

I've been giving you four Cs—four virtuous visions of leadership. But let me give you four more Cs—four leadership vices I call *the cycle of compulsion.*

Without a God-centered vision and deep convictions about who we are, our flesh can seduce us into the *comparison* game. We're afraid we don't measure up and we're not competent enough. We may claim to embrace a righteousness that comes by faith, but deep within there is an inordinate level of shame—a deep sense of inadequacy. We find ourselves walking on the road to Capernaum asking, "Who is the greatest in the kingdom" (Matt. 18:1; cf. Mark 9:33–34; Luke 9:46)? We may even find ourselves passing judgment—needing to rate others and impose our standards on them (and maybe even calling it "benchmarking").[6] Like Peter, in his most performance-driven moments, we promise more

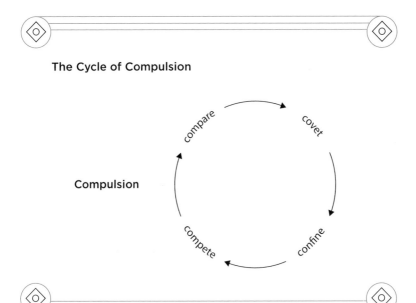

The Cycle of Compulsion

Compulsion

compare → covet → confine → compete (cycle)

than we can fulfill: "Even if everyone else deserts you, I will never desert you" (Matt. 26:33 NLT).

The next step after comparison is *coveting*. In fear of missing out, we find ourselves adding a little *too much* value. You know you have this problem if you have an overwhelming desire to add your opinion to every discussion. Our vision of what a ministry kingdom should look like can be driven by fleshly desires for success and power. When I was on the board of the Acts 29 Network, its early days of fast-paced growth swept me up. The region I led stretched from the Midwest into Louisiana. I had never been given so much leadership responsibility, and never had I been so unaware of my own soul fatigue. When we're coveting, we're always afraid we won't be able to maintain the level of success we've enjoyed. I love the way the King James Version phrases Jesus's response to Peter's ambitions: "Thou savourest not the things that be of God, but those that be of men" (Matt. 16:23). If we're comparing and coveting, we're savoring the wrong things.

When we live as compulsive leaders, we find our direction by comparing and coveting instead of living from conviction and creativity. We also *confine* the mission to a manageable size rather than taking courageous initiative. You know this is your attitude when you seek out ministry ideas with which you're comfortable or which you can control over ministry challenges.

When we live as compulsive leaders, we also *compete* rather than practice collaboration. We see friends as opponents rather than allies. In Mark 9:38, John demonstrates this attitude when he said, "Teacher, we saw someone casting out demons in your name, and we tried to stop him, because he was not following us." Jesus's response was classic: "Do not stop him. . . . For the one who is not against us is for us" (Mark 9:39–40). When leaders are competing, we feel the need to win at all costs and in all situations—as Marshall Goldsmith says, "when it matters, when it doesn't, and when it's totally beside the point."[7]

Do you find yourself making destructive comments, needless sarcasms, and cutting remarks that make you sound sharp and witty? Do you find it difficult to praise and reward others and give proper recognition? Do you find yourself claiming credit you don't deserve, failing to express gratitude, or failing to listen? Do you find yourself becoming defensive easily?

The business world clamors for compulsive workers. We call it effectiveness or getting things done. But comparing, coveting, seeking comfort, and competing leave us isolated from others. Psychologists aren't so positive about being compulsive. They call it *narcissism*. In theology, we call it *functional atheism*—living our lives as if we don't need God. It's blindness. And no matter what you call it, it always ends in a crash. The compulsive life just keeps comparing, keeps coveting, keeps competing, keeps driving—until it all comes crashing down. Our isolation leads to apathy about God and others. Our apathy leads to inaction. And inaction leads to atrophy. We find ourselves weak, spent, and unable to function.[8]

When I came back from our Florida vacation, I found two seasoned pastors who started tag-teaming my soul with good spiritual direction and gospel-saturated therapy. They counseled me to take a whole

Narcissism

Narcissistic Personality Disorder (DSM-4)*

A pervasive pattern of grandiosity (in fantasy or behavior), perceived need for admiration, and lack of empathy, beginning by early adulthood and present in a variety of contexts, as indicated by five (or more) of the following:

1. Has a grandiose sense of self-importance (e.g., exaggerates achievements and talents, expects to be recognized as superior without commensurate achievements).
2. Is preoccupied with fantasies of unlimited success, power, brilliance, beauty, or ideal love.
3. Believes that he or she is "special" and unique and only can be understood by, or should associate with, other special or high-status people (or institutions).
4. Requires excessive admiration.
5. Has a sense of entitlement, that is, unreasonable expectations of especially favorable treatment or automatic compliance with his or her expectations.
6. Is interpersonally exploitative, that is, takes advantage of others to achieve his or her own ends.
7. Lacks empathy: is unwilling to recognize or identify with the feelings and needs of others.
8. Is often envious of others or believes that others are envious of him or her.
9. Shows arrogant, haughty behaviors or attitudes.

* The *Diagnostic and Statistical Manual of Mental Disorders*, 4th ed. (DSM-4) is published by the American Psychiatric Association (2000).

month off of work. As I rested, my muscles unclenched, the fog lifted from my mind, and I started to breathe. I wish I could say that at the end of the month my tank was full and I was ready for another five years of swinging hard. The opposite was true. I felt twice my age. I was still spinning and empty. God used that season as well as rest times that followed to tutor me in my own frailty.

Compulsive leaders all eventually crash. It might come in the midst of your career so that you find yourself begging for a sabbatical. It might come on your deathbed. It might not come full circle in your church or organization until you're long gone. But comparing, coveting, and competing always bring death. The cycle of compulsion is a cycle of futility. It's what the author of Ecclesiastes calls "a chasing after the wind" (e.g., Eccles. 1:14, 17; 2:11, 17, 26 NIV). It's a failure to wake up and see that we are created for more.

Why do we see so much failure in ministry? Why do we see so many burned-out Christians? It's because we're living in the cycle of compulsion. Ask yourself. What are you chasing after? How is it working for you? How long do you think you can keep everything going?

Receive God's Presence

There's good news for leaders stuck in a cycle of compulsion. God wants you to put down your performance and be fully awake to his presence. God has a better way. Instead of burnout, God invites leaders to participate in communion with him. Contemplative leaders receive God's transforming presence. They are fully awake to it. And as a result, they give their transforming presence to others.

Leadership Vision 5: The Contemplative Leader

Contemplative leaders are fully awake to God.

They consistently make room for God's transforming presence in their lives, and then they give their transformed presence to others.

We struggle to find joy and rest. However, God lives in eternal rest and perpetual joy. Crack open your Bible, and you'll see the members of the Trinity loving, serving, and enjoying one another. The Father loves the Son and appoints him to a place of honor (Pss. 2:7; 110:1). He celebrates the Son and gives him the name that is above every name (Phil. 2:9–11). The Son and the Spirit joyfully submit to the Father (John

17:5, 24; 1 Cor. 11:3). The Father sends the Son into the world (1 John 4:10), and the Son happily obeys (Phil. 2:6–8). Then, at the end of time, when the Son has put all of his enemies under his feet, he lovingly gives the kingdom back to his Father and becomes a subject in his kingdom (1 Cor. 15:24, 28). The three persons graciously serve one another as a happy divine family.[9]

Trinitarian Doctrine 5: Communion

God lives in communion—eternal rest and perpetual joy. Father, Son, and Holy Spirit graciously serve one another as a happy divine family.

Joy and happy rest characterize their fellowship, and the best news is that we're invited to share in it. Paul teaches us that our union with Christ has brought us into the intra-Trinitarian life: "Through [Christ] we both have access in one Spirit to the Father" (Eph. 2:18). God pulls us close. This is an ongoing mystery. Christians never arrive in perfect communion with God in this life, though every group of Christians has tried to crack the riddle. With the help of Puritan pastor John Owen (1616–1683), we will try to advance the conversation. His work *Communion with the Triune God*, explains how, through Christ, we can experience intimate fellowship with each member of the Trinity:

- We can know the Father's love.
- We can know the Son's acceptance.
- We can know the Spirit's presence.

The Father's Love

"To know God as our father—as our almighty, loving Father—is the highest, richest, and most rewarding aspect of our whole relationship with him," writes J. I. Packer.[10] Even the best fathers leave us with daddy issues. The wounds may be unintentional, but they are unavoidable. Donald Miller describes our longing to know and belong: "As I look at humanity, I can only describe the human personality as one designed for relationship with something from which it has been separated."[11]

A few years ago, I was working with a small group of pastors. While teaching, I went off script and asked, "How many of you grew up without knowing your father?" Hands crept upward, slowly and with apprehension, around the room. Many men within the theologically driven church-planting movement are looking for answers because they didn't have any answers while growing up. These men want purpose because they had no one to show them what mattered in life. God is using the broken soil of a fatherless generation to bring radical missionary shifts to his church.

But achieving great things for God won't fill the void in our hearts. We need to receive God's love. How much of your life is lived to receive a nod from your earthly father? How often do you long to hear, "I am proud of you"? Our daddy issues are bigger than whether or not we have a human father. Only our Father in heaven can fill our longing to be known and loved. As John Owen says: "Going to God as a Father . . . gives us the rest which he promises; for the love of the Father is the only rest of the soul."[12] A. W. Tozer famously remarked, "What comes into our minds when we think about God is the most important thing about us."[13] However, there's a more comforting truth. The most important thing is what our Father thinks of us. God loves us with an eternal, free, and abundant love.

Eternal. He imagined you in eternity past. The way a mother thinks of her child while he still forms in the womb, God thought of you with an infinite, gracious, tender, and compassionate love (Ex. 34:6–7; Psalm 139). He draws near to craft each new child personally and yet has the power to bring life into dust. Owen tells us that God's eternal love fixed on us before the world's foundation: "Before we were, or had done the least good, then were his thoughts upon us."[14] The Father blessed us in the heavenly realms with every spiritual blessing in Christ. In love, he predestined us to be adopted as his sons (Eph. 1:3–4).

Free. The Father gives us his love "*through* Jesus Christ, *according to* the purpose of his will" (Eph. 1:5). Owen explains, "God loves us because he will; there was, there is, nothing in us for which we should be loved."[15] God demonstrated his love for us like this: When we were still sinners, Christ died for us (Rom. 5:8). Our performance means nothing. God's love is unchangeable and fixed. As Owen says, "Though we change every day, yet his love changeth not."[16] The impassive Father is impassioned for you with a fixed and forever love.

Abundant. He is present with you. He is not stingy, absentminded, or uncommitted. The love of the greatest human father is a mere drop in the bucket compared to the love with which the Father has loved you. You might resist his gentleness because you think about his power, justice, and wrath. British theologian Michael Reeves describes the trouble we sometimes feel:

> Much of what purports to be holiness has the aura of prickliness and prudery. People even say things like, "Yes, God is love, but he is *also* holy"—as if holiness is an unloving thing, the cold side of God that stops God from being *too* loving.
>
> Balderdash! Poppycock! Or at least, it is if you are talking about the holiness of the Father. . . .
>
> What is holiness, then? The words used for holiness in the Bible have the basic meaning of being "set apart." But there our troubles begin, because naturally I think I'm lovely. . . .
>
> [God's] holiness looks like a prissy rejection of my happy, healthy loveliness.
>
> Dare I burst my own bubble now? I must. For the reality is that *I* am the cold, selfish, vicious one, full of darkness and dirtiness. And God is holy—"set apart" from me—precisely in that he is *not* like that.[17]

Christians often fear and fret that the Father's love has something rough in it. Owen instructs us to imagine God's love as the most tender and compassionate affection devoid of imperfection or rough edges. He is like "a father, a mother, a shepherd, a hen over chicks."[18] The

Father's love is like an ocean.[19] Imagine a walk along the beach with warm waves breaking over your feet. As you wade out, the vastness of the ocean can be overwhelming. It envelops you. In the same way, the Father's love surrounds us. It cleans us and clears us. It causes us to forget ourselves. Like a current, God pulls us in. God's love toward us moves us to love in return (John 14:23; 1 John 4:19). We're swept into God's love, joy, and fellowship. In response to Christ's love, we seek, obey, enjoy, and adore.[20]

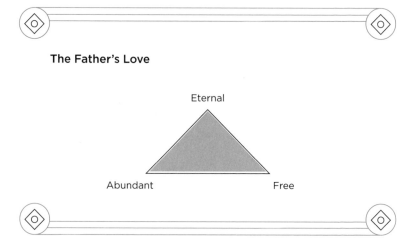

The Father's Love

Eternal

Abundant   Free

The Son's Acceptance

When we enter into loving fellowship with God the Father, we are also united with the Son. We become a part of his family and citizens in his kingdom (Eph. 2:19). We share in Christ's story (Gal. 2:20). We are members of Christ's body (Rom. 12:4–5). Plass and Cofield describe it this way:

> It is hard to get our minds and hearts around what it means to share Christ's life, to be identified with him, to participate in him. We live in a culture of radical autonomy and individualism that makes it hard to comprehend being completely identified with someone or something other than our self. Probably the best our society can muster is to par-

ticipate in the life of our favorite sports team or movie star. But that is a far cry from the very real participation we share in Christ.[21]

The Bible's most powerful images of union are the ones that describe us being made parts of his family: adoption and marriage. Paul writes, "Therefore a man shall leave his father and mother and hold fast to his wife, and the two shall become one flesh. This mystery is profound, and I am saying that it refers to Christ and the church" (Eph. 5:31–32). The marriage union is just a picture—just a taste—of what we have in union with Christ. In a healthy marriage couples share their hearts, minds, bodies, and lives with one another. They participate in each other's lives in a unique way, but marriage is only an analogy of what we're meant to experience.

Paul used the prepositions *in, into, with,* and *through* over 170 times to explain our relationship with Christ. John writes, "We know that the Son of God has come and has given us understanding, so that we may know him who is true; and we are in him who is true, in his

Union versus Communion: "Our Relationship with God"*

Union Cannot Change	*Communion* Can Change
Our sonship	Our fellowship
God's desire for our welfare	Our experience of God's blessing
God's actual affection for us	Our assurance of God's love
God's love for us	God's delight in our actions
Our destiny	God's discipline
Our security	Our sense of guilt

* Bryan Chapell, *Holiness by Grace: Delighting in the Joy That Is Our Strength* (Wheaton, IL: Crossway, 2011), 196.

Son Jesus Christ. He is the true God and eternal life" (1 John 5:20). As Peter stated boldly, "He has granted to us his precious and very great promises, so that through them you may become partakers of the divine nature" (2 Pet. 1:4).[22]

Union is our position *in* Christ. It speaks to the legal and vital realities we share because we are joined to him—our justification, adoption, and regeneration. If we are united with Christ, we cannot be separated from him. Our acceptance, destiny, and status as God's children are all secure. As Romans 8:30 makes clear, "Those whom he called he also . . . glorified." Paul describes this future event as if it has already happened. It's a sure thing.

Communion is our experience *of* Christ—our fellowship, holiness, and daily walk. Kingdom fellowship has been purchased for the believer by Christ's work on the cross. We can activate that fellowship only by God's grace.

CROSS

We receive communion with the Father freely, but we must not think it comes without a cost. Christ's acceptance of us begins at the cross. We have been bought with a price that only God could pay (1 Cor. 6:20). Jesus paid that price. We receive the Father's love through his work. Owen tells us, "The Father's love is an ocean but the faucet of this fount is Christ. We will never experience even the slightest droplet of the Father's love without Christ's life and work."[23]

True union with God—a true connection to the life and love the persons of the Trinity share—is found only through wholly resting in Jesus (John 17:1–3, 22–23). As Jesus said, "I am the way, and the truth, and the life. No one comes to the Father except through me" (John 14:6).[24]

KINGDOM

Through Jesus's work, we enter into kingdom fellowship with God. Jesus is our gateway to the Father's love. He's not like the self-righteous older brother in the parable of the prodigal son (Luke 15:11–32). The older brother was angry that his father loved his rebellious sibling.

He pouted about the loss of a shared inheritance. He refused to join the party when the lost son came home. Jesus is the opposite. Jesus is our *rejoicing* older brother. He knows all about us (Heb. 2:10–11). He knows all our lumps—all of our rottenness—but he sympathizes with our weakness (Heb. 4:15). He doesn't reject us. His affection is set. In love he lays down his life for us and calls us friends (John 10:10–11; 15:15). He is not bitter. He welcomes us into the Father's fellowship. He endured the cross for the joy set before him. *We* are his joy (Heb. 12:2).

Here's how John Owen celebrates the fellowship we receive as part of Christ's kingdom family:[25]

- Fellowship in name; we are called sons of God [John 1:12–13; Rom. 8:23; Gal. 4:5; Eph. 1:5].
- Fellowship in title and right; we are heirs, co-heirs with Christ [Rom. 8:17].
- Fellowship in likeness and conformity; we are predestinated to be like the firstborn of the family [Rom. 8:29].
- Fellowship in honor; he is not ashamed to call us brethren [Heb. 2:11].
- Fellowship in sufferings; he learned obedience by what he suffered, and every son is to be scourged that is received [Heb. 12:6].
- Fellowship in his kingdom; we shall reign with him [2 Tim. 2:12].

GRACE

We maintain this fellowship in the same way that we began, by grace from first to last (Gal. 3:2). God supplies all we lack. We are one in union and communion with him—not because of anything we've done but because his dying and rising count for us.

You can never have too much of this grace. Sometimes we think about the gospel in dry and transactional terms, but grace is always a personal invitation (Eph. 2:4–14; Titus 2:11–14). Jesus is inviting you to drink deeply. Because of God's grace, we are free to do what God desires, and we are free to receive the joy that comes only from obedience. We stop desiring a licentious life. God brings more joy. We daily turn from sin, because we know that fellowship with God is where life is found.

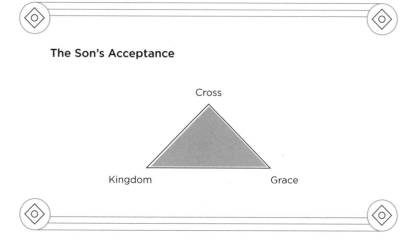

The Son's Acceptance

Cross

Kingdom   Grace

We can enjoy sweet communion with God by obediently depending upon his grace, but communion can also be broken. We can walk out of fellowship with him. There are times when we sense his presence and blessing, and there are times when we feel no assurance of his love or his delight in our actions. There are times when we feel our guilt and God's discipline more profoundly. Struggling believers aren't at risk of forfeiting their *union* with Christ, but there are certainly times when their intimate *communion* with God feels blocked.[26]

The Spirit's Presence

Union with Christ gives every believer access into the intra-Trinitarian life. Communion is experienced by living in step with the Holy Spirit. It should be normal for every believer. Every Christian needs a moment-by-moment awareness of God's presence. And communion with the Spirit is particularity important for church leaders. A failed pneumatology, an under-developed and under-utilized doctrine of the Holy Sprit, can lead to discouragement and depression. Christian leaders who don't commune with the Holy Spirit are miserable.

The Spirit speaks a better word into our desperation. That's good news for leaders stuck in the cycle of compulsion. God wants you to put down your performance and be fully awake to his presence. God dwells in you permanently (Eph. 1:13), so you can come needy and weary back to him even though you've sinned and failed. As Jesus said, "Come to me, all who labor and are heavy laden, and I will give you rest" (Matt. 11:28). Contemplative leaders maintain a life of communion by remembering God's presence, by trusting his promises to forgive and restore, and by seeking the Spirit's work (John 7:37–39; Luke 11:12–13; Gal. 3:2, 14). Such leaders receive peace, joy, and hope when they stop to hear the Spirit's voice and faithfully follow his promptings again. You may feel beaten, bedraggled, and lost, but contemplative leaders trust and obey even when the emotions aren't there. The moment you feel most downcast is when you need to actively trust God again.

The Holy Spirit communes with obedient leaders, and he brings us into a fuller communion with the Father and the Son.[27] He does this in at least three ways. The Holy Spirit gives witness to Christ, comforts our souls, and gives us power for mission.

Witness to Christ. The Spirit brings to mind Jesus's words (John 14:26). He makes much of Jesus (John 16:14). He reminds us of God's promise to forgive and accept us in Christ. The Spirit reminds us of the security of our union. Owen says, "He shows to us mercy, grace, forgiveness, righteousness, acceptance with God; [and] lets us know that these things are of Christ, which he has procured for us."[28]

Comfort for our souls. The Spirit pours the Father's love into our hearts (Rom. 5:5). He tells us we are God's children (Rom. 8:15–16). He seals our faith (Eph. 1:13; Rev. 7:4), providing the down payment for our future inheritance (2 Cor. 1:22; 5:5; Eph. 1:13–14). When we're downcast and depressed, he reminds us that his way is good and our reward is sure.

Power for mission. The Spirit anoints us, setting us apart for ministry (2 Cor. 1:21; 1 John 2:20, 27). He fills what is lacking in our prayers (Rom. 8:26–27). The Holy Spirit fills us with the fruit of love (Gal. 5:22), and he spreads his love abroad through us (Rom. 5:5). After we obey him, we can look back and see that he supplied our obedience. He is the one who made our work fruitful. When we see that evidence of his work, we can rejoice.

The Spirit's Presence

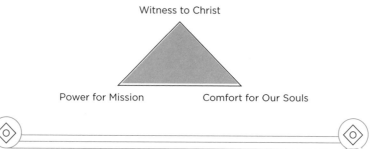

Witness to Christ

Power for Mission   Comfort for Our Souls

The Cycle of Communion

When I first became a Christian, getting away for silence and solitude was normal. My mentor would take weeklong wilderness retreats, and he instructed me to do so as well. When I was young and raw, I often wandered out alone to hike the Chattahoochee River near Atlanta, where I spent my high school and college years. The wilderness and solitude made room for my soul. It provided space and quiet, unfettered moments with God.

Seven years removed and four hundred miles away from those walks, I needed retreat again. Sojourn's first five years might have killed me if I hadn't found a little monastery near Bardstown, Kentucky. We didn't have the money to pay for counseling, so I drove out past fields and farmhouses to be alone and nurture my soul. The monastery never yielded a mystical moment. Instead, it gave me painful, deafening solitude. I meditated as the monks moved about, sung the evening vespers, and ate their simple meals. I walked. I slept. I read. I prayed. I hoped. I cried.

In that space, God drew me near. Soon, I discovered a nun named Joan Chittister, and her writings mentored me. Her words became a cool breeze for my weary soul: "Prayer is an opening of the self so that the Word of God can break in and make us new. Prayer unmasks. Prayer converts. Prayer impels. Prayer sustains us on the way. Pray for the grace it will take to continue what you would like to quit."[29]

Through Chittister's writings and those times of sweet communion with God, my understanding of ministry moved from duty to desire. God used those sweet times to preserve me. The longer and more often I stayed out there, the steadier I grew in my communion with God. I learned that being a leader required me to be present to God, and I learned that as God changed me, he would use my transformed presence in the lives of others.

Plass and Cofield tell us that communion is the "particular and penetrating presence of one with another."[30] Communion requires synergy. It only works when two people actively participate with each other. Distractions may cause a husband to neglect intimate relations with his spouse just as a Christian may neglect the fellowship of God. Though such neglect doesn't annul the union, it deeply affects their intimacy.[31] A contemplative leader is a man or woman who is fully awake to—who consistently practices—God's presence. This leader makes room for God in his life and, as a result, he can give his transformed presence to others.

Some might argue that "being present" is just Zen. Executive presence is trendy. But I believe there is a way to understand presence that is biblical. The key biblical term for this is fellowship (*koinōnia*), which is used some twenty times in the New Testament. It means sharing or participation with someone in something specific. The first occurrence is in Acts 2:42: "And they devoted themselves to the apostles' teaching and the *fellowship*, to the breaking of bread and the prayers." Philippians 2:1–2 declares, "If there is any encouragement in Christ, any comfort from love, any *participation* in the Spirit, any affection and sympathy, complete my joy by being of the same mind, having the same love, being in full accord and of one mind." The term, according to Stephen Seamands, "implies an intensely close relationship with one another beyond mere human camaraderie."[32] Paul teaches us that we not only share fellowship with one another as believers, but have been called into fellowship with Christ (1 Cor. 1:9) In fact, according to John, our communion and fellowship with each other is rooted in our communion with Christ. First John 1:6–7 says, "If we say we have *fellowship* with him while we walk in darkness, we lie and do not practice the truth. But if we walk in the light, as he is in the light, we have *fellowship* with one another, and the blood of Jesus his Son cleanses us from all sin" (cf. 1 John 1:3).

Jesus himself, in his High Priestly Prayer, grounds our unity and communion with one another in the mutual indwelling of the Father, Son, and Spirit. Our relationship with Christ should be a penetratingly rich personal connection[33] that fuels us to be present with others. Twenty to thirty years from now, people won't remember the sermons I preached. They will remember my presence in suffering. I hope they remember how my presence pointed them to commune with God.

Sometimes I don't hear what people say because I'm thinking more about my iPhone, the football game I watched last night, or a relational conflict at work. My presence is just pathetic. In the same way, our communion with God can come and go. How do we cultivate a life of presence? How do we cultivate a life of communion?

You've been reading about it through this entire book. The previous four Cs of the leadership mosaic—conviction, creativity, courage, and collaboration—provide a cycle of leadership that helps us commune with God. When a leader hears God's voice, he's moved from a life of coveting and comparing to one of creatively applying deep convictions. When we make room to experience God's presence, we see that he is big and people are small. There's no reason to compete or confine, so we collaborate with courage. Through communion with God, we can step out of our compulsions.

Contemplative leaders enter into the presence of God through this cycle of communion. When we taste just a bit of Trinitarian communion, we are changed. We are moved to give our own transformed presence—a receptive life that both rejoices in God and rejoices in his people. I'm convinced that's the greatest thing we can give to the people we lead—the kind of life-giving presence that pursues joy in God and others. This gift must undergird all our leadership.

God's Penetrating Presence

Circumincessio, circumcessio, circumcession, perichoresis, and *coinherence* are technical terms for the mutual indwelling of the persons of the Trinity—the Father in the Son and the Son in him (John 10:38; 14:10–11, 20; 17:21), both in the Spirit, and the Spirit in both (Rom. 8:9).* To see Jesus is to see the Father (John 14:9), for he and the Father are one (10:30). When Jesus departs from the earth, he "comes" in the Spirit to be with his people (John 14:18). According to Stephen Seamands, the terms convey a number of ideas—"reciprocity, interchange, giving to and receiving from one another, being drawn to one another and contained in the other, inter-penetrating one another by drawing life from and pouring life into one another."† We can also use several different images to describe the doctrine:

> It is like three sources of light in the same room, interpenetrating each other so that the resulting light is single yet somehow remains multiple. Or like the three notes of a major triad, which when played together indwell each other and create the one sound of the chord even while retaining their distinct identities. Or like the three dimensions of physical objects, height, depth, and width. Each dimension implies the other two, so that changing any one of the three changes the whole.‡

Remarkably, Jesus also draws an analogy between the mutual indwelling of the members of the Trinity and the unity of believers with one another (John 17:21–23). Our oneness, like our union with Christ, is mysterious and deep. It is *like* the unity and coinherence within the Trinity itself. Jesus prays "that they may all be one, just as you, Father, are in me, and I in you" (John 17:21). This is, of course, an analogy, not an identity: we cannot be one *exactly* as God is one. We are not the Trinity—but somehow our communion with one another *images* the Trinity. As the Father is in the Son, and the Son in the Father, and as the Father, Son, and Spirit are in us, and we in them, so we are to be *in* one another! I in you, and you in me.§

---

* John M. Frame, *Systematic Theology: An Introduction to Christian Belief* (Phillipsburg, NJ: P&R), 479.
† Stephen Seamands, *Ministry in the Image of God: The Trinitarian Shape of Christian Service* (Downers Grove, IL: InterVarsity Press, 2005), 142.
‡ Ibid., 143.
§ John Frame, "Working Together," May 30, 2012, http://frame-poythress.org.

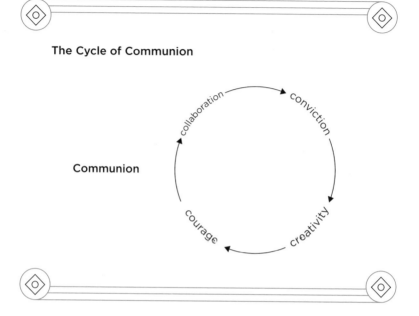

The Cycle of Communion

Communion

collaboration

conviction

creativity

courage

Rest in God and Rejoice in His People

Living in step with the Holy Spirit is the way to activate the cycle of communion and escape a life of compulsion. One question remains. What does that look like practically? What are the means I must consciously choose to have communion with God? The question centers on how we enter into God's rest: How do I position myself to experience God's joyful presence? In a way, this is mysterious. No one can force God's presence. But we can seek him. We put ourselves in a receptive position before God when we practice the spiritual disciplines. Here are three ways I regularly step off the treadmill of my compulsions to seek his sweet comfort and fellowship—trust, stop, and enjoy.

TRUST

It may sound like a given, but it's not. We must trust that God will speak to us. We must trust that God will hear us. Communion is often activated simply by trusting God for times of fruitful Bible reading and prayer. The Holy Spirit makes this possible (John 16:13–16; Rom. 8:26–27; Eph. 6:18).[34]

We live in a world that's constantly pushing more information. There's one more blog post to read. There's one more commentary to consult. The balance of our "quiet times" with God sometimes leans toward active Bible study and away from quiet reflection. We need to put it all down and do the trusting work of quiet meditation instead.

"Meditation," writes Adele Calhoun, "is a long ardent gaze at God, his work and his Word."[35] Begin with ten minutes every morning. Bring only your Bible and maybe a journal. Keep your task list, text messages, and email far away. Slow down, stretch, breathe deep—really, *breathe*—and then give your undivided attention to one passage of Scripture. Calhoun writes, "Meditation is a way we train our minds to stay put so that we can explore appropriate associations."[36] Pick one psalm, one narrative account, or one paragraph of an epistle. Attentively dwell on that passage with the goal of hearing God's voice. Mull over it. Say it over and over again in your head. Chew and ruminate on what God is saying. Write down your questions and reflections. Ask yourself: "Do I really believe this? What is God inviting me to feel through this passage?" God will speak to you through his Spirit. If the Spirit prompts you to confess a sin, write it down. If the Spirit prompts you to approach a coworker about something that's been bothering you, write that down too. As more comes to your mind, write it down and then keep thinking the passage through. When you get distracted, simply express to God your desire to pay attention and then return to your text.

Another way of trusting is by practicing the discipline of retreat. Retreats are "specific and regular times apart for quietly listening to God and delighting in his company."[37] Retreats remove us from the daily pressures of ministry into times of refreshing renewal. As Jesus said to his disciples, "Come with me by yourselves to a quiet place and get some rest" (Mark 6:31 NIV). Start by scheduling a daily walk into your calendar. Unplug from your phone and computer and go outside. Don't put in your ear buds. Simply dwell on what you see around you. Take time, as the Belgic Confession encourages us, to read creation as "a most elegant book, wherein all creatures, great and small, are as so many characters leading us to see clearly the invisible things of God" (art. 2). Ask the Lord, "What do you want to teach me through the world you've made?" A next step is to schedule two days away each month at a retreat center or monastery. Many of us are great at getting away to conferences filled with lectures, late nights, and constant activity. Such "retreats" aren't evil, but that's not the kind of retreat I'm talking about. Instead of getting away to get more information, get away to be with God and gaze at him. Don't try to catch up on reading or email. Instead take a nap and go to bed early. I find it's helpful to go to a place where I don't even have access to the Internet. Make meditation and rest your work just for a day or two and see what new perspective God may provide.

STOP

We begin to step off the treadmill of compulsion by going to God in his Word and prayer, but we need to cease running altogether. We need to stop—stop working and stop talking. We need to embrace Sabbath and silence.

Sabbath is particularly difficult for leaders in church ministry. After all, Sunday is the pinnacle of the ministry week. You've been preparing for it all week long. Some ministers feel the need to debate the Sabbath, but I'd rather take one. God has commanded his people: "Remember the Sabbath day, to keep it holy. Six days you shall labor, and do all your work, but the seventh day is a Sabbath to the LORD your God" (Ex. 20:8–10). For those in ministry, it may be that this command cannot be kept on Sunday, but it must be kept.

When God rested on the seventh day, he stooped to our level. He didn't need to stop, but he modeled stopping. He spoke to us in words we can understand—showing us that we are made for rest. Stopping teaches us that we are not God. Leaders often want work to revolve around them like a restless hurricane, but hurricanes always break up in the end—leaving only damage in their wake. Consider this warning from Calhoun:

When you get indignant over how seemingly incompatible Sabbath is with the tiring and relentless demands already facing you, consider what your tiredness means. Animals don't think about how tired they are. And they don't have a Sabbath *they* set aside for rest. It's humans who recognize the difference between work and rest. The fact that we make distinctions between being tired and rested is an indication we need to do both.[38]

Busyness is the enemy of stopping. Its hand turns up our compulsive speed dial. Its foot steps on the gas. Laziness may be evil, but regularly setting aside a twenty-four-hour period to stop is not idleness. Sabbath both acknowledges our human limits and submits to Christ's lordship (Heb. 4:1, 9–11). Stopping for rest is an opportunity to say, "God, I trust you with my whole life." We can stop working because God never slumbers or sleeps (Psalm 121).

Sabbath doesn't depend on our readiness to stop. We don't stop when we've finished our project, zeroed our inbox, and checked every voice mail. That would be like continuing to search for manna on a day God isn't providing it (Ex. 16:27–30). We stop because it's time to stop. The workweek is over, and we must rest. Sabbath reminds us we are not human *doings*. We are human *beings*. Regular and recuperative rest is something we need (Mark 2:27). Sabbath is God's way of saying, "Stop. Notice your limits. Don't burn out." We wake on our Sabbath day to a world we didn't make and a friendship with God we didn't earn.[39]

Here is how to practice the Sabbath. Set aside one regular day each week to rest and worship. Don't make a to-do list for your Sabbath day. Refrain from anything competitive that heightens your anger or stress. That might mean turning off the football game. Plan restful activities. Go on a walk. Take your family for a picnic. Take an afternoon nap. Plan a phone conversation with someone you love. Plan tea or coffee with a friend. Pull the board games out of the closet and give the gift of presence to your kids for twenty-four hours. Let go of things that stress you out. Let the difficult conversations happen another day. Honor the way God made you by living a healthy and intentionally rested life. Delight in God, family, the seasons, and a good meal. Trust God to take care of all the things you're not doing.

ENJOY

Many of us struggle with stopping because we don't know what to do once we have stopped. Some men fear retirement because they simply do not know what to do once they have stopped working. We simply feel lost without work.

God wants more for us. We stop and trust in order to enjoy. There are some pervasive myths about joy in contemporary Christianity. Have you heard these?

- God is concerned not with your happiness but with your holiness.
- Joy is an attitude, not an emotion.
- Happiness is tied to happenstance, but joy is beyond your circumstances. It should be unfettered from something positive happening to me.

Joy is more complex than these myths. The Bible tells us that holiness is the pathway to joy (Heb. 12:2). In fact, Jesus is concerned with our holiness precisely *because* he wants to make us happy (John 15:10–11). Joy *is* an attitude commanded by God (Phil. 4:4), but it is also an emotional reaction experienced in community with others (Luke 1:41; 6:23; 15:5–7, 9–10, 23–24; 1 John 1:3). When your wife looked at you for the first time and said, "We are going to have a baby," you felt joy. The first time you heard the words, "I'm proud of you," you felt joy. Joy is a virtue to cultivate in view of future hope (John 16:22; Rom. 12:12; James 1:2). Joy is a gift of the Spirit (Ps. 4:7; Acts 13:52; Rom. 14:17; Gal. 5:22).

Psalm 16 tutors us in rejoicing. First, it tells us God is the source of joy. The second verse declares,

> I say to the Lord, "You are my Lord;
> I have no good apart from you."

David goes on:

> The LORD is my chosen portion and my cup;
>   you hold my lot.
> The lines have fallen for me in pleasant places. (16:5–6)

David is saying, "Lord, you set me up with a house and yard. Thank you." Scholars struggle with saying that every Christian can claim a verse like this. It sounds dangerously close to a prosperity gospel, but it's not. David isn't telling us to name and claim a Mercedes. But he is telling us to be thankful and enjoy what God has given us (Phil. 4:4–7). We shouldn't feel low-grade guilt if God has given us something good. A weekend at a friend's lake house with fishing and jet skis doesn't have to include a guilt-ridden drive home for having "too much fun." Paul picks up on this truth: "For everything created by God is good, and nothing is to be rejected if it is received with thanksgiving" (1 Tim. 4:4). Paul's counsel here and throughout the New Testament is to enjoy God's gifts. In fact, he gives this instruction with a warning. When someone tells us we can't enjoy the good things God has made, he is teaching a doctrine from hell:

> But the Spirit explicitly says that in later times some will fall away from the faith, paying attention to deceitful spirits and doctrines of demons, ... men who forbid marriage and advocate abstaining from foods which God has created to be gratefully shared in by those who believe and know the truth (1 Tim. 4:1, 3 NASB).[40]

If we find ourselves trying to avoid enjoyment in created things, then we have fallen prey to the Devil's lies. Sometimes the most deadly teachings of Satan masquerade as the most holy.

We can enjoy all of God's gifts with thanksgiving. Pastor-theologian Joe Rigney asks, "Why did God make a world full of good friends, sizzling bacon, the laughter of children, West Texas sunsets, Dr. Pepper, college football, marital love, and the warmth of wool socks?"[41] God gives them for our joy. Pastors often quote the first part of 1 Timothy 6:17 as a rebuke to American consumerism: "As for the rich in this present age, charge them not to be haughty, nor to set their hopes on the uncertainty of riches." Rarely do we preach the

Do You Enjoy God's Gifts?

Here are some questions adapted from Joe Rigney's wonderful book *The Things of Earth** to help evaluate if you struggle with anxiety or guilt over enjoying God's gifts:

- Do I feel a low-grade sense of guilt when having or immediately after a fun activity?
- Am I overly suspicious of created things, unsure whether they are too precious for me?
- Do I have the sense that as I progress in holiness, my enjoyment of things ought to diminish?
- Do I regard certain activities such as prayer, worship, and Bible reading as more holy than other activities?
- Do I feel a low-grade guilt rooted in a vague sense that I'm not enjoying God "enough"?
- Do I feel unable to enjoy with thanksgiving God's creation gifts out of fear of idolatry?

* Joe Rigney, *The Things of Earth: Treasuring God by Enjoying His Gifts* (Wheaton, IL: Crossway, 2015).

back half. It tells us from whom our possessions come and why they are given—"but [to set their hopes] on God, who richly provides us with everything to enjoy."

Psalm 16 goes on. It doesn't stop with instructing us to enjoy God's creation. It shows us how to rejoice in one another. David says,

> As for the saints who are in the land, they are the glorious ones
> in whom is all my delight. (Ps. 16:3 NIV1984)

When I preached on this passage recently, I had to reread that passage. Aren't those so-called "glorious ones" whom David delights in the source of 90 percent of my tension headaches? Aren't they the ones whose expectations *make me* so compulsive? The more I read and studied the passage, the more I grew convicted. If I have problems with the "glorious ones," I have problems with God. He made these people. He put them in my community and church. There is no joy in the self-centered leader who thinks people are problems. God designed it so that joy comes in communion with his people. We enjoy others because they are glorious. Each person I encounter is potential joy. When I encounter difficult people, that is my opportunity to believe Christ's promise, "It is more blessed to give than to receive" (Acts 20:35). Joy comes through giving your presence away and allowing others into your life.

One of the chief obstacles to finding joy in others is the marauding sin of criticism. God freely praises far-from-perfect people, and we should as well. There may be bad things in their past, their present, *and* their future, but God praises his children, and he inspired the biblical authors to record his praise.[42] About Noah, who would later succumb to drunkenness and incest, God said, "You are righteous before me in this generation" (Gen. 7:1). About Job, who would come near to blaspheming him, God said, "There is none like him on the earth, a blameless and upright man, who fears God and turns away from evil" (Job 1:8). When Nathanael doubted salvation could ever come from Nazareth, Jesus at least praised his honesty: "Behold, an Israelite indeed, in whom there is no deceit!" (John 1:47). Jesus told the Canaanite woman, a former prostitute, "O woman, great is your faith!" (Matt. 15:28).[43] And Lot, for all his flaws, is called "righteous Lot" in 2 Peter 2:7.

David Murray observes, "Part of being perfect as our Father in heaven is perfect is imitating Him in verbally affirming others."[44] Pay attention to those inner promptings when the Holy Spirit is spotlighting your self-promotion. Own your pride and brokenness and rest in his grace. Then, having received from God's abundant stores, celebrate the ways he's poured out those stores in others.

Rejoicing in others will change your leadership. A leader recognizes the contributions made by each member of the team. Kouzes and Posner help us see that "belief in others' abilities is essential to making extraordinary things happen."[45] As Christian leaders, we can go a step further. Because we make much of Christ, we can make much of Christ in the people we lead.[46] If we believe the Holy Spirit indwells his church, then our interest in others (and what God is doing in them) will be piqued. Show your followers you believe Christ is at work in them (Phil. 1:6).

The first step is simply drawing near. Being receptive to others requires being in close proximity to them.[47] The next step is slowing down. Be among the people you lead. Take time to walk around and be present in their workspace. Presence, empathic listening, and intentional appreciation are the pathway to gratitude. Lay down your busy schedule and give your life to serving the brothers and sisters on your team. Be more interested in others and less interested in yourself. Be open to the gifts God has given them. Then intentionally thank them. Write regular thank-you notes to coworkers and family. That's a proven way to spur them on to love and good deeds.

Calhoun defines gratitude as a sensitivity to the Holy Spirit's prompting "to live with a grateful heart, cognizant of God's work in my life and my abundant resources."[48] Paul instructs us, "Rejoice always, pray without ceasing, give thanks in all circumstances; for this is the will of God in Christ Jesus for you" (1 Thess. 5:16–18). Begin by writing one thank-you note each week to a different coworker or ministry volunteer, or keep a gratitude journal that records the many gifts God has given you in your team. Go one step further and throw the team a party. This is more than just taking them bowling or doing trust exercises. It requires noticing the specific contributions each team member has made and celebrating how those outcomes accomplish God's vision for your church. Find ways to honor the people around you, and you will remind them that they matter. They are the glorious ones.

We can rejoice because God's gifts are good. We can rejoice because God wants to give us joy in his people. In addition to these, David gives us one more reason to rejoice. Near the end of Psalm 16 are these lines:

> *For* you will not abandon my soul to Sheol,
>   or let your holy one see corruption. (16:10)

David acknowledges that death and decay are coming. This world is broken. In this life, there's an abundance of reasons to feel

Schedule Your Celebrations*

- *Cyclical celebrations and milestones.* Celebrate the movements of the Christian year, your church's anniversary, as well as individual birthdays, marriages, and reunions.
- *Recognition ceremonies.* Celebrate by giving public honor and applause for a job well done. When a vision outcome is accomplished or an employee is promoted, take time to celebrate.
- *Celebrations of triumph.* Celebrate collective wins as well. When Easter services go well or a new initiative is launched, take time to give thanks to God and celebrate together with your team.
- *Rituals for comfort and letting go.* Suffering comes before glory. Not everything that happens in the church is about victory. There is the pain of church discipline or a fallen ministry leader. A ceremony or special meeting to help the team lament, grieve, and let go may be necessary to mark such an occasion.
- *Personal transitions.* Celebrate entrances and exits. This can be as simple as "hello" and "goodbye" when someone enters and leaves the room. It may also be a ceremony to mark initiation or separation as individuals enter and leave the church.
- *Celebrate going above and beyond.* Church staff are always serving. Be sure to notice and celebrate when your teams go above and beyond their call. Maybe this is serving diligently in a ministry area where they have no responsibility or sacrificially opening their home.
- *Play.* Finally, it's important to make celebrations fun. Energizing meetings with games and laughter are essential for encouraging the heart of your team.

* Adapted from James M. Kouzes and Barry Z. Posner, *The Leadership Challenge: How to Make Extraordinary Things Happen in Organizations* (San Francisco: Jossey-Bass, 2012), 325.

depressed. Our world is full of suffering and tragedy and sinning—racism, sex trafficking, abortion, disasters, systemic injustice, disability, oppression of women, pornography, cancer, death, and the list goes on. Are joyful Christians simply numb to these realities? Not necessarily. Busy Christians who endlessly seek explanations and solutions certainly numb their emotions. Contemplative leaders do not. They've made room in their lives to feel hurt and anguish.

They are awake to brokenness in themselves and in the world around them.

Yet David knows that even if joy can't be felt in the moment, joy will come. Christians can fight for joy and even count suffering as joy because they have a firm hope that inexpressible joy waits in the end (Heb. 12:1–2; James 1:2–4; 1 Pet. 1:3–9). David's words show up again as part of Peter's sermon in Acts 2. Then Peter explains how we should understand them:

> Brothers, I may say to you with confidence about the patriarch David that he both died and was buried, and his tomb is with us to this day. . . . He foresaw and spoke about the resurrection of the Christ, that he was not abandoned to Hades, nor did his flesh see corruption. This Jesus God raised up, and of that we all are witnesses. (Acts 2:29, 31–32).

Joy wasn't some honeymoon phase in the early church. Joy is the new standard made possible because of Jesus's resurrection. The resurrection tells us that the pain and betrayals of life will not get the last word. Joy will one day rise:

> You make known to me the path of life;
>> in your presence there is fullness of joy;
>> at your right hand are pleasures forevermore. (Ps. 16:11)

Leadership Skill Set 5: Receiving and Rejoicing

Being fully awake to God requires . . .

- *Receiving.* Open your heart to God. Hear his voice. Enter his rest.
- *Rejoicing.* Rejoice in his gifts. Celebrate God's work in others.

What would happen if people could say about you, "There goes the leader who lives calmly, sleeps soundly, and celebrates with wild joy"? Could leadership be any more countercultural? Our busyness causes

Cumulative Chapter Summary

Leadership begins with *knowing where people need to go*. When you combine *conviction* and *creativity*, you have vision to see the way forward.

Leadership Vision	Trinitarian Doctrine	Leadership Skills
Convictional leaders embody what they believe.	**Revelation:** God speaks. He makes himself known through his world, Word, and works.	Embodying what you believe requires . . . • *Listening.* Seek to hear God's voice in order to clarify your convictions. • *Living it out.* Practice what you preach, because people do what people see.
Creative leaders imagine the way forward.	**Creation:** God made everything. His creation work is a purposeful project of love.	Imagining the way forward requires . . . • *Dreaming.* Make creative connections between where you are and what God wants. • *Persuading.* Be winsome. Be a poet. Help your people dream.

Moving forward requires *courage, collaboration*, and *contemplation*. We *take initiative*, working *in God's way*—as part of a team—*and with God's power*—walking in step with the Spirit at every stage.

Leadership Vision	Trinitarian Doctrine	Leadership Skills
Courageous leaders take risks.	**Mission:** God moves out in love to rescue his children. The Father's mission plan is accomplished through the work of the Son and by the agency of the Holy Spirit.	Taking risks requires . . . • *Seeking.* Look for where God is working. Opportunities are invitations. • *Joining.* Speak up, step out, and act. God is inviting you to join him in his work.

| Collaborative leaders empower the team. | Covenant: an agreement that either creates or confirms a family relationship. God makes promises both to himself and to his people, and he keeps these agreements with loyalty and love. | Empowering the team requires . . .
• *Serving.* Be humble. Value others as more important than yourself.
• *Supporting.* Give your team what they need to grow through ministry challenges. |
| Contemplative leaders are fully awake to God. | Communion: God lives in eternal rest and perpetual joy. Father, Son, and Holy Spirit graciously serve one another as a happy divine family. | Being fully awake to God requires . . .
• *Receiving.* Open your heart to God. Hear his voice. Enter his rest.
• *Rejoicing.* Rejoice in his gifts. Celebrate God's work in others. |

our focus to narrow and our anxieties to grow, but the great call of Scripture is to draw near to God so we might enjoy him forever.

Learning to receive God's presence and give a restful and loving presence to others is a process. It isn't an easy one, because the life God invites us into is different from anything we know.

Having a transformed and transforming presence in a busy world takes work. Maybe that seems counterintuitive. In the evangelical world, we often think a new paradigm is enough to change our leadership: if you can just adopt a "grace-centered" or "gospel-centered" way of *thinking*, you'll grow and change. But as Dallas Willard once wrote, "Grace is not opposed to effort. It is opposed to earning."[49] That is true in all of leadership. We can't *think* or *talk* our way into better leading. We must *walk* with Jesus. We *practice* our way into better leadership. That's my invitation to you. Do you desire to be a better leader? Draw near to God. Draw near to your team. Be fully awake to God's presence and give your transformed presence to others.

Exercises

Here is a selection of ideas and activities to help you practice contemplative leadership. Pick out one or two and incorporate them into your regular leadership rhythms.

1. If *silence and solitude* are new for you, begin with five minutes. As you become quiet, what do you hear: voices, traffic, your breath, wind, your heart, distracting thoughts? Let the noise go. Let the quiet deepen. Be with God. After your time is finished, reflect on what it was like for you to simply become still enough to hear the background.

2. Meditate on Psalm 37:4—"Delight yourself in the Lord / and he will give you the desires of your heart." What desires has God put into your heart? What does God say to you about your desires?

3. Plan a twenty-four-hour Sabbath with your family. Ask, "How will we intentionally leave the school- and work-week behind?" Let each family member tell one thing he or she would love to do on the day of rest. The night before, ask God to guide your Sabbath day. Go to bed early. Pray for refreshing sleep and commit your dreams to the Lord. Plan personal things that will nourish you—attending worship, taking a nap, making love, walking, reading, playing with your children, meeting with a friend. Plan plenty of margin in your day for each activity.

4. Begin a gratitude journal. Keep a record of God's gifts. Next to each gift write what it means to you to have a God who interacts and intervenes in your life.

5. Notice your tendency to make comparisons that result in feelings of discontent or entitlement. Abstain from comparative statements about what you don't have. Instead give thanks for what you *do* have.

6. Find out about people's stories—what they are doing to make your church or ministry successful. Write them down in a journal to make sure you capture them. Identify some people who you think could use some encouragement to keep going.

7. End each of your ministry team's meetings with a round of public praise. What are some other ways that you can create a culture of celebration and appreciation?

Prayer

Go forth into the world in peace; be of good courage; hold fast that which is good; render to no man evil for evil; strengthen the faint-hearted; support the weak; help the afflicted; honour all men; love and serve the Lord, rejoicing in the power of the Holy Spirit. And the blessing of God Almighty, the Father, the Son, and the Holy Ghost, be upon you, and remain with you for ever.[50]

It is most true of the Blessed Trinity, *Satis amplum alter alteri theatrum sumus* [each is to the other a theater large enough].

Robert Leighton, *A Practical Commentary upon the First Epistle of Peter*

Conclusion

THE LEADERSHIP MOSAIC

Summary: *Sinful leaders often divide things God reveals as a whole. We see problems but then overreact by exaggerating one aspect of doctrine or leadership while neglecting or compartmentalizing others. Jesus revealed a better way. He shows us how our fractured ideas about leadership fit together. Jesus's crucified and resurrected life makes his role among the divine persons unique. Yet, through his work, the Son shows us God's unity. He reveals the divine essence and shows us how the divine persons work together in harmony and love. God welcomes divided leaders and conforms them into Christ's image. The Trinity invites leaders to put the pieces together. He calls leaders into communion and collaboration. He wants to fill them with conviction, creativity, and courage. That's the holistic vision of leadership God intended—a beautiful mosaic.*

Christian theologians have understood the Trinity in two primary ways.[1] One stream of thinking has focused on the eternal relationships between the divine persons—the *immanent* Trinity. The other stream emphasizes God's revelation and work in human history—the *economic* Trinity:

- According to the *immanent* perspective, God's social reality helps us understand his work in the world.[2] God is a social community of three persons. Created humanity reflects this social reality when we love, serve, and relate to one another. Relating is a basic part of the *imago Dei* (Gen. 1:26). The church also reflects God's social reality. God designed it as a collaborative communion to display the self-giving unity of his own mutual indwelling. Christian community reflects intra-Trinitarian communion. Jesus prayed "that they may all be one, just as you, Father, are in me, and I in you" (John 17:21).[3]
- The *economic* perspective focuses on God's united work. Father, Son, and Holy Spirit are united and work together to create and redeem. God created the heavens and the earth through the Son (Col. 1:16) and by the agency of the Spirit (Gen. 1:2). It is this same creation, now fallen, that God redeems. The entire Godhead—Father, Son, and Spirit—are dynamically involved in God's grand rescue mission.[4] The Father sent the Son into the world to accomplish salvation (John 3:17; 5:36; 6:57; Gal. 4:6; 1 John 4:9). The Father and Son send the Spirit (John 14:26; 15:26) to empower the church and lead it to participate in God's mission (Matt. 28:18–20; Acts 1:8; 2:33).[5]

Both streams of thought express important truths about God. Kevin Vanhoozer describes the relationship between the immanent and economic Trinity by saying, "The economic Trinity is, or rather communicates, the immanent Trinity."[6] Yet some theologians and pastors overemphasize and exaggerate one view at the expense of the other:

- Those who focus solely on the *immanent* Trinity may end up preaching generous, servant-hearted love for the church while neglecting pastoral authority and missionary initiative.[7] The churches and movements they lead grow inward. They fail to live with the boldness required to fulfill the Great Commission.
- Those who exaggerate the *economic* perspective might move the mission forward while creating an oppressive work environment and missing love and grace as the true motivation for Christian work.[8] New converts and churches may spring up fast but quickly wither or get choked out by the world's cares. They weren't planted in the relational soil necessary to sustain faith.

Sometimes I'll ask leaders on our team, "Are we more about the community or about the cause?" I know we're finding balance when it's hard to tell. There is no need to make this an either–or argument. These are twin truths we want to hold in dialogue with each other.[9] God wants more for followers than shallow and fractured ways of being and believing. He wants us to see the truth in the whole.

Our Divided Leadership Visions

Leaders see problems and look for solutions. That's the gift of leadership. It's also an occupational hazard, because one leader can't see every issue. A civil engineer sees a river that needs to be crossed. He tests the banks and traffic patterns to find the most appropriate place for a bridge. He determines the kinds of materials necessary to make it safe. His vision defines reality for the construction crew. The plan is seamless until the engineer sits down with a city planner. Her perspective is different. She's focused on conflicting realities: How will the large metal structure look against the city skyline? Would a suspension bridge be less obtrusive? How will the noise affect business in an adjacent neighborhood? Could we move it a few miles upstream? They work together and collaborate. Then an environmentalist walks in. He sees the potential damage to the ecosystem and asks, "Do we even need a bridge?"

It's tempting to surround ourselves with leaders who are just like us. A convictional leader has a tendency to marginalize a creative one. He loves his own style, so he clamors for more stalwart and dogmatic young leaders to join his team. In the process, he misses the complementary perspectives his followers really need.

Evangelicals tend to run in tribal packs. Culture-making creative leaders join the church downtown near the gallery district. Justice-seeking courageous leaders move into the poorest neighborhoods. Executives build a comfortable church in the suburbs. What emerges is a church made in the image and likeness of its leaders.

God imagines something better than our tribalism. He envisions holistic leaders who embody each aspect of the leadership mosaic. And he imagines all kinds of leaders working together to create a beautiful mosaic. He wants us to sharpen one another so that every leader grows in conviction, creativity, courage, collaboration, and contemplation—whether it's our strength and preference or not. No leader and no aspect of leadership should be forfeited.

To work together, we need humility. We embrace our strengths as God's gifts. We also embrace our weaknesses; they show us our need for others.

The convictional leader is strong. He has something to live for, and he's willing to die for it. His danger is becoming part of the "frozen chosen." Exaggerated dogmatism stifles innovation. Frozen in time, the convictional leader misses out on fresh ideas he'd learn by collaborating with others. When a dogmatic leader lacks humility, he demonizes creativity and spontaneity. He loses the power to communicate his convictions with beauty and love. If he doesn't take risks, he quenches the Spirit. He misses opportunities to win souls to the truth.

The creative leader keeps things fresh and exciting. She breathes new life where there was only dust. She transforms dead declarations into lyrics the whole church can sing. Her temptation will be to place too much value on what's original and "cutting edge." If her dreams aren't rooted in reality, her team accomplishes nothing.

The courageous leader rises to challenges and takes the hill. He fights to the finish. He perseveres until the team tastes victory. The trouble is that sometimes the courageous leader isn't leading the mission so much as running over everyone else. Daring leaders are dangerous when they lack compassion. The brave leader needs to look behind him—not just ahead. He needs a collaborative friend to help bring his followers along.

The collaborative leader builds consensus and mobilizes an army. When she leads, every party feels respected and heard. Every player—from the janitorial staff to the financial accountability team—owns the mission and knows his role. The collaborative leader's temptation is a lack of urgency. If a team becomes a bureaucracy, decisions come at a glacial pace. If they focus on one another more than results, the mission stagnates.

The contemplative leader never loses his first love. Even in the coldest season of life and ministry, his heart is warm. He practices God's presence, and when he's healthy, he comforts and shepherds the flock with care. If he's not healthy, contemplation warps and bends inward. He may become an experience junkie—filling his calendar with retreats and little else. He may lose himself in navel gazing, asking, "How do I get out of this prayer labyrinth?"

The courageous leader who can't work alongside a creative leader falls flat before problems that are too big for boldness. But where brute strength fails, a little ingenuity can pave the way. If a convictional pastor can't see the value of having a contemplative leader on staff, dry orthodoxy may kill his church. But a little love brings truth to life.

We must acknowledge our narrow gifts and perspective and allow others to challenge us. We are one body with many parts (Rom. 12:4; 1 Cor. 12:12). We want God to work through our gifts and shine his glory through our weakness (2 Cor. 12:9)—even if that means our strengths fade into the background.

Making All Things Beautiful

Inside the basilica in Istanbul known as Hagia Sophia, one of the seven wonders of the medieval world, is a stunning collection of Byzantine mosaics. The Deësis, which dates from 1261, may be the most stunning. It's widely considered the finest in the basilica because of its soft tones and the emotional realism on the faces of its figures.[10] The Deësis was commissioned to mark the return of Hagia Sophia to the Eastern Orthodox faith after fifty-seven years of Roman Catholic use. It pictures two saints who are revered by the Eastern Church, Mary and John the Baptist, entreating Christ to pray for humanity on judgment day.

If you look closely, you'll discover that what forms the beautiful image are shards of deep blue and golden glass. Each has a different shape and hue, but the differences work together to make the whole. In fact, the variegated tesserae in a mosaic like the Deësis *must* differ from one another not only in color but also in shape and size—otherwise, there is no picture. Part of the beauty of a mosaic is that, unlike other mediums, its components are distinct and visible. The "big picture" is beautiful, but part of what makes it amazing is that it's made up of small bits that are meaningless on their own.

Leadership, like a mosaic, hinges on our ability to hold together the one and the many. We need one purpose but many gifts. Where can we look for a model?

The answer is the Trinity. God is one, God is three, and God is three in one—a diversity in unity. Christian leadership stands or falls with our ability to cling to and live out these beautiful truths.[11]

First, God is *one*. To say that God is one is to say that he is the only being with his unique nature.[12] There is no one like him. No other gods can stand before him. He is God alone. And as the only God, he demands absolute devotion: "Hear, O Israel: The LORD our God, the LORD is one. You shall love the LORD your God with all your heart and with all your soul and with all your might" (Deut. 6:4–5). Through the prophet Isaiah, God declares,

> I am the LORD, and there is no other,
>> besides me there is no God;
>> I equip you, though you do not know me,
> that people may know, from the rising of the sun
>> and from the west, that there is none besides me;
>> I am the LORD, and there is no other. (Isa. 45:5–6)

To say that God is one is also to say that God is unified in his nature. Classically, theologians have called this the doctrine of God's simplicity. Carl Henry defines it this way: "God is not compounded of parts; he is not a collection of perfections, but rather a living center of activity pervasively characterized by all his distinctive perfections."[13] When John tells us that "God is spirit" (John 4:24) or "God is light" (1 John 1:5) or "God is love" (1 John 4:8, 16), he's not telling us that God is some cosmic cocktail of one part light, one part love, and one part spirit mixed together. No. Being spirit is essential to God's nature. God *is* light all the way through. He *is* love (if we could ever plumb the depths) right down to the bottom. In his essence, he is one.

But God is also *three*. Each of the persons of the Trinity is distinct from the others. The New Testament speaks clearly of the Father, Son, and Holy Spirit. They exist eternally as distinct persons. Jesus came from the Father (John 16:28), and he sent the Spirit from the Father (John 15:26).[14] The persons of the Trinity act with a unity of purpose and nature, but the Bible distinguishes their actions and interactions. In the work of creation, the Spirit hovers (Gen. 1:2), the Father speaks (Gen. 1:3), and the Son is the Word through whom all things are made (John 1:3) and sustained (Col. 1:17). In the work of redemption, the Father elects (Eph. 1:4–5), the Son purchases (Eph. 1:6–7), and the Spirit seals (Eph. 1:14–15). In 1 Peter 1:1–2, the Father chooses and foreknows, the Son sprinkles with his blood, and the Spirit sanctifies. John Frame says, "This is a useful generalization about the distinctive roles of the persons: the Father plans, the Son executes, and the Spirit applies."[15]

Finally, God is *three in one*. The action of the Trinity in history tells a beautifully harmonious story.[16] God is relational and communitarian. When we see God's harmony in both his universality and particularity, we see his beauty. Jeremy Begbie describes how the heart of the Trinity is most visible in God's redemptive work in the world:

> Divine beauty is discovered not in the first instance by reference to a doctrine (still less to a philosophy of beauty) but by strict attention to a movement in history enacted for us—supremely the story of Jesus Christ the incarnate Son, living in the Father's presence in the power of the Spirit. Trinitarian beauty has, so to speak, been performed for us. . . .
> God's beauty is not static structure but the dynamism of love.[17]

The story we tell about God's actions in history show us the dynamic way we should experience him today. The *economic* Trinity provides a window into the life of the *immanent* Trinity.[18] As Jesus said, "If you had known me, you would have known my Father also" (John 14:7). In other words, Jesus's story should inform and control our understanding of who God is.

Jesus is our model for leadership because he revealed the God who leads. There's no doubt Jesus's crucified and resurrected life makes his role among the divine persons unique, but Jesus didn't come to earth and go rogue. The Bible reiterates his relational dependence on the Father.[19] Jesus can only do what he sees the Father doing (John 5:19). Though the Father has entrusted judgment to him (John 5:22), Jesus only judges as he hears from the Father and seeks, he says, "not my own will but the will of him who sent me" (John 5:30). Through his dependent work, the Son reveals for us God's harmonious plan.

Jesus's story is good news for divided leaders because through Christ's work, we are changed. God welcomes and invites divided leaders to come and be conformed into Christ's image. God fashions our broken stories after the pattern of Jesus's life: crucifixion, death, and then resurrection. God calls us to hardship (2 Tim. 2:3; 4:5; Heb. 12:7), to face pressure (2 Cor. 11:28), to kill sin (Rom. 8:12–13; Col. 3:5), to have faith in the midst of a civil war of the soul (Rom. 7:23), and to take up our cross (Matt. 10:38; 16:24; Mark 8:34; Luke 9:23; 14:27). Transition, hardship, and loss are overwhelming, but God doesn't want us to get lost in the broken pieces. He wants to show us the goodness and glory that exist in the midst of sorrows. He wants to show us how the divine persons work together to make all things beautiful in their time (Eccles. 3:11). Like a father lifting up his son so he can take in all the flavors at an ice cream shop or putting his daughter on his shoulders at a wedding reception so she can see everyone dancing, God wants to lift you up and give you a glimpse at the beauty of his redemptive purposes. We relish glory, joy, and love because they are gifts from God, but what we experience now is only a foretaste of what is to come. When we see that better things are coming, we can lay down our leadership preferences and follow a more holistic vision.

Jesus shows us the way. He demonstrates that a cruciform life makes a beautiful leader. His death and resurrection put every broken piece in its place. In this way, Jesus provides a window into God's mosaic of leadership.

I have a selective memory about Christ's words in Matthew 16.

Jesus brought the disciples into Caesarea Philippi. The city was a regional epicenter of pagan ritual and worship. Its people bowed to Baal in the Old Testament era and Pan—the goat god of fertility—under the Greeks. They renamed the city Caesarea as a nod to the Romans and the imperial cult. Right there, at what must have felt like the very gates of hell, Peter confessed Christ: "You are the Christ [Messiah], the Son of the living God" (Matt. 16:16).

Sometimes, I misremember Jesus's famous response. I think it says, "Peter, you will build my church," and I translate that to "Daniel, you will build my church." But Jesus gave Peter (and me) more than personal encouragement and a commission. Jesus gave Peter a promise: "I [*not you*] will build my church, and the gates of hell shall not prevail against it" (Matt. 16:18). Jesus builds the church, and he builds it in his own cruciform image. Suffering is the pathway to glory. Whoever wants to be Jesus's disciple must also take up his cross (Matt. 16:24).

Jesus Holds Us Together

I drove fast and frustrated out into the Kentucky countryside for our annual campus pastors' retreat. The white and yellow lines of pavement slipped by underneath my car's hood. My mind raced as I sipped coffee and listened to NPR. I thought about my plan for our time together. I wanted it to be intimate and authentic. Why had the team been holding back over the past few months? Where was the deep friendship we once enjoyed?

A day or two into the retreat, we sat on the front porch of the cabin. I had spent the time asking questions, probing, and pontificating, but I wasn't self-aware.

In a few months, we would bring on a new lead pastor for Sojourn's Midtown campus. Jamaal Williams would be our first African-American staff member. He's an answer to our prayers for greater diversity, and he's the right leader to lead our main campus forward in a historically black neighborhood. I sensed that Jamaal would lead our church to a new era of fruitfulness and faithful obedience. I couldn't be happier or more thankful for him. When someone brought up the idea of Jamaal's upcoming transition to lead pastor, I immediately expressed my genuine joy.

But then I broke. Without warning my neglected emotions started to flow. I thought about the many leaders and members I'd poured into over the past decade and a half. Memories flickered by like a carousel in my mind. I had baptized them, married them, dedicated their children. I had leaned over them in a hospital to pray with them. I had mentored them, given them career advice, stuck with them through church discipline.

Now I was passing them on to a new leader.

They would no longer need me in the same way. The transition felt like the culmination of a painful dethroning of self. Over the past five years, Sojourn had transitioned to a multisite church. My closest friends moved out of the city to roomier houses and better school systems for their growing families. In the process, they left the campus where I served. Leaders that I had trained now led their own campuses, churches, businesses, and parachurch ministries with little to no input from me. I wanted to lead a releasing and sending church, but now it seemed like everyone was released and sent. In God's gracious plan, they increased, and I decreased.

In that moment at the cabin, I felt the full weight of being superfluous. I had been uprooted from a position I held with pride and gratitude for fifteen years. Now everything was changing. Even though I was still present with the staff at Midtown and serving as the teaching pastor of Sojourn, giving up the lead-pastor role felt like a free fall.

I found freedom in the humiliation of shedding tears in front of my friends. "Am I overreacting? Am I this egotistical? What did I think would happen? Wasn't this the goal of all my dreams and prayers since I was twenty-five?" The tears flowed all around. One of the other pastors turned toward me. He gathered himself, slid a hand on my back, and said, "Daniel, this is why we follow you. It's not because you are a vision machine or because you have all the theological answers. We follow you because you are in touch with your brokenness, and you lead us with vulnerability. We are glad to follow this Daniel."

Giving away the ministry I loved meant dying to self. God's only route to resurrection power in leadership is dying again and again. Suffering is the pathway to glory because, when we die, only Jesus can hold us together. Whoever wants to be Jesus's disciple must also take up his cross again and again (Matt. 16:24). In obedience to the Father, we must follow Jesus's example. It's only when we follow Jesus to the cross that we have confidence the Spirit will bring life (Phil. 2:5–8).

"We Cannot Forget That Beauty"

God invites leaders to put the pieces together. He wants us to find in him what unites every vision of leadership from East to West. The Trinity calls leaders into communion and collaboration. He wants to fill them with conviction, creativity, and courage. That's the holistic vision of leadership God intended—a beautiful mosaic.

At the end of the tenth century, the Russian people converted to Christianity under Prince Vladimir the Great (ca. 956–1015). During the early years of his reign, he built temples to various gods, commissioned numerous idols, and gave particular devotion to the thunder god Perun. Vladimir erected a statue cast in gold with a moustache made of silver. According to legend, the prince sent out envoys in 987 to investigate the faiths of neighboring regions. Those who visited the Muslim Bulgars returned complaining about the joylessness of their religion, but those who attended a glorious divine liturgy at Hagia Sophia in Byzantium reported the following: "Then we went to the Greeks and they led us to the place where they worship their God, and we knew not whether we were in earth or heaven, for on earth there is no such vision nor beauty, and we do not know how to describe it; we only know that God dwells among men. We cannot forget that beauty."[20] Vladimir was captivated by God's beauty. He converted, took a Christian name, and destroyed the Russian idols. He threw the statue of Perun into the river Dnieper.

If we follow Jesus, we lead others to be his disciples (Matt. 28:18–20). Since you picked up this book, you are probably a church leader of some variety. Let today's seekers and explorers who search for truth find the beauty of God in us (Col. 1:27). The world says we need strong, effective, and future-thinking leadership. God says we need him. There's true beauty in the presence of God. We must not forget that beauty. We will participate in it with him forever. The psalmist yearned for that day: "So shall the king greatly desire thy beauty" (Ps. 45:11 KJV).

My prayer for every leader who reads this book is movement from "How do we get this done?" to "What's the most beautiful way to accomplish this?" In ages past, Father, Son, and Spirit collaborated in just this way. Now God is calling you to collaborate *with* him.

In 1943, C. S. Lewis had the challenge of explaining the doctrine of the Trinity in a brief radio broadcast over the BBC. He met the challenge with the following words:

> You may ask, "If we cannot imagine a three-personal Being, what is the good of talking about Him?" Well, there isn't any good talking about Him. The thing that matters is being actually drawn into that three-personal life, and that may begin at any time—tonight, if you like.
>
> What I mean is this. An ordinary simple Christian kneels down to say his prayers. He is trying to get into touch with God. But if he is a Christian he knows what is prompting him to pray is also God: God, so to speak, inside him. But he also knows that all his real knowledge of God comes through Christ, the Man who was God—that Christ is standing beside him, helping him to pray, praying for him. You see what is happening. God is the thing to which he is praying—the goal he is trying to reach. God is also the thing inside him which is pushing him on—the motive power. God is also the road or bridge along which he is being pushed to that goal. So that the whole threefold life of the three-personal Being is actually going on in that ordinary little bedroom where an ordinary man is saying his prayers.[21]

That ordinary man is being caught up into a higher kind of life—the life of the Trinity. And what is true about that ordinary man's participation in God's life through prayer can be true for our leadership as well.

May the Triune God—Father, Son, and Holy Spirit—fill your bedroom and board room. May he frustrate your plans, deepen your conviction, and expand your vision.

May he give you empowering grace to express yourself as an image bearer reborn for kingdom creativity. May he enlarge your heart and engage your hands with his mission in the world. May you experience the same oneness with your colleagues and coworkers that the Son experiences with the Father. And may the Spirit draw you further up and further into the mystery and beauty of Triune communion. Amen.

May the infinite and glorious Trinity, the Father, the Son, and the Holy Spirit, direct our life in good works, and after our journey through this world, grant us eternal rest with the saints.

Seventh-century Mozorabic liturgy

O Lord, one God, God the Trinity, whatsoever I have said in these books that comes of thy prompting, may thy people acknowledge it: for what I have said that comes only of myself, I ask of thee and of thy people pardon.

Augustine, *On the Trinity*

ACKNOWLEDGMENTS

Daniel: *Leadership Mosaic* is a mosaic in every sense of the word. There are literally hundreds of books, lectures, podcasts, experiences, and articles we have gleaned from, and their notable impacts are seen throughout the endnotes. But it's the personal pieces of our mosaic that matter most, including the people and pastors of Sojourn family and beyond. Some of our fellow workers on this project need special mention.

I am thankful for my Mandy. She is always patient with me and the first one to hear my ideas. Her feedback and support have been preeminent in my life for the past nineteen years. I am thankful for Jared Kennedy as a cowriter and a pastor at Sojourn for the past decade. Jared is a brilliant writer, thinker, and leader of Sojourn Kids. His fingerprints are all over Sojourn and consequently this book. I am thankful for coconspirator Justin Karl, who shepherded this project with dreaming, research, testing, editing, writing, and care.

I am thankful for invaluable early editing, feedback, and research on the manuscripts from Mike Cosper, Timothy Paul Jones, Kelly Kapic, Justin Taylor, Michael Wilder, Amy Kratzsch, Megan Kennedy, Luke Barker, Brad House, Amanda Edmondson, Nick Weyrens, Brad Bell, Jason Read, Robert Cheong, Ryan Hopkins, Josh Richerson, Bryan Burgess, and Grant Flynn. Crossway and our editor, Thom Notaro, have been great partners in bringing this work to fruition.

I am thankful you have read through *Leadership Mosaic* and made it to the acknowledgments. I hope and pray this resource will help in your own leadership journey and experience of the gospel.

———

Jared: My wife, Megan, and our three daughters gave up a lot of time with husband and father over a two-year span so I could be a part of this project. I am in their debt. In addition, Megan read over the entire manuscript and gave really helpful feedback on every chapter. And it was truly a joy to get to know, serve alongside, and become friends with Justin Karl as he managed our writing from beginning to end.

Finally, I'm so grateful to have had this opportunity to write with Daniel Montgomery. He has been my lead pastor for ten years now. I have worked with Daniel as a member, staff person, and elder at Sojourn Community Church. And I've grown as a leader while watching him lead with integrity, vulnerability, regular repentance, and relentless missionary passion. I am privileged to help share his leadership vision with readers. I praise God for him and the insight God has given him. As the prophet said:

> Praise be to the name of God for ever and ever;
>   wisdom and power are his. . . .
> He gives wisdom to the wise
>   and knowledge to the discerning. (Dan. 2:20–21 NIV)

Appendix

FOUR DEFINITIONS OF LEADERSHIP

Leadership Mosaic, by Daniel Montgomery	The Marks of a Spiritual Leader, by John Piper	The Leadership Challenge, by James M. Kouzes and Barry Z. Posner	Transforming Leadership, by James MacGregor Burns
Convictional leaders embody what they believe. • *Listening.* Seek to hear God's voice in order to clarify your convictions. • *Living it out.* Practice what you preach, because people do what people see.	"I define spiritual leadership as knowing where God wants people to be . . ."	**Model the Way** • Clarify values by finding your voice and affirming shared values. • Set the example by aligning actions with shared values.	**Values:** "Leaders embrace values; values grip leaders. The stronger the values systems, the more strongly leaders can be empowered and the more deeply leaders can empower followers" (211).
Creative leaders imagining the way forward. • *Dreaming.* Make creative connections between where you are and what God wants. • *Persuading.* Be winsome. Be a poet. Help your people dream.		**Inspire a Shared Vision** • Envision the future by imagining exciting and ennobling possibilities. • Enlist others by appealing to shared aspirations.	**Creativity:** "At its simplest, creative leadership begins when a person imagines a state of affairs not presently existing" (153).

Leadership Mosaic, by Daniel Montgomery	The Marks of a Spiritual Leader, by John Piper	The Leadership Challenge, by James M. Kouzes and Barry Z. Posner	Transforming Leadership, by James MacGregor Burns
Courageous leaders take risks. • *Seeking.* Look for where God is working. Opportunities are invitations. • *Joining.* Speak up, step out, and act. God is inviting you to join him in his work.	. . . and taking the initiative . . .	**Challenge the Process** • Search for opportunities by seizing the initiative and looking outward for innovative ways to improve. • Experiment and take risks by constantly generating small wins and learning from experience.	**Conflict:** "While Christ enjoined men to 'do good to them that hate you,' he also warned that he had come 'not to send peace, but a sword' and foresaw grimly the conflict his message of love and forgiveness would inspire. . . . Conflict—especially nonviolent conflict—may be the key to opening up crucial dimensions of leadership" (187).
Collaborative leaders empower the team. • *Serving.* Be humble. Value others as more important than yourself. • *Supporting.* Give your team what they need to grow through ministry challenges.	. . . to use God's methods to get them there . . .	**Enable Others to Act** • Foster collaboration by building trust and facilitating relationships. • Strengthen others by increasing self-determination and developing competence.	**Empowerment and Efficacy:** "Instead of exercising power over people, transforming leaders champion and inspire followers" (26).
Contemplative leaders are fully awake to God. • *Receiving.* Open your heart to God. Hear his voice. Enter his rest. • *Rejoicing.* Rejoice in his gifts. Celebrate God's work in others.	. . . in reliance on God's power."	**Encourage the Heart** • Recognize contributions by showing appreciation for individual excellence. • Celebrate the values and victories by creating a spirit of community.	**Pursuit of Happiness:** "This is a large claim, based on the proposition that transforming leadership begins on people's terms, driven by their wants and needs, and must culminate in expanding opportunities for happiness" (230).

NOTES

Introduction: The Complexity of Leadership and Our Triune God

1. On August 27, 2014, Timothy Paul Jones and I debated Austin Fischer and Brian Zahnd on the Calvinistic understanding of the doctrines of grace. The debate was hosted by the Sojourn Network and moderated by Mark Galli of *Christianity Today*. I am thankful for all these men. You can view parts 1 and 2 of the debates on YouTube.

2. The questions in this paragraph and the following ones are adapted from Gordon McDonald, *A Resilient Life: You Can Move Ahead No Matter What* (Nashville: Thomas Nelson, 2004), 53–58, and Wayne Cordeiro, *Leading on Empty: Refilling Your Tank and Renewing Your Passion* (Minneapolis: Bethany House, 2009), 196–98.

3. George Cladis, *Leading the Team-Based Church: How Pastors and Church Staffs Can Grow Together into a Powerful Fellowship of Leaders* (New York: Josey-Bass, 1999), 3.

4. The *gentleman theologian*, according to Craig Van Gelder, "Theological Education and Missional Leadership Formation: Can Seminaries Prepare Missional Leaders for Congregations?," in *The Missional Church and Leadership Formation: Helping Congregations Develop Leadership Capacity*, ed. Craig Van Gelder (Grand Rapids, MI: Eerdmans, 2009), 17–20, is an image of the Christian leader born out of the free and enlightened thinking of America's revolutionary period. In the early days of our country, a new democratic spirit extended to every area of life. This included religious beliefs. The church, which since Constantine had been part of the establishment, was now a voluntary organization (Van Gelder, "An Ecclesiastical Geno-Project: Unpacking the DNA of Denominations and Denominationalism," in *The Missional Church and Denominations: Helping Congregations Develop a Missional Identity*, ed. Craig Van Gelder [Grand Rapids, MI: Eerdmans, 2008], 17–20). The fastest growing churches in this period of American life were the free churches—ones like the Baptists, Methodists, and Churches of Christ, who adopted democratic and congregational governing structures.

   The Christian leader in this period embodied two great cultural ideals: (1) He was a thinking man—an intellectual. Within the church, schools were seen as the primary means of cultural and personal change. Glenn T. Miller observes, "Protestants staked the future of their movement on the ability of teachers to transform patterns of thought" (*Piety and Intellect: The Aims and Purposes of Ante-Bellum Theological Education, 1870–1970* [Grand Rapids, MI: Eerdmans, 1990], 17, quoted in Van Gelder, "Theological Education," 14). So Christians founded schools like Harvard (1636) and Yale (1701) for training ministers in classical study. (2) In addition, the colonial pastor was a personable gentleman. He was faithful to challenge his congregants in their personal and individualized walk with God. After the two Great Awakenings, "revival and personal conversion became a deep and enduring value within U.S. Christianity" (Van Gelder, "Theological Education," 14). Pastors in this period were challenged with managing the polarity of how to shape both minds and hearts.

5. Van Gelder, "Theological Education," 27.

6. The *innovator* and *activist* both find their roots in the entrepreneurial church leader of the 1980s, 1990s, and 2000s. In recent years, our society has become more culturally diverse, and "company man" loyalty to denominations has declined. Church members have become church shoppers. Standardized denominational curriculums have gone into decline, and many of their publishers have already either merged or gone out of business. Revenue coming into national church offices is dramatically down, and this has led to the downsizing of national agencies. There is an emphasis in growing evangelical churches on congregations starting congregations—churches planting churches and doing missions instead of agencies planting churches and doing missions (ibid., 40; Van Gelder, "Ecclesiastical Geno-Project," 40–41).

With the decline of denominations came the rise of parachurch societies. Significant college campus organizations such as Campus Crusade (now Cru), InterVarsity, and the Navigators came into prominence in the late 1970s. Leaders or participants in these organizations migrated with age to be pastors and church members, and they brought with them the ethos of parachurch leadership into the church.

Following the parachurch lead, many growing churches are adopting strategies that do not require the primary leadership of national and regional denominational structures—strategies such as becoming seeker-sensitive, developing small groups, and using contemporary worship. We've seen the rise of the self-sufficient and full-service mega-church. And other independent congregations known by generic names such as community churches, fellowship churches, Bible churches, and so forth are growing as well. Growing evangelical groups are often influenced by what might be labeled as market-driven or mission-driven models of church. The purpose-driven model of Saddleback Community Church, led by Rick Warren, is a prime example.

These churches have formed networks—like the Willow Creek Association and the Acts 29 Network—that cross traditional denominational lines. The unity of these networks doesn't ignore doctrine, but it is based more in pragmatic and methodological affinity. Van Gelder observes, "Expansive approaches to starting new congregations have led many out of the more evangelical churches to reshape pastoral identity in yet another new direction: the *entrepreneurial leader*. This approach draws heavily on secular business models that place an emphasis on visionary leadership" (Van Gelder, "Theological Education," 40).

7. The *good manager* finds his roots in America's cultural focus on industry and efficiency in the post–Civil War era. In the late 1800s and early 1900s, the American church became more organized and sectarian. Leading the way was the denominational franchise—with its distinctive identities and practices that drew upon then-in-vogue principles of scientific management. Denominations bloomed and grew by adding agencies like mission boards, Sunday school boards, and publishing houses. In this period, "most churches began to take on a more comprehensive and programmatic approach to ministry ... that would deal with its members from cradle to grave" (Van Gelder, "Ecclesiastical Geno-Project," 34).

In the post–World War II era, this organized church thrived in America's newly developed suburbs—"the good life of the American dream was packaged and commodified into the suburban ideal" (Van Gelder, "Theological Education," 27). The Christian leader in the organized suburban church was a true professional. He was a "company man." He stood by his denomination's standardized programming. He stood by his church's political agenda. Before the Civil War, he stood against abolition. In the late nineteenth century, he stood for the temperance and women's suffrage movements. Even as the church's political influence on society began to wane, his fervor for what became known as the "culture war" did not.

The good manager has often stood loyally by the convictional theologian in a commitment to truth. He stood for the addition of the phrase "under God" to the Pledge of Allegiance in 1954. He stood with the Moral Majority and pro-life movement in the 1980s. And he stands for traditional marriage. Van Gelder observes, "There is an expectation among most U.S. denominations that they are responsible to help shape public behavior, and they often seek to use the democratic political process to achieve this end" ("Ecclesiastical Geno-Project," 30). When higher criticism challenged the Bible's authority as divine revelation and the modernist-fundamentalist split led to the division of many churches and denominations, these leaders valiantly stood for truth.

8. "America's Changing Religious Landscape: Christians Decline Sharply as Share of Population; Unaffiliated and Other Faiths Continue to Grow," *Pew Research* Center, May 12, 2015, http://www.pewforum.org/2015/05/12/americas-changing-religious -landscape.

9. Nick Bogardus, "People > Everything Else (Adapting Your Leadership and Ministry Philosophy to Change)," *Sojourn Network*, October 19, 2015, http://www.sojourn network.com/blog/what-counterinsurgency-tactics-can-teach-you-about-volunteer -management-in-your-church.

10. Stanley A. McChrystal et al., *Team of Teams: New Rules of Engagement for a Complex World* (New York: Portfolio/Penguin, 2015), Kindle edition, chap. 3.

11. Donella H. Meadows, *Thinking in Systems: A Primer*, ed. Diana Wright (White River Junction, VT: Chelsea Green, 2008), 181–82.

12. Cladis, *Leading the Team-Based Church*, 3–4.

13. Paul S. Fiddes, *Seeing the World and Knowing God: Hebrew Wisdom Literature and Christian Doctrine in a Late-Modern Context* (Oxford: Oxford University Press, 2013), 139.

14. Herman Bavinck, *The Doctrine of God*, trans. William Hendrickson, Students Reformed Theology Library (Carlisle, PA: Banner of Truth, 1978), 329.

15. Michael Reeves, *Delighting in the Trinity: An Introduction to the Christian Faith* (Downers Grove, IL: IVP Academic, 2012), 24.

16. "You know what happens when a portrait that has been painted on a panel becomes obliterated through external stains. The artist does not throw away the panel, but the subject of the portrait has to come and sit for it again, and then the likeness is re-drawn on the same material. Even so was it with the All-holy Son of God. He, the image of the Father, came and dwelt in our midst, in order that He might renew mankind made after Himself, and seek out His lost sheep, even as He says in the Gospel: 'I came to seek and to save that which was lost'" (St. Athanasius, *On the Incarnation of the Son of God* 3.14 [trans. Penelope Lawson]; compare *Against the Arians* 14.2).

17. Alexander quietly allowed the young deacon Athanasius to speak for him during the council. He would transfer his role as lead pastor to the young man after his death the next year.

18. Van Gelder, "Ecclesiastical Geno-Project," 43.

19. See John Piper, "The Marks of a Spiritual Leader," January 1, 1995, http://www
    .desiringgod.org/articles/the-marks-of-a-spiritual-leader, accessed on January 16,
    2015.

Chapter 1. The Convictional Leader: Embodying What You Believe

1. Norman Crane et al., "Leadership Imperatives for the Information Age," in *Proceed-
   ings of the 5th International Conference on Intellectual Capital, Knowledge Management, and Organizational Learning, New York Institute of Technology, 9–10 October
   2008* (New York: Academic, 2008), 220–21.

2. David Shenk, "Information Overload, Concept of," in *Encyclopedia of International
   Media and Communications*, vol. 2 (New York: Elsevier Science, 2003), 395–405.

3. Richard Saul Wurman, *Information Anxiety*, 2nd ed. (Indianapolis: Hayden/Que,
   2000), 15.

4. SINTEF, "Big Data, for better or worse: 90% of the world's data generated over the
   last two years," *ScienceDaily*, May 22, 2013, http://www.sciencedaily.com/releases
   /2013/05/130522085217.htm.

5. Jonathan B. Spira, "The Knowledge Workers Day: Our Findings," *Basex*, November
   4, 2010, http://www.basexblog.com/2010/11/04/our-findings.

6. "What Is Information Overload?" James C. Jernigan Library, Texas A&M University–Kingsville, accessed June 30, 2015, http://libguides.tamuk.edu/content.php?pid
   =176524&sid=1620069.

7. Quoted in Evgeny Morozov, *To Save Everything, Click Here: The Folly of Technological Solutionism* (Philadelphia: Public Affairs, 2013), Kindle edition, chap. 1, under
   "Solutionism and Its Discontents."

8. Ibid., introduction, and chap. 1, under "The Will to Improve (Just about Everything)."

9. Ibid., introduction. We should remember that Radiohead's recording was a parody
   about a kind of societal solutionism. The track "Fitter Happier" is about "a pig in a
   cage on antibiotics."

10. Morozov, *To Save Everything*, chap. 1, under "The Will to Improve (Just about
    Everything)."

11. Ibid.

12. Ibid., chap. 8, under "Monkeys, Sex, and Predictable Duress."

13. Ibid., chap. 1, under "The Will to Improve (Just about Everything)."

14. Andy Johnson, "Pragmatism, Pragmatism Everywhere!," *9Marks Blog*, February 26,
    2010, http://9marks.org/article/pragmatism-pragmatism-everywhere. I don't agree
    with all of Andy Johnson's conclusions about contextualization. In some situations,
    I believe that de-engineering a missional strategy from desired results is wise. But
    I believe he's hit the nail on the head about the contemporary evangelical church's
    focus on results at the expense of deeply held convictions.

15. James MacGregor Burns, *Transforming Leadership: A New Pursuit of Happiness*
    (New York: Grove, 2003), 147.

16. James M. Kouzes and Barry Z. Posner, *The Leadership Challenge: How to Make Ex-
    traordinary Things Happen in Organizations* (San Francisco: Jossey-Bass, 2012), 51.

17. R. Albert Mohler, *The Conviction to Lead: 25 Principles for Leadership That Matters*
    (Minneapolis: Bethany House, 2012), 21.

18. Gene Wood and Daniel Harkavy, *Leading Turnaround Teams* (St. Charles, IL: Church
    Smart Resources, 2004), 28.

19. This section is adapted from John Starke's interview with Nathan Ivey, "How to
    Start and Persevere in Inner-City Ministry," *The Gospel Coalition Blog*, January 9,

2014, http://www.thegospelcoalition.org/article/how-to-start-and-persevere-with
-inner-city-ministry.

20. Simon Sinek, *Start with Why: How Great Leaders Inspire Everyone to Take Action* (New York: Portfolio/Penguin, 2011).

21. Esther Lightcap Meek, *A Little Manual for Knowing* (Eugene, OR: Cascade, 2014).

22. David Allen, *Getting Things Done: The Art of Stress-Free Productivity* (New York: Penguin, 2015); Brian Tracy, *Eat That Frog! 21 Great Ways to Stop Procrastinating and Get More Done in Less Time* (San Francisco: Barrett-Kohler, 2007); Stephen R. Covey, *The 7 Habits of Highly Effective People: Powerful Lessons of Personal Change* (New York: Simon and Schuster, 2013).

23. John M. Frame, *Systematic Theology: An Introduction to Christian Belief* (Phillipsburg, NJ: P&R), 656–58.

24. Mohler, *Conviction to Lead*, 21.

25. Wayne Grudem, *Bible Doctrine: Essential Teachings of the Christian Faith* (Grand Rapids, MI: Zondervan, 1999), 56–58, 485. See Gayne J. Anacker and John R. Shoup, "Leadership in the Context of the Christian Worldview," in *Organizational Leadership: Foundations and Practices for Christians*, ed. John S. Burns, John R. Shoup, and Donald C. Simmons Jr. (Downers Grove, IL: IVP Academic, 2014), 50–54, for an argument for the priority of the doctrine of revelation in any Christian theology of leadership.

26. Colin E. Gunton, *A Brief Theology of Revelation* (London: T&T Clark, 1995), 33, argues that the way systematic theology creates lines of demarcation between general and special revelation has contributed to our misguided secular-sacred divide. I would argue that even the title "doctrine of revelation" itself skews our thinking a bit. It nominalizes what the Bible speaks about in active tenses and hides God as the subject of the action. It's better to simply say, "God speaks through the world he has made."

27. Ibid.

28. Abraham Kuyper, *Lectures on Calvinism* (repr., New York: Cosimo, 2009), 79.

29. Richard Lints, *The Fabric of Theology: A Prolegomenon to Evangelical Theology* (Grand Rapids, MI: Eerdmans, 1993), 23.

30. Donella H. Meadows, *Thinking in Systems: A Primer*, ed. Diana Wright (White River Junction, VT: Chelsea Green, 2008), 183.

31. Gunton, *Brief Theology of Revelation*, 30.

32. See John S. (Jack) Burns, "The Leadership River: A Metaphor for Understanding the Historic Emergence of Leadership Theory," in Burns, Shoup, and Simmons, *Organizational Leadership*, 94–99.

33. Abraham Kuyper, inaugural address at the opening of the Free University of Amsterdam, October 20, 1880, quoted in *Abraham Kuyper: A Centennial Reader*, ed. James D. Bratt (Grand Rapids, MI: Eerdmans, 1998), 488.

34. Mark Schlabach, *Heisman: The Man behind the Trophy* (New York: Howard, 2012).

35. Though the sentiment is characteristic of the High Middle Ages, the description of theology as "queen of the sciences" may have originated with Martin Luther. See Luther H. Martin, *Deep History, Secular Theory* (Berlin: de Gruyter, 2014), 13.

36. Geerhardus Vos, *Biblical Theology* (Grand Rapids, MI: Eerdmans, 1948), 17, quoted in Lints, *Fabric of Theology*, 64.

37. I'm making essentially the same argument as Anacker and Shoup, "Leadership in the Context of the Christian Worldview," 35–64. To everything they write about the Christian worldview and leadership, I give a hearty "Amen."

38. Frame, *Systematic Theology*, 618. That is, Scripture provides all the norms we need to apply to ourselves—our minds and hearts—in our situations. But knowing the

facts of our situation is vital to making any sort of life application. See Frame's full discussion on 618–29.

39. John Piper, "Thoughts on the Sufficiency of Scripture: What It Does and Doesn't Mean," *desiringGod*, February 9, 2005, http://www.desiringgod.org/articles/thoughts -on-the-sufficiency-of-scripture.

40. D. A. Carson, *Christ and Culture Revisited* (Grand Rapids, MI: Eerdmans, 2008), 228.

41. See Lints's critique in *Fabric of Theology*, 22ff.

42. Ibid., 64.

43. Timothy Paul Jones, *Family Ministry Field Guide: How Your Church Can Equip Parents to Make Disciples* (Indianapolis: Wesleyan, 2011), 72. The title of this volume is deceiving, because while there is a focus on equipping parents, the volume is Jones's manual for helping churches plan strategic alignment for their ministries in light of God's goals for both the family and the church.

44. The roots of leadership as discussed in Jack Burns ("The Leadership River," in Burns, Shoup, and Simmons, *Organizational Leadership*, 94–99) parallels the basic relationship structure we see in the Old Testament—covenant and contract. Cf. Peter J. Gentry and Stephen J. Wellum, *Kingdom through Covenant: A Biblical-Theological Understanding of the Covenants* (Wheaton, IL: Crossway, 2012), 129–45.

45. Rick Langer, "Toward a Biblical Theology of Leadership," in Burns, Shoup, and Simmons, *Organizational Leadership*, 77.

46. Ibid., 70.

47. Lints, *Fabric of Theology*, 59–62. Lints unpacks how the Bible is God's Word incarnated for us. God speaks "to and through people and in and through history. The speech of God has entered into time and space. It comes clothed in a cultural history and addresses itself to people across different cultural histories" (59–60).

48. Kouzes and Posner, *Leadership Challenge*, 45–47.

49. Ibid.

50. For a good book on listening, see Adam S. McHugh, *The Listening Life: Embracing Attentiveness in a World of Distraction* (Downers Grove, IL: InterVarsity Press, 2015).

51. Lints, *Fabric of Theology*, 58.

52. Ibid., 59.

53. Abraham Kuyper, *Principles of Sacred Theology*, trans. J. Hendrik DeVries (Grand Rapids, MI: Eerdmans, 1954), 110.

54. Lints, *Fabric of Theology*, 60.

55. Ibid., 69.

56. Kuyper, *Principles of Sacred Theology*, 111.

57. Ibid., 61.

58. Lints, *Fabric of Theology*, 77.

59. Ibid., 59.

60. Michael Winters, "After Six Years of the 930—Was It Worth It?," *Daniel Montgomery: Preach the Gospel, Die, Be Forgotten*, July 31, 2012, http://daniel-montgomery -sojourn.com/after-six-years-of-the-930-art-center-was-it-worth-it.

61. "Smells Like Holy Spirit," *LEO (Louisville Eccentric Observer) Weekly*, April 8, 2008, http://www.leoweekly.com/2008/04/smells-like-holy-spirit.

62. Kouzes and Posner, *Leadership Challenge*, 17.

63. Martin Luther, "Preface to the Wittenberg Edition of Luther's German Writings (1539)," in *Martin Luther's Basic Theological Writings*, ed. Timothy F. Lull (Minneapolis: Augsburg Fortress, 1989), 67.

64. Ibid.

65. Søren Kierkegaard, *The Diary of Søren Kierkegaard* (New York: Citadel, 2000), 126.
66. John Kotter, *Leading Change* (Watertown, MA: Harvard Business, 2012), 90.
67. Wood and Harkavy, *Leading Turnaround Teams*, 31.
68. Mohler, *Conviction to Lead*, 22.
69. These activities and reflections are adapted from Kouzes and Posner, *Leadership Challenge*, 68–69, 96–97; and Adele Ahlberg Calhoun, *Spiritual Disciplines Handbook: Practices That Transform Us* (Downers Grove, IL: InterVarsity Press, 2005), 166–69, 172–75.
70. Stanley Hauerwas, *Prayers Plainly Spoken* (Eugene, OR: Wipf & Stock, 2003), 26.

Chapter 2. The Creative Leader: Imagining the Way Forward

1. Kevin Cawley, "Creativity" (a presentation for Sojourn Network's "From Ashes to Beauty" conference, November 2014).
2. James MacGregor Burns, *Transforming Leadership* (New York: Grove, 2003), 153.
3. Avi Dan, "The 3 Things That Steve Jobs Taught Us about Creative Leadership," *Forbes*, October 31, 2011, http://www.forbes.com/sites/avidan/2011/10/31/the-3-things-that-steve-jobs-taught-us-about-creative-leadership/#2595fa8a542d.
4. Carmine Gallo, "Why Larry Ellison Calls Steve Jobs Another Picasso and What It Teaches Us about Creativity," *Forbes*, September 16, 2013, http://www.forbes.com/sites/carminegallo/2013/09/16/why-larry-ellison-calls-steve-jobs-another-picasso-and-what-it-teaches-us-about-creativity.
5. Ibid.
6. Ibid.
7. Gary Wolf, "Steve Jobs: The Next Insanely Great Thing, The Wired Interview," *Wired*, February 1, 1996, http://archive.wired.com/wired/archive/4.02/jobs.html.
8. Gallo, "Why Larry Ellison."
9. See Daniel Montgomery and Timothy Paul Jones, *PROOF: Finding Freedom through the Intoxicating Joy of Irresistible Grace* (Grand Rapids, MI: Zondervan, 2012).
10. See Lindsey Blair, Timothy Paul Jones, and Jonah Sage, *PROOF Pirates: Finding the Treasure of God's Amazing Grace Family Devotional* (Greensboro, NC: New Growth, 2015); and Jared Kennedy et al., *PROOF Pirates: Finding the Treasure of God's Amazing Grace, Bible Club and VBS Curriculum* (Greensboro, NC: New Growth, 2015).
11. Twyla Tharp, *The Creative Habit: Learn It and Use It for Life* (New York: Simon and Schuster, 2006), 103.
12. Tina Seelig, *inGenius: A Crash Course on Creativity* (New York: HarperOne, 2012), 15.
13. Eric Liu and Scott Noppe-Brandon, *Imagination First: Unlocking the Power of Possibility* (San Francisco: Jossey-Bass, 2011), 19.
14. J. K. Rowling, "The Fringe Benefits of Failure, and the Importance of Imagination" (commencement address, Harvard University, June 5, 2008), http://harvardmagazine.com/2008/06/the-fringe-benefits-failure-the-importance-imagination.
15. Liu and Noppe-Brandon, *Imagination First*, 19.
16. Anne Kreamer, "Creativity Lessons from Charles Dickens and Steve Jobs," *Harvard Business Review*, March 27, 2012, https://hbr.org/2012/03/creativity-lessons-from-charle.
17. Liu and Noppe-Brandon, *Imagination First*, 21.
18. Ibid., 22.
19. Tom and David Kelley, *Creative Confidence: Unleashing the Creative Potential within Us All* (New York: Crown Business, 2013), 2–3.
20. Liu and Noppe-Brandon, *Imagination First*, 23.

21. Ibid.
22. Bruce Nussbaum, *Creative Intelligence: Harnessing the Power to Create, Connect, and Inspire* (New York: Harper Business, 2013), 6–7.
23. Ibid.
24. Tharp, *Creative Habit*, 6.
25. C. S. Lewis, *Mere Christianity* (New York: HarperCollins, 2001), 151–52.
26. Colin E. Gunton, *The Triune Creator: A Historical and Systematic Study* (Grand Rapids, MI: Eerdmans, 1998), 12–13.
27. Troy Bronsink, *Drawn In: A Creative Process for Artists, Activists, and Jesus Followers* (Brewster, MA: Paraclete, 2013), 23.
28. Ibid., 26.
29. Daniel J. Treier, "Creation," in *Dictionary for Theological Interpretation of the Bible,* ed. Kevin J. Vanhoozer (Grand Rapids, MI: Baker Academic, 2005), 144–45.
30. Michael Reeves, *Delighting in the Trinity: An Introduction to the Christian Faith* (Downers Grove, IL: IVP Academic, 2012), 51.
31. Ibid., 145.
32. Bronsink, *Drawn In*, 38.
33. Catherine F. Vos, *A Child's Story Bible* (Grand Rapids, MI: Eerdmans, 1977), 3.
34. Harold M. Best, *Creative Diversity, Authenticity, and Excellence* (Washington, DC: Heldref, 1994), accessed May 23, 2014, http://leaderu.com/offices/haroldbest /diversity.html on.
35. Brandon Stanton, introduction to *Humans of New York* (New York: St. Martin's, 2013).
36. Peter J. Gentry and Stephen J. Wellum, *Kingdom through Covenant: A Biblical-Theological Understanding of the Covenants* (Wheaton, IL: Crossway, 2012), 200.
37. This is implied by Gen. 5:1–3: "This is the book of the generations of Adam. When God created man, *he made him in the likeness of God.* Male and female he created them, and he blessed them and named them Man when they were created. When Adam had lived 130 years, *he fathered a son in his own likeness,* after his image, and named him Seth"; and it is confirmed by Luke 3:38: ". . . the son of Enos, the son of Seth, the son of Adam, *the son of God."* Sonship is developed throughout the Old Testament. Israel inherits the role of Adam and Eve and is specifically called the son of God (Ex. 4:22–23). Later the role of divine sonship is given particularly to the king in the Davidic covenant (2 Sam. 7:14–15).
38. Gentry and Wellum, *Kingdom through Covenant*, 181–202.
39. In the beginning, God provided humanity with a creation mandate to "be fruitful and multiply and fill the earth and subdue it" (Gen. 1:28). "Be fruitful and multiply" suggests cultivation of the social world—calling humanity to build families, churches, schools, cities, governments, laws. "Subdue the earth" includes stewardship of the natural world—calling us to plant crops, build bridges, design computers, fling paint onto canvases, turn ink and paper into books, compose music, construct houses. See Nancy Pearcey, *Total Truth: Liberating Christianity from Its Cultural Captivity* (Wheaton, IL: Crossway, 2004), 19; and Michael Wilder and Timothy Paul Jones, *The God Who Goes Before Us* (Nashville: B&H, 2016), chap. 2.
40. Michael Horton, *God of Promise: Introducing Covenant Theology* (Grand Rapids, MI: Baker, 2006), 10.
41. I agree with J. Todd Billings, who writes, "While we are to cherish and utilize these God-given ways of portraying how God relates to the world, we should also avoid thinking that 'love,' 'grief,' 'wrath,' or 'jealousy' mean exactly the same thing for God as they do for us. . . . Unlike the love, grief, wrath, and jealousy that we see and experi-

ence with other humans, God's affections are perfect, self-derived expressions of his faithful covenant love" (*Rejoicing in Lament: Wrestling with Incurable Cancer and Life in Christ* [Grand Rapids, MI: Brazos, 2015], 157).

42. Bruce Ware, *Big Truths for Young Hearts* (Wheaton, IL: Crossway, 2009), 64–65. It is key to see that God plans everything to show his glory and to do good for his people. If God were the King of everything but not wise and loving, we would worry that he would rule the world in ways that are not good or best. But the Bible teaches us that God rules over everything with wisdom and love. We know this because God has shown us his wisdom and love in Jesus Christ. Because he is wise and good, we should praise God. At the end of time, all of creation will praise him. His creatures will say, "You are worthy, our Lord and God! You are worthy to receive glory and honor and power. You are worthy because you created all things. They were created and they exist. That is the way you planned it" (Rev. 4:11, my paraphrase).

43. Andy Crouch, *Culture Making: Recovering Our Creative Calling* (Downers Grove, IL: InterVarsity Press, 2013), 22.

44. Ibid., 21.

45. Ibid., 22, 106.

46. Best, *Creative Diversity*.

47. Andy Stanley, *Visioneering: God's Blueprint for Developing and Maintaining Vision* (Colorado Springs, CO: Multnomah, 1999), 18.

48. James M. Kouzes and Barry Z. Posner, *The Leadership Challenge: How to Make Extraordinary Things Happen in Organizations* (San Francisco: Jossey-Bass, 2012), 17–19.

49. Ibid., 103.

50. Ibid., 105.

51. Tharp, *Creative Habit*, 8.

52. Introduction to *Dictionary of Biblical Imagery*, ed. Leland Ryken, James C. Wilhoit, and Tremper Longman III (Downers Grove, IL: IVP Academic, 1998), xiii.

53. Ibid. Also see Lisa Cron, *Wired for Story: The Writer's Guide to Using Brain Science to Hook Readers from the Very First Sentence* (New York: Ten Speed, 2012).

54. Brian Godawa, *Word Pictures: Knowing God through Story and Imagination* (Downers Grove, IL: InterVarsity Press, 2009), 16.

55. Ibid., 16–18.

56. A. W. Tozer, *Born after Midnight* (Chicago: Moody Press, 2015), chap. 22.

57. John Hodgman, interview by Elizabeth Gilbert, "John Hodgman on 'The Question of What Comes Next,'" podcast episode 10 of *Magic Lessons with Elizabeth Gilbert*, September 5, 2015, https://www.youtube.com/watch?v=zumtQuvjcn4.

58. Brené Brown, "The Power of Vulnerability," June 2010, *TEDxHouston*, https://www.ted.com/talks/brene_brown_on_vulnerability.

59. These activities and reflections adapted from Kouzes and Posner, *Leadership Challenge*, 125–26, 152–53; Bronsink, *Drawn In*, 25–26; and Adele Ahlberg Calhoun, *Spiritual Disciplines Handbook: Practices That Transform Us* (Downers Grove, IL: InterVarsity Press, 2005), 56–58.

60. Anselm, "Proslogion," in *A Scholastic Miscellany: Anselm to Ockham*, ed. Eugene R. Fairweather (Philadelphia: Westminster, 1961), 73.

Chapter 3. The Courageous Leader: Taking Risks

1. Brené Brown tells this story in her book *Daring Greatly: How the Courage to Be Vulnerable Transforms the Way We Live, Love, Parent, and Lead* (New York: Avery, 2012), 12–16, and in an interview with Tim Ferriss, "Brené Brown on Vulnerability

and Home Run TED Talks," *The Tim Ferriss Show*, August 28, 2015, http://www
.stitcher.com/podcast/tim-ferriss-show/the-tim-ferriss-show/e/bren-brown-on
-vulnerability-and-home-run-ted-talks-40298967.

2. Brown, *Daring Greatly*, 13.
3. Ibid., 13–14.
4. Ibid., 112.
5. Dick Keyes, *True Heroism in a World of Celebrity Counterfeits* (Colorado Springs: NavPress, 1995), 146.
6. Nik Ripken, "Is God Insane?," *Nik Ripken Ministries*, December 16, 2013, http:// ripken25.rssing.com/chan-23108274/all_p2.html.
7. Ibid.
8. Ross Hastings, *Missional God, Missional Church: Hope for Re-evangelizing the West* (Downers Grove, IL: IVP Academic, 2012), 84–85.
9. Paul Stevens, *The Other Six Days: Vocation, Work, and Ministry in Biblical Perspective* (Grand Rapids, MI: Eerdmans, 2000), 194. See John R. Franke, "God Is Love: The Social Trinity and the Mission of God," in *Trinitarian Theology for the Church: Scripture, Community, Worship*, ed. Daniel J. Treier and David Lauber (Downers Grove, IL: InterVarsity Press).
10. See Hastings, *Missional Church, Missional God*, 80–117.
11. Leanne Van Dyk, "The Church's Proclamation as a Participation in God's Mission," in Treier and Lauber, *Trinitarian Theology for the Church*, 229.
12. Stephen Seamands, *Ministry in the Image of God: The Trinitarian Shape of Christian Service* (Downers Grove, IL: InterVarsity Press, 2005), 160–61; Andreas J. Köstenberger and Peter T. O'Brien, *Salvation to the Ends of the Earth: A Biblical Theology of Mission* (Downers Grove, IL: InterVarsity Press, 2001), 268–69. Köstenberger and O'Brien state:

> God's saving plan for the whole world forms a grand frame around the entire story of Scripture. His mission is bound up with his salvation, which moves from creation to new creation. Its focus is on God's gracious movement to save a desperately needy world that is in rebellion against him and which stands under his righteous judgment. The Lord of the Scriptures is a missionary God who reaches out to the lost, and sends his servants, and particularly his beloved Son, to achieve his gracious purposes of salvation.

13. Seamands, *Ministry in the Image of God*, 120.
14. This outline is adapted from Daniel Montgomery and Timothy Paul Jones, *PROOF: Finding Freedom through the Intoxicating Joy of Irresistible Grace* (Grand Rapids, MI: Zondervan, 2014), 31–41.
15. Franke, "God Is Love," 118.
16. Van Dyk, "The Church's Proclamation," 229.
17. Keyes, *True Heroism*, 175.
18. Ibid.
19. Martin Luther King Jr., speech at the "Great March on Detroit," June 23, 1963, http:// kingencyclopedia.stanford.edu/encyclopedia/documentsentry/doc_speech_at_the _great_march_on_detroit.1.html.
20. Seamands, *Ministry in the Image of God*, 168–69.
21. Zach Bradley, *The Sending Church Defined* (Knoxville, TN: Upstream Collective, 2015), 15.
22. Here I am echoing language from J. R. R. Tolkien, *The Hobbit*.

23. Alan Hirsch, *The Forgotten Ways: Reactivating the Missional Church*, 5th ed. (Grand Rapids, MI: Brazos, 2009), 193–95; see also James M. Kouzes and Barry Z. Posner, *The Leadership Challenge: How to Make Extraordinary Things Happen in Organizations* (San Francisco: Jossey-Bass, 2012), 159, and Ichak Adizes, *Corporate Lifecycles: How and Why Corporations Grow and Die and What to Do about It* (Santa Barbara, CA: Adizes Institute, 1990), 87–109.

24. Seamands, *Ministry in the Image of God*, 165.

25. Oswald Chambers, "The Place of Ministry," in *My Upmost for His Highest* (October 3), accessed July 9, 2015, http://utmost.org/the-place-of-ministry.

26. Henry Blackaby, Richard Blackaby, and Claude King, *Experiencing God: Knowing and Doing the Will of God*, rev. ed. (Nashville: B&H, 2008), 72.

27. Hirsch, *The Forgotten Ways*, 195.

28. Keyes, *True Heroism*, 46.

29. Ibid., 30.

30. The Amazon author ranking can be the Devil incarnate to inflate or deflate a writer's ego. Lord, have mercy.

31. This turn of phrase is adapted from Count Nicolaus Zinzendorf as quoted in A. J. Lewis, *Zinzendorf the Ecumenical Pioneer* (London: SCM, 1962), 59.

32. This included a place to live (Gen. 2:8), food (Gen. 1:29; 2:9), water (Gen. 2:10–14), responsibility (Gen. 1:28; 2:15), boundaries for his protection (Gen. 2:16–17), and companionship (Gen. 2:18, 21–25).

33. Curt Thompson, *The Soul of Shame: Retelling the Stories We Believe about Ourselves* (Downers Grove, IL: InterVarsity Press, 2015), 24.

34. Mike Wilkerson, *Redemption: Freed by Jesus from the Idols We Worship and the Wounds We Carry* (Wheaton, IL: Crossway, 2011), 88–89.

35. Gary L. McIntosh and Samuel D. Rima Sr., *Overcoming the Dark Side of Leadership: The Paradox of Personal Dysfunction* (Grand Rapids, MI: Baker, 1997), 50–51.

36. Ibid.

37. Ibid.

38. Edward T. Welch, *Shame Interrupted: How God Lifts the Pain of Worthlessness and Rejection* (Greensboro, NC: New Growth, 2012), 135–36.

39. Thompson, *Soul of Shame*, 119.

40. Quoted in Brian J. Dodd, *Empowered Church Leadership: Ministry in the Spirit according to Paul* (Downers Grove, IL: InterVarsity Press), 79.

41. C. John Miller, *Saving Grace: Daily Devotions from Jack Miller* (Greensboro, NC: New Growth, 2014), 72.

42. Seamands, *Ministry in the Image of God*, 22.

43. James MacGregor Burns, *Transforming Leadership: A New Pursuit of Happiness* (New York: Grove, 2003), 183.

44. Ibid., 187.

45. Eugene Peterson, *Leap Over a Wall: Earthly Spirituality for Everyday Christians* (San Francisco: HarperSanFrancisco, 1998), 101, 234–35.

46. Kouzes and Posner, *Leadership Challenge*, 169–70, emphasis mine.

47. Ross Hastings, *Missional God, Missional Church: Hope for Re-evangelizing the West* (Downers Grove, IL: IVP Academic, 2012), 116.

48. Portions of this paragraph were adapted from Craig Van Gelder, *The Ministry of the Missional Church: A Community Led by the Spirit* (Grand Rapids, MI: Baker, 2007), 41–46.

49. Questions adapted from Rick Langer, "Toward a Biblical Theology of Leadership," in *Organizational Leadership: Foundations and Practices for Christians*, ed. John S. Burns, John R. Shoup, and Donald C. Simmons Jr. (Downers Grove, IL: IVP Academic, 2014), 85.
50. Seamands, *Ministry in the Image of God*, 28.
51. This wording is adapted from Michael Crawford, pastor of Freedom Church, Baltimore, Maryland.
52. Seamands, *Ministry in the Image of God*, 175.
53. This wording is adapted from Michael Crawford as well.
54. Jared and I are really thankful for Barbara Miller-Juliani, Jack Miller's daughter, who at the time of writing is editorial director for New Growth Press. Barbara helped us edit this section and tell her dad's story. To learn more about the missionary efforts of Serge, check out their website at www.serge.org.
55. These activities and reflections are adapted from Kouzes and Posner, *Leadership Challenge*, 182–83, and Adele Ahlberg Calhoun, *Spiritual Disciplines Handbook: Practices That Transform Us* (Downers Grove, IL: InterVarsity Press, 2005), 161.
56. From *The Worship Sourcebook*, 2nd ed., ed. Emily R. Brink and John D. Witvliet (Grand Rapids, MI: Calvin Institute of Christian Worship; Faith Alive Christian Resources; Baker, 2013), 711

Chapter 4. The Collaborative Leader: Empowering the Team

1. Peter J. Gentry and Stephen J. Wellum, *Kingdom through Covenant: A Biblical-Theological Understanding of the Covenants* (Wheaton, IL: Crossway, 2012), 129–45.
2. Timothy Keller, *The Meaning of Marriage: Facing the Complexities of Commitment with the Wisdom of God* (New York: Dutton, 2011), 81.
3. Ibid.
4. Ibid., 81–82.
5. Michael Horton, *God of Promise: Introducing Covenant Theology* (Grand Rapids, MI: Baker, 2006), 10.
6. John R. Franke, "God Is Love: The Social Trinity and the Mission of God," in *Trinitarian Theology for the Church: Scripture, Community, Worship*, ed. Daniel J. Treier and David Lauber (Downers Grove, IL: InterVarsity Press, 2009), 118.
7. Josh Sanburn, "Millennials: The Next Greatest Generation?," *Time*, May 9, 2013, http://nation.time.com/2013/05/09/millennials-the-next-greatest-generation.
8. Stephen A. Macchia, *Becoming a Healthy Team: 5 Traits of Vital Leadership* (Grand Rapids, MI: Baker, 2005), 28–31, cites example after example of teamwork in the Bible.
9. Brad House, *Community: Taking Your Small Group off Life Support* (Wheaton, IL: Crossway, 2011), 34.
10. Horton, *God of Promise*, 10.
11. Thom S. Rainer, "The Dangerous Third Year of Pastoral Tenure," June 18, 2014, http://thomrainer.com/2014/06/dangerous-third-year-pastoral-tenure.
12. Gerald Chaliand and Arnaud Blin, "Zealots and Assassins," in *The History of Terrorism and Guerilla Warfare: From Antiquity to Al Qaeda*, ed. Gerald Chaliand (Berkeley: University of California Press, 2007), 55.
13. John Edmund Kaiser, *Winning on Purpose: How to Organize Congregations to Succeed in Their Mission* (Nashville: Abingdon, 2006), 81.
14. Larry Osborne, *Sticky Teams: Keeping Your Leadership Team and Staff on the Same Page* (Grand Rapids, MI: Zondervan, 2010), 28–34.

15. Ibid.
16. Kaiser, *Winning on Purpose*, 82.
17. Randy Nabors, "Mission to the Poor" (presented at the Sojourn Network "Ashes to Beauty" National Conference, Louisville, Kentucky, November 4, 2014).
18. John Maxwell, *The 17 Indisputable Laws of Teamwork* (Nashville: Thomas Nelson, 2001), 42.
19. John Maxwell, *Teamwork 101: What Every Leader Needs to Know* (Nashville: Thomas Nelson, 2008), 19.
20. Timothy S. Lane and Paul David Tripp, *Relationships: A Mess Worth Making* (Greensboro, NC: New Growth, 2006).
21. Maxwell, *17 Indisputable Laws of Teamwork*, 210.
22. Larry Osborne, *The Unity Factor: Developing a Healthy Church Leadership Team* (Vista, CA: Owl Concepts, 1989), 52.
23. See the section on social power in A. Scott Moreau, Evvy Hay Campbell, and Susan Greener, *Effective Intercultural Communication: A Christian Perspective* (Grand Rapids, MI: Baker Academic, 2014), 165–70.
24. Maxwell, *17 Indisputable Laws of Teamwork*, 39.
25. Ibid., 33.
26. Ibid., 117ff.
27. See Robert Cheong, *God Redeeming His Bride: A Handbook for Church Discipline* (Fearn, Ross-Shire, UK: Christian Focus, 2013).
28. James MacGregor Burns, *Transforming Leadership: A New Pursuit of Happiness* (New York: Grove, 2003), 26.
29. Rick Langer, "Toward a Biblical Theology of Leadership," in *Organizational Leadership: Foundations and Practices for Christians*, ed. John S. Burns, John R. Shoup, and Donald C. Simmons Jr. (Downers Grove, IL: IVP Academic, 2014), 68.
30. Florence Whiteman Kaslow and Marvin B. Sussman, *Cults and the Family* (Binghamton, NY: Haworth, 1982), 34.
31. Ron Friedman, "The Collaboration Paradox: Why Working Together Often Yields Weaker Results," *99u: insights on making ideas happen*, accessed July 10, 2015, http://99u.com/articles/27941/the-collaboration-paradox-why-working-together -often-yields-weaker-results.
32. George Cladis, *Leading the Team-Based Church: How Pastors and Church Staffs Can Grow Together into a Powerful Fellowship of Leaders* (San Francisco: Jossey-Bass, 1999), 133. Cladis references research from Thomas J. Peters and Robert H. Waterman, a pair of management gurus from the 1980s, and their landmark work *In Search of Excellence: Lessons from America's Best-Run Companies* (New York: Harper & Row, 1982).
33. David G. Benner, *Soulful Spirituality: Becoming Fully Alive and Deeply Human* (Grand Rapids, MI: Brazos, 2011), 131.
34. Ronald Heifetz, Alexander Grashow, and Marty Linsky, *The Practice of Adaptive Leadership: Tools and Tactics for Changing Your Organization and the World* (Boston, MA: Harvard Business Press, 2009), 29.
35. Thomas Merton, *The Intimate Merton: His Life from His Journals*, ed. Patrick Hart and Jonathan Montaldo (New York: HarperCollins, 1999), 171–72.
36. Claudio Fernández-Aráoz, "21st Century Talent Spotting: Why Potential Now Trumps Brains, Experience, and 'Competencies,'" *Harvard Business Review* 92, no. 6 (June 2014).

37. Ichak Adizes. *Corporate Lifecycles: How and Why Corporations Grow and Die and What to do About It* (Englewood Cliffs, NJ: Prentice Hall, 1988), 4.

38. Will Welch, "The Survivors: Jack White," *GQ* (music issue), November 7, 2011, http://www.gq.com/entertainment/music/201111/jack-white-gq-music-issue.

39. James M. Kouzes and Barry Z. Posner, *The Leadership Challenge: How to Make Extraordinary Things Happen in Organizations* (San Francisco: Jossey-Bass, 2012), 21.

40. These activities and reflections adapted from ibid., 238–40, 268–69, and Adele Ahlberg Calhoun, *Spiritual Disciplines Handbook: Practices That Transform Us* (Downers Grove, IL: InterVarsity Press, 2005), 118–20, 144–47.

41. Stanley Hauerwas, *Prayers Plainly Spoken* (Eugene, OR: Wipf & Stock, 2003), 102.

Chapter 5. The Contemplative Leader: Waking Up to Reality

1. C. S. Lewis, *Surprised by Joy: The Shape of My Early Life* (New York: Harcourt Brace Jovanovich, 1966), 207–8.

2. Josh Levs, "Overscheduled Kids, Anxious Parents," *CNN*, March 10, 2013, http://www.cnn.com/2013/03/08/living/overscheduled-busy-children.

3. Carolyn Gregoire, "Happiness Index: Only 1 in 3 Americans Are Very Happy, according to Harris Poll," *The Huffington Post*, June 1, 2013, http://www.huffingtonpost.com/2013/06/01/happiness-index-only-1-in_n_3354524.html.

4. "Statistics in the Ministry," *Pastoral Care, Inc.*, accessed July 10, 2015, http://pastoralcareinc.com/WhyPastoralCare/Statistics.php.

5. Jack Wellman, "Why We Are Losing So Many Churches in the United States," *Christian Crier*, October 26, 2013, http://www.patheos.com/blogs/christiancrier/2013/10/26/why-we-are-losing-so-many-churches-in-the-united-states.

6. This section, "Cycle of Compulsion," was adapted from Jim Cofield and Rich Plass, "Three Emotions That Drive Your Compulsions," March 4, 2013, http://www.sojournnetwork.com/news/compulsions; and Marshall Goldsmith, *What Got You Here Won't Get You There* (New York: Hyperion, 2007), 40.

7. Goldsmith, *What Got You Here*, 40.

8. I'm indebted to Sojourn Network church planter Dustin Crawford for insights in this paragraph.

9. I'm following Jonathan Edwards, who departed from the Western Trinitarian tradition by rejecting its over-emphasis upon divine simplicity. As Michael J. McClymond and Gerald R. McDermott, *The Theology of Jonathan Edwards* (Oxford University Press, 2012), 199, point out:

> The social analogy, which was articulated by the medieval thinker Richard of St. Victor, conceives of God as a society or family of persons. This analogy did not gain much traction until recent times because of the strong commitment to divine simplicity in Western or Latin theology. Each person, it was thought, was only modally distinct from the divine essence. More emphasis was placed on the concurrence of all three persons in every divine act than on distinct roles for each. As Plantinga-Pauw has shown, the Reformed tradition in particular placed divine simplicity at the head of theology and tended to "tailor the doctrine of the Trinity to fit with divine simplicity." But in a "startling departure," Edwards rejected this trend by developing "an alternative conception of divine oneness that revolved around the notions of excellency, harmony and consent." He presented God (in his words) as "three persons of the Trinity . . . act[ing] as a society" in the great affair of redemption. Their mutual love makes for a "fountain of happiness" that

renders the Trinity an "infinitely sweet and glorious society." William Danaher suggests that even Edwards's use of the psychological model was social because he thought of God's unity as mutual participation in an identical idea. For the tradition that developed the psychological model, personhood is individuality, love is an individual's governing disposition, and the *imago dei* is found in consciousness. But for Edwards, personhood is relationality and dialogue, love is communal and interpersonal, and the *imago dei* is found in relationships.

Another contemporary writer who follows Edwards's social Trinitarianism is Peter J. Leithart, *Traces of the Trinity: Signs of God in Creation and Human Experience* (Grand Rapids, MI: Brazos, 2015), 151–52. He shows how the biblical writers use familial language for God's intra-Trinitarian relationships:

> God oversaw the formation of human families and politics, and as he did so, he directed them so that "fathers" and "kings" depict in various ways how Yahweh relates to his creation, to human beings, and to his people in particular. Ultimately, he designed the world so that fathers and sons would point toward the eternal Father who loves his eternal Son. . . . There is no impropriety in . . . suggesting that there are analogies between father-son relations and the eternal relation of the Father and Son. Though "Father, Son, and Spirit" is an unrevisable name, Scripture sometimes, for example, uses maternal analogies to describe God's relation to his people: "as one whom his mother comforts, so I will comfort you" (Isa. 66:13). There would seem to be no obstacle to extending these analogies, provided we recognize when we leave behind definite statements of Scripture and begin to speculate.

10. J. I. Packer, *In God's Presence: Daily Devotions with J. I. Packer* (Wheaton, IL: Shaw, 2000), 7.
11. Donald Miller and John MacMurray Jr., *To Own a Dragon: Reflections on Growing Up without a Father* (Colorado Springs: NavPress, 2006), 183.
12. John Owen, *Communion with the Triune God*, ed. Kelly Kapic and Justin Taylor (Wheaton, IL: Crossway, 2007), 112.
13. A. W. Tozer, *The Knowledge of the Holy* (New York: HarperOne, 2009), 1.
14. Joel R. Beeke and Mark Jones, *A Puritan Theology: Doctrine for Life* (Grand Rapids, MI: Reformation Heritage, 2012), 107.
15. Ibid.
16. Owen, *Communion with the Triune God*, 107.
17. Michael Reeves, *Delighting in the Trinity: An Introduction to the Christian Faith* (Downers Grove, IL: IVP Academic, 2012), 114–15.
18. Kelly M. Kapic, *Communion with God: The Divine and the Human in the Theology of John Owen* (Grand Rapids, MI: Baker, 2007), 170. Kapic quotes *Owen's Works*, 2:22 with references to Pss. 23:1; 103:13; Isa. 40:11; 63:16; Matt. 6:6; 23:37.
19. Kapic, *Communion with God*, 172.
20. Ibid., 172; Owen, *Communion with the Triune God*, 113.
21. Richard Plass and James Cofield, *The Relational Soul: Moving from False Self to Deep Connection* (Downers Grove, IL: InterVarsity Press, 2014), 73.
22. Ibid., 74.
23. Owen, *Communion with the Triune God*, 117.
24. Ibid.

25. Ibid., 352.
26. Kapic, *Communion with God*, 152; cf. 176–92.
27. Beeke and Jones, *Puritan Theology*, 111–12. They are summarizing Owen, *Communion with God*, in *Works*, 2:236–53, as follows: (1) the Spirit helps the believer remember the words of Christ and teaches what they mean; (2) the Spirit glorifies Christ; (3) he pours out the love of God in the Christian's heart; (4) he witnesses to the believer that he or she is a child of God; (5) the Spirit seals faith in the Christian; (6) as the earnest of our inheritance, he assures the believer of salvation; (7) he anoints the believer; (8) as the indwelling Spirit he sheds the love of God abroad in the believer's heart; and (9) he becomes to him the Spirit of supplication (Acts 9:31; Rom. 14:17; Gal. 5:22; 1 Thess. 1:6). What I'm calling "power for mission," Owen called "consecration for experiential holiness."
28. Owen, *Communion with the Triune God*, 377.
29. Joan D. Chittister, *In a High Spiritual Season* (Liguori, MO: Triumph, 1995), 26.
30. Plass and Cofield, *Relational Soul*, 75.
31. Kapic, *Communion with God*, 153.
32. Stephen Seamands, *Ministry in the Image of God: The Trinitarian Shape of Christian Service* (Downers Grove, IL: InterVarsity Press, 2005), 150.
33. Plass and Cofield, *Relational Soul*, 75.
34. Owen, *Communion with God*, in *Works*, 2:245.
35. Adele Ahlberg Calhoun, *Spiritual Disciplines Handbook: Practices That Transform Us* (Downers Grove, IL: InterVarsity Press, 2005), 172–75.
36. Ibid., 173.
37. Ibid., 166–69.
38. Ibid., 42.
39. Ibid., 41.
40. This demonic teaching that we should reject God's material world finds its origins in the garden of Eden. God made Adam and Eve, placed them in a beautiful garden, and put them in charge over everything. He prohibited only their eating from the tree of the knowledge of good and evil lest they surely die (Gen. 2:16–17). God gave them one *no* in a world full of *yes*. The Demon of demons came along and he distorted God's command. He poisoned our human understanding of creation and the Creator. He said, "Did God actually say, 'You shall not eat of *any* tree in the garden'?" (Gen. 3:1). One of Satan's tactics, from the very beginning, has been to distort who God is in the eyes of humanity. Satan does not want us to see God as a loving Father. He does not want us to see God as the giver of every good and perfect gift. His version of God is a ruthless forbidder, a cosmic killjoy, who creates enjoyable things and then denies us from partaking. Asceticism isn't holy. It's a rejection of the gifts and the giver.
41. Joe Rigney, *The Things of Earth: Treasuring God by Enjoying His Gifts* (Wheaton, IL: Crossway, 2015), 25.
42. David Murray, *The Happy Christian: Ten Ways to Be a Joyful Believer in a Gloomy World* (Nashville: Thomas Nelson, 2015), 124.
43. Ibid.
44. Ibid.
45. James M. Kouzes and Barry Z. Posner, *The Leadership Challenge: How to Make Extraordinary Things Happen in Organizations* (San Francisco: Jossey-Bass, 2012), 276.
46. Lance Witt, *Replenish: Leading from a Healthy Soul* (Grand Rapids, MI: Baker, 2011), 149–50.

47. Kouzes and Posner, *Leadership Challenge*, 288.
48. Calhoun, *Spiritual Disciplines Handbook*, 29.
49. Dallas Willard, "Live Life to the Full," *Christian Herald*, April, 14, 2001, http://www.dwillard.org/articles/artview.asp?artID=5.
50. Church of England, Book of Common Prayer, with the additions and deviations proposed in 1928.

Conclusion: The Leadership Mosaic

1. Craig Van Gelder, "Missiology and the Missional Church in Context," in *The Missional Church in Context: Helping Congregations Develop Contextual Ministry*, ed. Craig Van Gelder (Grand Rapids, MI: Eerdmans, 2007), 28–29; J. Scott Horrell, "The Eternal Son of God in the Social Trinity," in *Jesus in Trinitarian Perspective: An Intermediate Christology*, ed. Fred Sanders and Klaus Issler (Nashville: B&H Academic, 2007), 47.
2. Ibid., 29.
3. Craig Van Gelder, *The Essence of the Church: A Community Created by the Spirit* (Grand Rapids, MI: Baker, 2000), 96.
4. Ibid.
5. Van Gelder, "Missiology," 29.
6. Kevin Vanhoozer, *Remythologizing Theology* (Cambridge: Cambridge University Press, 2010), 294. This is Vanhoozer's reappropriation of the well-known dictum by Roman Catholic theologian Karl Rahner, "The 'economic' Trinity is the 'immanent' Trinity and the 'immanent' Trinity is the 'economic' Trinity" (*The Trinity*, trans. J. Donceel [New York: Crossroad, 1997], 22).
7. One expression of this exaggeration seems to deny that intra-Trinitarian communion has any order at all. Horrell ("The Eternal Son of God in the Social Trinity," 62) calls this perspective *egalitarian*. Millard Erickson calls it the "equivalent-authority" position. One ardent proponent is Kevin Giles (*The Trinity and Subordinationism: The Doctrine of God and the Contemporary Gender Debate* [Downers Grove, IL: InterVarsity, 2002]). Fred Sanders outlines Giles's argument and offers a brief critique in "The State of the Doctrine of the Trinity in Evangelical Theology," *Southwestern Journal of Theology* 47, no. 2 (Spring 2005): 165–67. According to Erickson, who is also a proponent (*Christian Theology*, 2nd ed. [Grand Rapids, MI: Baker, 1998], 361), a member of the Trinity might take a subordinate role for a time, but that doesn't tell us there's an eternal hierarchy within the Godhead. Erickson contends that there is not necessarily "epistemological identity" between what God is on earth and what he is in heaven: "There is a rather obvious sense in which we can say that the immanent Trinity and the economic Trinity are the same. That would be the metaphysical identity, whereby they are not two different Trinities. The epistemological identity is something quite different, however" (*God in Three Persons: A Contemporary Interpretation of the Trinity* [Grand Rapids, MI: Baker, 1995], 309).

From one point of view, Erickson's explanation is understandable. Though the Bible indicates that the Son submits to the Father while the Son is incarnate (John 5:19; 12:49) and that he continues to do so into the future (1 Cor. 15:24–28), it is silent (or, at the very least, ambiguous) about any submission in eternity past.

Still, it is important to affirm that our experience of God in revelation, creation, and redemption bears witness to who God is and how he relates *ad intra*. In other words, the way the Father, Son, and Holy Spirit work—in particular, the Son submitting to the Father's authority after the incarnation—still reflects the order of their subsistence. It was fitting for Son to become the incarnate Mediator (John 20:21), because that action in history testified to God's essence—that the Father has eternally generated the Son (John 1:1). We call the Father the *first* person of the Trinity, and we are right to do so.

8. One expression of this exaggeration is a *functional subordinationism*. This view overstates hierarchy and minimizes divine mutuality. We concur with Robert Letham (*The Holy Trinity: In Scripture, History, Theology, and Worship* [Phillipsburg, NJ: P&R, 2004], 480–82, 492–93), and with Horrell ("The Eternal Son of God in the Social Trinity," 73), who put it this way: "The term *subordination* immediately implies hierarchy, top-down authority, power over another, subjugation, repression, and inequality," and it should be rejected. With Horrell, we affirm the generous preeminence of the Father, the joyous collaboration of the Son, and the ever-serving activity of the Spirit (44). However, we disagree with the view that the Son in eternity past submits to and obeys the Father, as represented in Bruce Ware, "Does Affirming an Eternal Authority-Submission Relationship in the Trinity Entail a Denial of *Homoousios?*," in *One God in Three Persons: Unity of Essence, Distinction of Persons, Implications for Life*, ed. Bruce A. Ware and John Starke (Wheaton, IL: Crossway, 2015), 237–48, because this would imply (even if it is denied) two wills in God before the incarnation. For more on this debate, see Andrew Wilson's excellent summary of the issues at stake, "Eternal Submission in the Trinity: A Quick Guide to the Debate," *Think*, June 13, 2016, http://thinktheology.co.uk/blog/article /submission_in_the_trinity_a_quick_guide_to_the_debate, and his helpful reflections in "Complementarianism in Crisis?," *Think*, July 6, 2016, http://thinktheology .co.uk/blog/article/complementarianism_in_crisis.

9. Fred Sanders, *The Deep Things of God: How the Trinity Changes Everything* (Wheaton, IL: Crossway, 2010), 15–19.

10. "Deësis," *Hagia Sophia*, accessed September 4, 2015, http://hagiasophia.com.

11. Sanders, "The State of the Doctrine of the Trinity," 175.

12. John M. Frame, *Systematic Theology: An Introduction to Christian Belief* (Phillipsburg, NJ: P&R), 423.

13. Carl F. H. Henry, *God, Revelation, and Authority*, vol. 5 (Waco, TX: Word, 1982), 131.

14. Frame, *Systematic Theology*, 441.

15. Ibid., 480.

16. Ibid., 489–90.

17. Jeremy S. Begbie, "Created Beauty: The Witness of J. S. Bach," in *The Beauty of God: Theology and the Arts*, ed. Daniel J. Treier, Mark Husbands, and Roger Lundin (Downers Grove, IL: IVP Academic, 2007), 22.

18. Horrell, "The Eternal Son of God in the Social Trinity," 47.

19. John R. Franke, "God Is Love: The Social Trinity and the Mission of God," in *Trinitarian Theology for the Church: Scripture, Community, Worship*, ed. Daniel J. Treier and David Lauber (Downers Grove, IL: IVP Academic, 2009), 116.

20. Story and quotation from David Bentley Hart, *The Story of Christianity: An Illustrated History of 2000 Years of the Christian Faith* (London: Quercus, 2007), 130–32.

21. C. S. Lewis, *Mere Christianity* (New York: HarperCollins, 2001), 162–63.

LEADERSHIP BIBLIOGRAPHY

THE TRINITY

Allberry, Sam. *Connected: Living in Light of the Trinity.* Phillipsburg, NJ: P&R, 2012.

Chester, Tim. *Delighting in the Trinity: Why Father, Son and Spirit Are Good News.* Epsom, UK: Good Book, 2010.

Cunningham, David S. *These Three Are One: The Practice of Trinitarian Theology.* Malden, MA: Blackwell, 1998.

Grenz, Stanley J. *The Social God and the Relational Self: A Trinitarian Theology of the Imago Dei.* Louisville: Westminster John Knox, 2001.

Gunton, Colin E. *The One, the Three, and the Many: The 1992 Bampton Lectures.* New York: Cambridge University Press, 1993.

————. *The Promise of Trinitarian Theology.* 2nd ed. Edinburgh: T&T Clark, 1997.

————. *The Triune Creator: A Historical and Systematic Study.* Grand Rapids, MI: Eerdmans, 1998.

Leithart, Peter J. *Traces of the Trinity: Signs of God in Creation and Human Experience.* Grand Rapids, MI: Brazos, 2015.

Owen, John. *Communion with the Triune God.* Edited by Kelly Kapic and Justin Taylor. Wheaton, IL: Crossway, 2007.

Reeves, Michael. *Delighting in the Trinity: An Introduction to the Christian Faith.* Downers Grove, IL: IVP Academic, 2012.

Sanders, Fred. *The Deep Things of God: How the Trinity Changes Everything.* Wheaton, IL: Crossway, 2010.

Seamands, Stephen. *Ministry in the Image of God: The Trinitarian Shape of Christian Service.* Downers Grove, IL: InterVarsity Press, 2005.

Treier, Daniel J., and David Lauber. *Trinitarian Theology for the Church: Scripture, Community, Worship.* Downers Grove, IL: IVP Academic, 2009.

GENERAL LEADERSHIP

Bell, Skip. *Servants and Friends: A Biblical Theology of Leadership.* Berrien Springs, MI: Andrews University Press, 2014.

Burns, James MacGregor. *Transforming Leadership: A New Pursuit of Happiness.* New York: Grove, 2003.

Burns, John S., John R. Shoup, and Donald C. Simmons Jr., eds. *Organizational Leadership: Foundations and Practices for Christians.* Downers Grove, IL: IVP Academic, 2014.

Forman, Rowland, Jeff Jones, and Bruce Miller. *The Leadership Baton: An Intentional Strategy for Developing Leaders in Your Church.* Grand Rapids, MI: Zondervan, 2004.

Kouzes, James M., and Barry Z. Posner. *Credibility: How Leaders Gain and Lose It, Why People Demand It.* San Francisco: Jossey-Bass, 2011.

———. *The Leadership Challenge: How to Make Extraordinary Things Happen in Organizations,* 5th ed. San Francisco: Jossey-Bass, 2012.

———. *The Leadership Challenge Workbook,* 3rd ed. San Francisco: Jossey-Bass, 2012.

———. *The Truth about Leadership: The No-Fads, Heart-of-the-Matter Facts You Need to Know.* San Francisco: Jossey-Bass, 2010.

Malphurs, Aubrey. *Being Leaders: The Nature of Authentic Christian Leadership.* Grand Rapids, MI: Baker, 2003.

Malphurs, Aubrey, and Will Mancini. *Building Leaders: Blueprints for Developing Leadership at Every Level of Your Church.* Grand Rapids, MI: Baker, 2004.

Stanley, Andy. *Visioneering: God's Blueprint for Developing and Maintaining Vision.* Sisters, OR: Multnomah, 1999.

CONVICTION

DeYoung, Kevin. *Taking God at His Word: Why the Bible Is Knowable, Necessary, and Enough, and What That Means for You and Me.* Wheaton, IL: Crossway, 2014.

Gunton, Colin E. *A Brief Theology of Revelation.* London: T&T Clark, 2005.

Lints, Richard. *The Fabric of Theology: A Prolegomenon to Evangelical Theology.* Grand Rapids, MI: Eerdmans, 1993.

McHugh, Adam S. *The Listening Life: Embracing Attentiveness in a World of Distraction.* Downers Grove, IL: InterVarsity Press, 2015.

Meadows, Donella H., and Diana Wright. *Thinking in Systems: A Primer.* White River Junction, VT: Chelsea Green, 2008.

Meek, Esther L. *Longing to Know: The Philosophy of Knowledge for Ordinary People*. Grand Rapids, MI: Brazos, 2003.

Mohler, Albert. *The Conviction to Lead: 25 Principles for Leadership That Matters*. Minneapolis: Bethany House, 2012.

Moore, T. M. *Consider the Lilies: A Plea for Creational Theology*. Phillipsburg, NJ: P&R, 2005.

Sinek, Simon. *Start with Why: How Great Leaders Inspire Everyone to Take Action*. New York: Portfolio/Penguin, 2011.

Sire, James W. *Habits of the Mind: Intellectual Life as a Christian Calling*. Downers Grove, IL: InterVarsity Press, 2000.

Smith, James K. A. *You Are What You Love: The Spiritual Power of Habit*. Grand Rapids, MI: Brazos, 2016.

Vanhoozer, Kevin J. *The Drama of Doctrine: A Canonical-Linguistic Approach to Christian Theology*. Louisville: Westminster John Knox, 2005.

Ward, Timothy. *Words of Life: Scripture as the Living and Active Word of God*. Downers Grove, IL: IVP Academic, 2009.

Willard, Dallas. *Hearing God: Developing a Conversational Relationship with God*. Downers Grove, IL: InterVarsity Press, 1999.

Wilson, Jonathan R. *God's Good World: Reclaiming the Doctrine of Creation*. Grand Rapids, MI: Baker Academic, 2013.

CREATIVITY

Bronsink, Troy. *Drawn In: A Creative Process for Artists, Activists, and Jesus Followers*. Brewster, MA: Paraclete, 2013.

Brueggemann, Walter. *The Practice of Prophetic Imagination: Preaching an Emancipating Word*. Minneapolis: Fortress, 2012.

Card, Michael. *Scribbling in the Sand: Christ and Creativity*. Downers Grove, IL: InterVarsity Press, 2002.

Crouch, Andy. *Culture Making: Recovering Our Creative Calling*. Downers Grove, IL: InterVarsity Press, 2008.

Fujimura, Makoto. *Refractions: A Journey of Faith, Art, and Culture*. Colorado Springs: NavPress, 2009.

Godawa, Brian. *Word Pictures: Knowing God through Story and Imagination*. Downers Grove, IL: InterVarsity Press, 2009.

Guthrie, Steven R. *Creator Spirit: The Holy Spirit and the Art of Becoming Human*. Grand Rapids, MI: Baker Academic, 2011.

Hendricks, Howard G. *Color Outside the Lines: A Revolutionary Approach to Creative Leadership*. Nashville: Word, 1998.

Nussbaum, Bruce. *Creative Intelligence: Harnessing the Power to Create, Connect, and Inspire.* New York: Harper Business, 2013.

Seelig, Tina L. *inGenius: A Crash Course on Creativity.* New York: HarperOne, 2012.

Shaw, Luci. *Breath for the Bones: Art, Imagination, and Spirit.* Nashville: Thomas Nelson, 2007.

Treier, Daniel J., Mark Husbands, and Roger Lundin. *The Beauty of God: Theology and the Arts.* Downers Grove, IL: IVP Academic, 2007.

Veith, Gene E., and Matthew P. Ristuccia. *Imagination Redeemed: Glorifying God with a Neglected Part of Your Mind.* Wheaton, IL: Crossway, 2015.

Wiersbe, Warren W. *Preaching and Teaching with Imagination: The Quest for Biblical Ministry.* Wheaton, IL: Victor, 1994.

COURAGE

Batterson, Mark. *In a Pit with a Lion on a Snowy Day: How to Survive and Thrive When Opportunity Roars.* Sisters, OR: Multnomah, 2006.

Brown, Brené. *Daring Greatly: How the Courage to Be Vulnerable Transforms the Way We Live, Love, Parent, and Lead.* New York: Avery, 2015.

——. *Rising Strong: The Reckoning. The Rumble. The Revolution.* New York: Spiegel & Grau, 2015.

Frost, Michael, and Alan Hirsch. *The Faith of Leap: Embracing a Theology of Risk, Adventure and Courage.* Grand Rapids, MI: Baker, 2011.

Greear, J. D. *Jesus, Continued . . . : Why the Spirit inside You Is Better than Jesus beside You.* Grand Rapids, MI: Zondervan, 2014.

Hastings, Ross. *Missional God, Missional Church: Hope for Re-evangelizing the West.* Downers Grove, IL: IVP Academic, 2012.

Lowney, Chris. *Heroic Leadership: Best Practices from a 450-Year-Old Company That Changed the World.* Chicago: Loyola, 2003.

Piper, John. *Don't Waste Your Life.* Wheaton, IL: Crossway, 2007.

Stone, Charles. *People-Pleasing Pastors: Avoiding the Pitfalls of Approval-Motivated Leadership.* Downers Grove, IL: InterVarsity Press, 2014.

Thompson, Curt. *The Soul of Shame: Retelling the Stories We Believe about Ourselves.* Downers Grove, IL: InterVarsity Press, 2015.

Van Gelder, Craig. *The Ministry of the Missional Church: A Community Led by the Spirit.* Grand Rapids, MI: Baker, 2007.

Welch, Edward T. *Running Scared: Fear, Worry, and the God of Rest.* Greensboro, NC: New Growth, 2007.

———. *Shame Interrupted: How God Lifts the Pain of Worthlessness and Rejection.* Greensboro, NC: New Growth, 2012.

COLLABORATION

Cladis, George. *Leading the Team-Based Church: How Pastors and Church Staffs Can Grow Together into a Powerful Fellowship of Leaders.* San Francisco: Jossey-Bass, 1999.

Hartwig, Ryan T., and Warren Bird. *Teams That Thrive: Five Disciplines of Collaborative Church Leadership.* Downers Grove, IL: InterVarsity Press, 2015.

Kaiser, John Edmund. *Winning on Purpose: How to Organize Congregations to Succeed in Their Mission.* Nashville: Abingdon, 2006.

Karlgaard, Rich, and Michael S. Malone. *Team Genius: The New Science of High-Performing Organizations.* New York: HarperCollins, 2015.

Lencioni, Patrick. *The Advantage: Why Organizational Health Trumps Everything Else in Business.* San Francisco: Jossey-Bass, 2012.

———. *The Five Dysfunctions of a Team: A Leadership Fable.* San Francisco: Jossey-Bass, 2002.

———. *Overcoming the Five Dysfunctions of a Team: A Field Guide for Leaders, Managers, and Facilitators.* San Francisco: Jossey-Bass, 2005.

Mallory, Sue. *The Equipping Church: Serving Together to Transform Lives.* Grand Rapids, MI: Zondervan, 2001.

Mallory, Sue, and Brad Smith. *The Equipping Church Guidebook.* Grand Rapids, MI: Zondervan, 2001.

Markova, Dawna, and Angie McArthur. *Collaborative Intelligence: Thinking with People Who Think Differently.* New York: Spiegel & Grau, 2015.

Maxwell, John C. *The 17 Indisputable Laws of Teamwork: Embrace Them and Empower Your Team.* Nashville: Thomas Nelson, 2001.

McChrystal, Stanley A., Tantum Collins, David Silverman, and Chris Fussell. *Team of Teams: New Rules of Engagement for a Complex World.* New York: Portfolio/Penguin, 2015.

Osborne, Larry W. *Sticky Teams: Keeping Your Leadership Team and Staff on the Same Page.* Grand Rapids, MI: Zondervan, 2010.

Tharp, Twyla, and Jesse Kornbluth. *The Collaborative Habit: Life Lessons for Working Together.* New York: Simon & Schuster, 2009.

Thune, Robert H. *Gospel Eldership: Equipping a New Generation of Servant Leaders.* Greensboro, NC: New Growth, 2016.

CONTEMPLATION

Allender, Dan B. *Leading with a Limp: Turning Your Struggles into Strengths.* Colorado Springs: WaterBrook, 2006.

Calhoun, Adele Ahlberg. *Spiritual Disciplines Handbook: Practices That Transform Us.* Downers Grove, IL: InterVarsity Press, 2005.

Dawn, Marva J. *Keeping the Sabbath Wholly: Ceasing, Resting, Embracing, Feasting.* Grand Rapids, MI: Eerdmans, 1989.

DeGroat, Chuck. *Toughest People to Love: How to Understand, Lead, and Love the Difficult People in Your Life—Including Yourself.* Grand Rapids, MI: Eerdmans, 2014.

———. *Wholeheartedness: Busyness, Exhaustion, and Healing the Divided Self.* Grand Rapids, MI: Eerdmans, 2016.

Eswine, Zack. *The Imperfect Pastor: Discovering Joy in Our Limitations through a Daily Apprenticeship with Jesus.* Wheaton, IL: Crossway, 2015.

Kouzes, James M., and Barry Z. Posner. *Encouraging the Heart: A Leader's Guide to Rewarding and Recognizing Others.* San Francisco: Jossey-Bass, 2003.

MacDonald, Gordon. *Building Below the Waterline: Shoring Up the Foundations of Leadership.* Peabody, MA: Hendrickson, 2011.

Miller, C. John. *The Heart of a Servant Leader: Letters from Jack Miller.* Phillipsburg, NJ: P&R, 2004.

Owen, John. *Communion with the Triune God.* Edited by Kelly Kapic and Justin Taylor. Wheaton, IL: Crossway, 2007.

Peterson, Eugene H. *The Pastor: A Memoir.* New York: HarperCollins, 2011.

Plass, Richard, and Jim Cofield. *The Relational Soul: Moving from False Self to Deep Connection.* Downers Grove, IL: InterVarsity Press, 2014.

Scazzero, Peter. *The Emotionally Healthy Leader: How Transforming Your Inner Life Will Deeply Transform Your Church, Team, and the World.* Grand Rapids, MI: Zondervan, 2015.

Witt, Lance. *Replenish: Leading From a Healthy Soul.* Grand Rapids, MI: Baker, 2011.

GENERAL INDEX

SCRIPTURE INDEX

Is the Christian life about **missions**, **discipleship**, **worship**, the **cross**, or the **kingdom**?

In *Faithmapping*, pastors Daniel Montgomery and Mike Cosper help us see that we don't have to choose. Rather, they encourage us to view the Christian life holistically—helping us understand how the *whole gospel* forms a *whole church* that is passionate about carrying the good news about Jesus to the *whole world*.

For more information, visit crossway.org.